# Shirley Jackson's American Gothic

# Darryl Hattenhauer

State University of New York Press

Published by

State University of New York Press, Albany

© 2003  State University of New York

All rights reserved

Printed in the United States of America

For information, address
State University of New York Press,
90 State Street, Suite 700, Albany, NY 12207

Production by Christine L. Hamel
Marketing by Patrick J. Durocher

Library of Congress Cataloging-in-Publication Data

Hattenhauer, Darryl.
    Shirley Jackson's American gothic / by Darryl Hattenhauer.
        p. cm.
    Includes bibliographical references and index.
    ISBN 0-7914-5607-2—ISBN 0-7914-5608-0 (pbk.)
    1. Jackson, Shirley, 1916–1965—Criticism and interpretation. 2. Horror tales,
American—History and criticism. 3. Gothic revival (Literature)—United States. I. Title.

PS3519.A392 Z7 2003
813'.54—dc21

                                                                                2002075874

10  9  8  7  6  5  4  3  2  1

*For Andy, John, Kim, and Laura*

# Contents

# Acknowledgments

Conversations with numerous fiction writers influenced this study: Russell Banks, Ron Carlson, Christina Garcia, Barry Hannah, William Kennedy, Steven Millhauser, Alberto Ríos, Marilynne Robinson, Lynn Sharon Schwartz, Mona Simpson, Will Weaver, James Welch, and Hilma Wolitzer.

Several participants in a National Endowment for the Humanities Summer Institute at the University of California at Berkeley strengthened this study's theoretical underpinning: Stuart Culver, Wai-Chee Dimock, Michael Fried, Gregory S. Jay, David Lubin, Walter Benn Michaels, Richard H. Millington, Ross Posnock, Mark Seltzer, and Christopher Wilson. Also influential were conversations with Eugenia C. DeLamotte, Teresa L. Ebert, Philip Furia, Jan Nordby Gretlund, Edward M. Griffin, Hamlin Hill, Julio Jeha, Arthur Kinney, Thais Morgan, David W. Noble, David Nye, Donna Przbylowicz, Douglas Robinson, Judith Sensibar, and Madelon Sprengnether.

Several colleagues read all or part of the manuscript: Dorothy Broaddus, Joseph Comprone, Victoria Hay, Ian Moulton, Arthur Sabatini, Cynthia Tompkins, Priscilla Van Dam, Eric Wertheimer, and William H. Young. The State University of New York Press' outside readers provided everything from sources of Shirley Jackson's allusions to rectifications of arguments.

At the Library of Congress, Alice L. Birney, James H. Hutson, and Mary Wolfskill were invaluable. At Arizona State University West's Fletcher Library, Joseph Buenker tracked down a lot of citation information missing from the newspaper clippings in the Shirley Jackson Papers; Dennis Isbell and Lisa Kammerlocher shepherded many literature searches; and Sondra Brough, Milli Herrschaft, and Sharon

Rhoades handled numerous interlibrary loans. Arizona State University West research grants supported this project.

Barbara Burley, Kathleen Grimes, and Stacey Kimbell solved the most astounding hardware and software snafus since the invention of the computer.

# SHIRLEY JACKSON AND PROTO-POSTMODERNISM

Jackson was a fabulist.

—Howard Nemerov, "Poet Nemerov
Appraises Shirley Jackson's Works"

In the 1940s, 1950s, and 1960s, Shirley Jackson was ranked among America's most highly regarded fiction writers. In 1944, when she was just getting started and "The Lottery" was four years away, an anthology of the leading new American writers included—out of a thousand submissions—Langston Hughes, Jane Bowles, Richard Wright, Arthur Miller, Norman Mailer, and Ralph Ellison, along with Jackson (Seaver). Similarly, an article in 1955 on the strength of contemporary American fiction listed her with J. D. Salinger, Ellison, Flannery O'Connor, Saul Bellow, William Styron, Carson McCullers, Eudora Welty, and Truman Capote ("U.S."). At the New School for Social Research in 1958, the required reading in a contemporary literature course included Jackson along with Kingsley Amis, Albert Camus, Allen Ginsburg, Mailer, Vladimir Nabokov, Salinger, and Jean-Paul Sartre.[1] A list of twelve books recommended by the *Saturday Review* in 1967 included *The Magic of Shirley Jackson* along with fiction by Bernard Malamud and Mailer, poetry by Donald Davidson and Adrienne Rich, and criticism by Frederick C. Crews and Richard Poirier.[2] Kurt Vonnegut's list of writers whom "highly literate people once talked enthusiastically about" included Jackson along with Salinger, John Cheever, and O'Connor (15). In 1968, Macmillan's Literary Heritage series included her with Edgar Allen Poe, Nathaniel Hawthorne, Herman Melville, Mark Twain, Henry

1

James, F. Scott Fitzgerald, Ernest Hemingway, William Faulkner, Willa Cather, John Steinbeck, Welty, and Ellison in its canonical anthology *The American Experience: Fiction*. She also won many awards.[3] And major critics in prestigious periodicals routinely reviewed her novels and anthologies.[4] In addition, renowned editors wanted to work with her. When she was published at Farrar et al., her editor was Robert Giroux; at Viking, Pascal Covici. Editors and publishers relied on Jackson as a judge of new talent. For example, Alfred Knopf Jr., requested her assessment of a manuscript by a new novelist named Anne Tyler (Shirley Jackson Papers [SJP Box 4]). (However, no record of Jackson's answer exists in her papers.) And new writers were compared to Jackson. When Joyce Carol Oates's first novel appeared, her publisher advertised her as "already compared to William Faulkner, Katherine Anne Porter and Shirley Jackson" (SJP Box 29).

This study argues that Jackson's reputation should be restored to the lofty position it occupied during her life. The main reason for this recuperation is that her writing is more varied and complex than critics have realized. She deserves recuperation not for her few works that readers have simplified as horror. Rather, she should be included with many of the other canonical writers of her time for many of the same reasons they are: she excels in a number of forms and themes. Her fiction shares many of the characteristics marking the most forward-looking writing of the 1940s and 1950s. John Barth calls such fiction "proto-postmodernist" (Plumley 14, 15). (Critics usually hold that the most significant anticipations of postmodern fiction written in America are to be found primarily in Nabokov, John Hawkes, William Gaddis, and Barth, but also in Jane Bowles, Paul Bowles, Ellison, O'Connor, and James Purdy.) While the term *proto-postmodernist* is a little infelicitous, it is nonetheless precise. This study follows Barth's use of the term to denote late modernist writing that shows traits of what will become postmodernism. As such, *proto-postmodernism* is a term useful not only for a focus on historical context, but also for studies addressing forms and themes. Indeed, for postmodernists form *is* theme. In other words, nonrealist forms such as disunified characterization, discontinuous plots, absurd settings, illegible narrative point of view, and self-reflexive style are more suitable for themes such as the divided subject, the seeming chaos of events, the incongruity of institutions, the undecidability of current epistemes, and the intertextuality of signification.[5] *Proto-postmodernism,* then, is an inclusive term that contains the specific terms used in the present study. Several characteristics of proto-postmodernism recur throughout Jackson's writing. Of course, the following traits of character, plot, narrative point of view, and setting exist before proto-postmodernism, but they occur more frequently and are more momentous in postmodernism.

Jackson's characterizations are one of her most prominent proto-postmodernist features. Her characters are usually disunified. Their psychological boundaries are usually violated by Others in a process that Rosemary Jackson (no relation) describes as "the slipping of object into subject" (82). Most of her protagonists are decentered, estranged from Others even as they consist of conflicting introjected Others.[6] Such protagonists are borne back ceaselessly into the Imaginary (the infant's sense of self).[7] They are reproductions of conflicting identities, traces of identifications with contradictory representations. Her characters rarely win, succeed, or transcend. They do not grow as much as they disintegrate. They are, in a word, entropic. Accordingly, Jackson's characterizations inconvenience notions of autonomous self-fashioning.[8]

Jackson's characters are not constitutive as much as they are constituted. They exemplify the move from the character as the creator or discoverer of meaning to the character as the captive of meaning. In this regard, she continues to endorse her Marxism of the thirties. As Frank Lentricchia says, "The central commitment of historicists, old and new, is to the self as product of forces over which we exercise no control—the self as effect, not origin" (100). Jackson features characters who have too little agency. Often they are victims of those empowered with too much agency, or of a Foucauldian system in which agency is unidentifiably diffuse. Either way, her characters experience agency as something from without. In addition, Jackson's characters are not only disunified but often flat. Similar to many of the other forerunners of postmodernism, she creates many caricatures that deflate realist notions about character.

Her plots are also sometimes disunified, although not as often as her characters. Where magical realists often begin with an absurd premise and develop it realistically, Jackson often begins with what seems to be mundane and unravels it—shows the character and sometimes the setting as they disintegrate along fault lines of internal contradictions. Sometimes her plots are radically implausible. But these implausible plots are always referential. As Barth and Philip Roth point out, both the gargantuan horrors of the twentieth century and the morass of petty absurdities in politics and mass culture have revealed not only that some real events and people are really unbelievable and simple but also that such incredible realities cannot be represented with realism.[9] In other cases, she truncates the plot. In *The Sundial,* the characters await what they believe is the imminent apocalypse, but the novel ends before they can know if their expectations are valid. In other words, the plot ends before the story does—before there is a resolution to the conflict. The effect is rather like that in Thomas Pynchon's *Crying of Lot 49,* which ends before the protagonist (and the reader) can know if the solution to the mystery is in the offing. Jackson's plots are inchoate postmodernism in other ways. For example, her questing heroines usually fail. Sometimes there is no epiphany. What is more unsettling is that often there is a revelation but it offers no salvation, or even delivers the character into perdition. Unable to complete the hero journey, they exemplify what Eugenia C. DeLamotte calls "the story of hero-journeys that fail to work. In these plots, the . . . knowledge discovered in the dark alien world is such that it renders a return to the daylight world meaningless or impossible" (54). In *The Haunting of Hill House,* for example, the protagonist keeps reciting to herself some lines from one of Shakespeare's ballads, "Journeys end in lovers meeting" *(Twelfth Night).* But her journey ends in suicide.

Jackson is also an inchoate postmodernist in her extensive and complex use of unreliable narration. As one would expect with fiction featuring decentered characters, her first-person narrators are often delusional. Moreover, her third-person narration often affords only a delusional focalization because so many of her characters are decentered. The result is a rather undecidable world. The reader does not stand outside the scene with a reliable view of it but rather is often inserted into the frame and shares the cloudy vision of the first- or third-person narrator. Such an ambiguous narrative point of view makes not only the characters but also the settings undecidable. In fact, Jackson manages to conflate the categories of character and setting. Her characters are sometimes so restricted by place that they start to merge with it. After the protagonist in *The Haunting of Hill House* discovers her self in the house, the unreliable third-person narration makes it seem impossible to differentiate the character from the house.[10] Some of her characters merge with sites of their interpellation (the process through which ideology imposes identity on a subject).[11] Whether in urban or sylvan scenes, these characters do not just reflect but rather embody the conflicting myths of capitalism and the pastoral. Her settings, then, trap her characters not only in space but also in time. Haunting is Jackson's recurrent figure for the ever-present past. Her use of ghosts and witchcraft, then, is not mystification but historicization. Arthur M. Saltzman writes that "in the wake of the notorious expulsion of history that characterized Modernist fiction, contemporary fiction ventures to reintroduce history by recognizing its availability to fictional devices" (33).

Her most proto-postmodernist trait is the intertextuality of her style. That Jackson's writing anticipates the postmodern self-consciousness of form is easy to miss because her syntax and diction alone rarely call attention to themselves; her surface features are like those of modernism in a realist mode. Anticipating postmodernism's writing about writing, she develops her characters, plots, narrators, and settings by using techniques from several non-realist modes. The nonrealist modes she reinscribes are, in descending order of importance in her fiction, the Gothic, fantastic, fabulist, allegorical, tragic, darkly comic, and grotesque.

Exemplifying Vijay Mishra's argument that Gothic is "an earlier moment of the postmodern," Jackson's decentering of the subject draws on Gothic characterization (17). As William Patrick Day says, one of the principles of Gothic is to undermine the notion of "the stability of personality and identity" (7). One hallmark of the decentered Gothic subject is the loss of agency. Tony Tanner notes the "growing tendency among American novelists to refer to ghosts, demons, occult powers, and all sorts of magic when it comes to offering some account of the forces at work in the real dream, or dreamed reality, of modern life" (348). Jackson uses demons and witchcraft to register her characters' lack of agency. Her settings, too, are Gothic. Often her settings at first appear ordinary but then emerge as extraordinary. As Kari J. Winter notes, "Female Gothic novelists uncovered the terror of the familiar" (21). Jackson's characters usually end up Gothic victims. As Day says of Gothic's disabling of the heroic romance, "There is no ascent from the underworld, nor is a New Eden established there" (7). Thus the hallmark of Gothic that Jackson reinscribes most is the motif of entrapment as a figure of power and powerlessness. Often she uses Gothic to figure entrapment that manifests its results psychologically—in private demons—but that traces back to the historical.

The fantastic, too, features Gothic entrapment. Also like Gothic, the fantastic relies on deceptive narration. But the fantastic technique she uses most is the implausible plot. As critics such as Jane Campbell and Hazel W. Carby have shown, the plausible plot is a culturally loaded conception. It fits the imagined reality of the successfully integrated white bourgeois but not Others, for example, poor African-Americans whose lives of domination in a sharecropper's shack or urban ghetto with threats from the likes of the Ku Klux Klan are quite consistent with the themes of domination in Gothic or the implausible events of the fantastic. In addition, to write the fantastic is not to write asocially. The binary opposition of fantasy and reality will not hold, especially now that we have works such as Lauren Berlant's *The Anatomy of National Fantasy*, which shows that the reality of American history is that it is, indeed, a fantasy. The new world, the new promised land, the new Eden, the virgin land, the American Adam, and the urban frontier—all of these are fantastic narratives.[12]

As Howard Nemerov contends, Jackson is also a fabulist. Sometimes her fiction is a morality tale. When it is, her protagonist may not perceive or benefit from an epiphany, but sometimes the reader can. Her most significant fabulation, *The Sundial,* is a narrative against the narrative of America as the new world.

And if she is a fabulist, then by definition there is some allegorical element as well, which is implicit in fable (she did not write full-fledged allegories). *The Sundial* is not only in part a dystopian political allegory like *The Plague, 1984, Animal Farm, The Trial, The Castle, Lord of the Flies,* and *Player Piano,* but also in part a cultural allegory like *The Scarlet Letter, Moby-Dick, Adventures of Huckleberry Finn,* and *The Great Gatsby.* Although not as great as those, *The Sundial* should have a place with the latter group as a text that reveals the tenets of the dominant culture. Its theme is the devolution of America's master narratives.

Although Jackson's usual mode is tragedy, with fated characters determined by history, when she is comic she is tragicomic. She anticipates the dark humor of postmodernism. As Joan Wylie Hall notes, Jackson's dark humor parallels the absurdism of postwar playwrights. Her comic protagonists are usually *alazons,* the victims of exploiters and tricksters. The *eirons,* who are the tricksters and victimizers, are usually antagonists. Jackson also anticipates the absurdism of postmodernism. However, she does not posit a thoroughgoing indeterminacy. In this regard, she holds to the Marxist notion of a largely determinate base underlying an apparently disordered surface. On the other hand, her demonstration of the difficulty of knowing and representing often approaches that of postmodernism.

Jackson uses the grotesque in two ways. The first is to figure the cause and effect of the abuses of power. In Jackson, the grotesque is a necessary result of the Gothic. In other writers, a text can begin with grotesqueries and not emphasize the Gothic origins of the grotesqueries, and even end without emphasizing the result when grotesque characters pass on their abuse and interpellation. Such a writer is Carson McCullers, who actually writes Southern grotesque more than Southern Gothic. By contrast, Jackson's grotesque characters are often psychological studies—accounts of the origins of the subject's formation in the Imaginary and the Symbolic. Thus Jackson exemplifies what Mary Russo calls "the grotesque as strange and uncanny" (7). This heteroglossic style drawn from various nonrealist modes also contributes to her themes. On the one hand, those themes are often found in some modernists and even naturalists, especially her historicist rendering of gender and class. On the other hand, she shares the post-modernist resistance to modernism's privileging, mystifying, and dehistoricizing of myth.

Another theme she shares with many postmodernists is subject formation. Jackson depicts interpellation by delineating the transition (or lack thereof) from the Imaginary to the Symbolic. Accordingly, she also probes the primary site of subject formation: the family. One of her most common family motifs is what Jane Gallop would later call "the phallic mother."[13] Jackson disrupts the notion that families make women more nurturing. She also figures the feminized father. Jackson, then, anticipates later discussions of the masculine and feminine as social positions. The depiction of subject formation through interpellation in the family accompanies her representation of the unconscious, which facilitates her creation of disunified characters. (According to Patricia Waugh, "To focus on an 'unconscious' immediately undercuts the very concept of a 'unitary' subject") (35). Anticipating Jacques Lacan, Jackson depicts the unconscious as linguistically constituted. Produced by the social text in general, Jackson's characters are interpellated primarily by literary texts, but also by all forms of representation—songs, paintings, statues, and so forth. Often she uses metonymic displacement to depict a character's unconscious. That is, her characters unconsciously associate part of one character or event or object with part of another character or event or object in a chain of signifiers. For example, *Hangsaman* is the study of the protagonist's insertion into the Symbolic by virtue of the metonymic chain of signifiers in her unconscious.[14] The result is a disunified character who is like a text with aporias; her behavior is more contiguous than continuous. Like other Jackson characters, she incorporates the ideology around her, and she exhibits one of the most cardinal traits of postmodern characters: schizoid paranoia. Jackson, then, is a political writer. She is a forerunner of those who Paul Maltby calls "dissident postmodernists."

Her heteroglossia, particularly her Gothicism, is one reason why she has been overlooked. She cannot be inserted into the myth of Southern Gothic, which holds that American Gothic is not of the dominant culture but of the South. However, as Teresa A. Goddu shows, Gothic applies to America as a whole. The fact is that, like Jackson, other post-war writers outside of the South also produced Gothic—for example Purdy, Hawkes, Bowles, and Nemerov. And their fiction has also been insufficiently studied.

This problem of classification also extends to the opposition of modernism/postmodernism. The forerunners of postmodernism become what Thomas Pynchon calls "the excluded middle" (136). The proto-postmodernists most studied are those who move back closer to realism and modernism as their careers develop, such as Welty and Salinger, or forward into postmodernism, such as Nabokov, Barth, and Vonnegut. But after critics concentrated on the first two waves of postmodernism—sixties dark humor and seventies metafiction—some of their attention has turned away from where postmodernism is going to how it arose. As a result, there will probably be more critical work done on *proto-post-modernism* (indeed Barth looked back and coined that term).

Another reason for the neglect of Jackson is that for the first twenty years after her death, American feminists privileged realism over postmodernism, asserted self-fashioning over historicism, and looked for role models rather than victims. But increasingly, feminists are moving away from realism. Similarly, Jackson's susceptibility to Lacanian elucidation should attract attention. Likewise, historicism and recent feminism have allowed critics to think of women as empowered, so attention should turn to Jackson's many phallic mothers. And now that feminism uses discourse theory to analyze the resistance by victims, Jackson's discourse should be a case study, for her writing bears traces of her resistance to social forces in general and to her husband in particular.

An additional reason why Jackson has not received sufficient critical attention is that her best writing is available only in out-of-the-way editions—for example, those by the Quality Paperback Book Club. Out of print are the major press editions of *The Sundial,* which reveals more about the myths of America's dominant culture than perhaps any other postwar novel, and *Hangsaman,* an outstanding psychological novel. An even better psychological novel, *The Bird's Nest,* is readily available only in an anthology, *The Magic of Shirley Jackson,* which is in print but rarely stocked. Her writing that is most available often does not show her to advantage, for example, her two collections of domestic narratives, *Raising Demons* and *Life among the Savages,* both of which Jackson wrote for the mass market.[15] Her three serious anthologies of short stories are in print, but a reader has only a one-in-three chance of getting the collection that shows her at her best, *The Lottery or, The Adventures of James Harris.* The only two novels in print and readily available in bookstores are *The Haunting of Hill House* and *We Have Always Lived in the Castle,* but they have been misread as literal-minded endorsements of witchcraft and the paranormal. Jonathan Lethem, winner of a National Book Critics Circle Award, notes that "an unfortunate impression persists . . . that her work is full of ghosts and witches" (2).

One of the most important correctives this study will offer is that Jackson did not literally believe in the supernatural, for example, witchcraft and psychic phenomena.[16] After her career was firmly established, she admitted that using anecdotes about her witchcraft and magic were promotional ploys. In addition, most of those who knew Jackson said she was not a literal believer.[17] Although her teenaged attempts to make magic work were literal-minded efforts to counteract her disempowerment and marginalization, if any of her adult attempts were literal-minded they appear to have been temporary regressions. Even during her nervous breakdown, her diaries and letters show that (unlike Eleanor in *The Haunting of Hill House*) she did not believe the voices she heard were actually coming from outside of her. Yet she took such experiences seriously, for both her self-understanding and her fiction (although taking the supernatural seriously is not the same as taking it literally). The supernatural referred to the possibility—in life and in her fiction—that the Marxist base was a doubtful foundation. Indeed, the totalism of her Marxism, never strong to begin with, diminished in the course of her life and writing. The anxiety resulting from this increasing instability of her episteme threatened her with regression to the anxiety of her youth (when indeed she did literally believe in the supernatural). But her prevailing adult attitude emerges in her ironic remark that her hex wouldn't work across state lines. Her humor should emerge for anyone not invested in mystification.

Taking supernaturalism literally, Judy Oppenheimer tries to claim that Jackson's alleged "psychic awareness" is not psychological: "Her psychic awareness was part of her individuality, not her madness; it was part of what made her who she was" (21). Jackson's "madness" was not part of who she was? In Oppenheimer's anxiety to literalize psychic awareness and separate it from psychology, she claims what she cannot know. She says of Jackson's psychic experiences, "It is highly unlikely that she even discussed them with the psychiatrist she went to late in her life" (21). She states that when Jackson saw and heard things that others did not, such phenomena were actually there: "Shirley was, in fact, psychic: she heard conversations, even music, that no one else heard; she saw faces no one else could see" (18). Thus for Oppenheimer as for the paranoid judges and teenagers Jackson condemns in *The Witchcraft of Salem Village*, spectral evidence is valid. Something is true if someone thinks it is true. Such assertions are not just laughably illogical. They are reactionary. They enable the sentimentalizing of Jackson as the purveyor of "private demons" and the erasure of Jackson as the complex political writer who compares with the best of her generation. And it sentimentalizes her by discussing her in terms of "madness." Jackson was neurotic, not psychotic. In her life as in her fiction, the ideology that masked reality broke down and enabled a clearer view of reality. She didn't break down and separate from reality.

Jackson did not experience the supernatural. She experienced the *fantastic* (in Tzvetan Todorov's classic definition of the term). That is, her consciousness was often in the ambiguous place between the seemingly supernatural and the real, where it seems hard to classify events as either supernatural or real because there seems to be evidence both ways. Jackson was not so simple as to believe that what seems true necessarily is true. Indeed, one of her anxieties is the common proto-postmodern one that what seems true is absurd. For Jackson, the supernatural—witchcraft, ghosts, spiritualism, and the paranormal—isn't a foray into her private demons. Rather it is a metaphor for reality: "I have had for many years a consuming interest in magic and the supernatural. I think this is because I find there so convenient a shorthand statement of the possibilities of human adjustment to what seems to be at best an inhuman world" and the "wickedness of human behavior" (Oppenheimer 125). She uses the supernatural in her fiction to depict the interpellation of unstable subjects into the dominant culture's myths and ideologies—particularly about class and gender—by exposing the roots of those myths and ideologies in witchcraft. (As Oates says in a similar vein, "Gothicism . . . is . . . a fairly realistic assessment of modern life") ("Writing" 108). Jackson's interest evolved from rituals of child's play through the modernist exploration of myth into various forms of nonrealist fiction, especially Gothic and the fantastic. In this process, she studied various aspects of the supernatural thoroughly. She didn't believe everything she read anymore than she endorsed every act she depicted. One can read tarot cards and tea leaves as well as fiction and even nonfiction without taking them literally. As a writer of intertextual fiction that both rehabilitated and parodied Gothic and fantastic elements, Jackson used such conventions to figure not only literature but also other aspects of reality.

Accordingly, all of Jackson's characters who appear to be in touch with the supernatural are either delusional or foolish—for example, the mad Eleanor Vance in *The Haunting of Hill House* and Merricat Blackwood in *We Have Always Lived in the Castle*, or the tellingly named Fanny Halloran in *The Sundial*. Regarding the novel unfinished at Jackson's death, Oppenheimer claims that the self-proclaimed psychic protagonist is Shirley (21). Oppenheimer elides the differences between the author and the character and overlooks the fact that Jackson's plots eventually undercut literal-minded characters. Jackson said of a purportedly nonfictional account of mesmerism, ghosts, and spiritualism by a group of ostensibly scientific researchers, "They thought that they were being terribly scientific and proving all kinds of things, and yet the story that kept coming through their dry reports was not at all the story of a haunted house, it was the story of several earnest, I believe misguided, certainly determined people" (Friedman 121). Jackson's novel *The Haunting of Hill House* draws on that account to parody such literal-minded attitudes toward the supernatural (even though such mystification was later used to market the book and the two movies based on it). Jackson satirizes spiritualism in the character of the obnoxious Mrs. Montague, a parody of Jackson's phallic mother, Geraldine, who told fortunes, read tea leaves, and showed Jackson how to use a Ouija board. But not even Jackson's mother could go as far as Jackson's grandmother, a Christian Scientist who introduced Geraldine to faith healing. As a child when Shirley was sick, this grandmother (who lived with Jackson's family) would sneak into Jackson's room at night and whisper in her ear for hours that her fevered mind would make her well. Jackson's mother, who contained the supernatural in the mystification of bourgeois respectability, prepared for her many parties by hiding the grandmother upstairs, thereby also preparing Jackson to read Gothic fiction as referential. Jackson's recurring figure of the madwoman in the attic is not derived solely from Gothic literary conventions.

Nonetheless, Jackson has been marketed as a genre writer. For example, her husband entitled the posthumous collection that he edited *The Magic of Shirley Jackson*. This image of magic, witchcraft, and the supernatural (along with the opposite image of her as a writer of massmarket domestic narratives in the age of Ozzie and Harriet) has presented a persona of someone who would not appear to be a significant writer. What helped her sell to the mass market has helped to put her best novels out of print. Her book jackets tell the reader less about the stories within than the story of her marketing. Her domestic narratives were (and still are) sold with covers that look as if they could have been done by Grandma Moses (whose paintings depicted Bennington, Vermont, where Jackson lived, and its surroundings). By contrast, the novels that are still in print have the sort of sensationalist covers of the bodice rippers at the supermarket.

Yet recently Jackson criticism has flourished. Since 1990, after Gary Scharnhorst predicted a Jackson "revival" (248), there have been over a dozen articles, two book chapters, several dissertations, a volume in Harold Bloom's series on short story writers, a book-length annotated bibliography, and a book about Jackson's first two anthologies of short stories. In addition, a third anthology of her short fiction appeared. Indicative of this restoration is S. L. Varnado's claim that among writers of twentieth-century Gothic, "first place unquestionably belongs to Shirley Jackson" (128). After critics of the eighties rehabilitated Gothic, excellent feminist criticism by Dale Frederick Bailey, Lynnette Carpenter,

Lorna Ellen Drew, Claire Kahane, Tricia Lootens, Judie Newman, Roberta Rubenstein, and Andrew J. Schopp has appeared on Jackson's two most Gothic novels, *The Haunting of Hill House* and *We Have Always Lived in the Castle*. Marta Caminero-Santangelo's reading of *The Bird's Nest* shows Jackson's deep understanding of psychology. Peter Kosenko published a brilliant Marxist analysis of "The Lottery." And Joan Wylie Hall's study of the short stories is a breakthrough. Significant studies of Jackson's other modes have also begun to appear. For example, James Egan has addressed Jackson's use of the fantastic, and both Anne LeCroy and Nancy A. Walker have analyzed her humor.

Yet however fine each of these may be, taken together they do not establish a footing for a wider variety of critics to establish a multivocal dialogue on all of Jackson's work. What is new in each of these studies is either an article, or a book introduction, or a book chapter, except for Hall's, and her book addresses only the short fiction and appeared before the publication of Jackson's third and longest short story anthology. Similarly, Egan examines only a few short stories, and Kosenko only one. Likewise, LeCroy and Walker examine only humor and only in Jackson's domestic narratives. In addition, most of the feminism continues to minimize Jackson's first four novels and to defer considerations of class and ethnicity. A sufficient body of Jackson criticism would include at least several volumes devoted to her oeuvre by approaches from within each of the following methods: poststructuralism, historicism, psychoanalysis, and genre study. Such an edifice is beyond the scope of the present study. But to encourage other scholars, the present study tries to demonstrate that each of these methods is important in showing that Jackson's achievement is much wider and deeper than the existing criticism implies. Focusing on one variable does not solve a complex equation. Using one method or theme, examining one form or text—these approaches miss Jackson's multivocality.

This study tries to capture her heteroglossia by using several methods to address several forms and themes. Beginning with a topically (not chronologically) organized overview of issues in Jackson's life, chapter 1 looks at her social position and family situation as they influenced Jackson's subject formation. Then comes a reading of the short stories followed by a reading of the novels. Chapters 2, 3, and 4 each address one of her three short story anthologies in the order in which they appeared: 1949, 1968, and 1996. When the chronological analysis of the novels begins, the organization circles back to a reading of her novels in chronological order. This organization shows that by the middle 1950s the novel takes over from the short story as the genre in which she makes her most noteworthy achievements.

This study follows the injunction of Jackson's friend Kenneth Burke that critics should use all that is there to use—that they should not necessarily stick with one method or theory. This injunction seems especially apt for a study that tries to show that several methods can and should be applied to Jackson. It is also apt because an overview of a heteroglossic oeuvre demands the use of different theories and methods.

## CHAPTER ONE

# SOME CONDITIONS OF PRODUCTION

How did Shirley Jackson become a writer of heteroglossic fiction with political themes?

She and her husband, Stanley Edgar Hyman, who was an eminent critic, knew many of the leading scholars, editors, and fiction writers of the 1940s and 1950s. Jackson's children recall playing baseball with J. D. Salinger. Ralph Ellison, who taught with Hyman at Bennington College and whom Hyman touted before *Invisible Man* appeared, was godfather to one of her children. Jackson and Hyman also knew Bernard Malamud when he taught at Bennington. Another Bennington faculty member, Howard Nemerov, was a close personal influence on Jackson. She refers to him often in her diary. Perhaps even more influential was another Bennington faculty member, Kenneth Burke, who hired Hyman. Hyman regarded Burke as the greatest critic ever, and following his example, Hyman was adept in psychoanalytics, formalism, myth criticism, and Marxism.

The greatest influence on Jackson was Hyman. This influence began in 1937 when they were both undergraduates at Syracuse University. One of their friends said, "Shirley had the highest respect for Stanley as a writer [and] as her critic" (Friedman 42). This New York Jewish Marxist radicalized this suburban Anglo daughter of a Republican businessperson. Following the lead of Hyman and his friend Walter Bernstein, she joined the Young Communist League. (Bernstein would be blacklisted as a screenwriter during the McCarthy era; much later he would be employed by Woody Allen as a screenwriter for *The Front*.) At Syracuse University, Jackson and Hyman coedited a radical literary journal, *Spectre*, named after Karl Marx's spectre haunting Europe. After Hyman wrote an essay on blues and Jackson wrote a sonnet and an editorial on racism, the university shut down their journal. Not until the late 1950s did her belief in the certainties of Marxism wane, apparently because of her growing prosperity and mental instability.

Hyman and Burke also mentored her in psychology. With their help, Jackson studied all of the major works on the multiple personality, such as *The Three Faces of Eve*, but primarily Morton Prince's work on the multiple personality, which influenced her fiction in general and *The Bird's Nest* in particular. About preparing for that novel, Jackson wrote to her parents, "i did a good deal of background reading before i wrote the book and one area of hysterical behavior i know backward and forward is the dissociated personality."[1] From such research, Jackson knew that the popular psychology used in the movie based on that novel was invalid, especially as it distorted her protagonist: "they have made her into a lunatic, which she can't be, by definition, and the doctor cures her with a very interesting combination of freudian analysis, pre-freudian hypnosis, jungian word-association, and rorshak inkblots. not one of these systems gets along with any of the others in real life, but i guess it is different in the movies."

Perhaps Hyman's greatest influence on Jackson was in the study of myth and ritual. Jackson drew on Hyman's knowledge of myth and ritual especially in the early years of her production. For example, a book he had given her about rituals of human sacrifice influenced her writing of "The Lottery." Hyman even originated the story's incantation, "Lottery in June, corn be heavy soon" (Oppenheimer 130). (However, Jackson's production increasingly undercut Hyman's increasingly ahistorical privileging of myth.)

In turn, Jackson came to influence Hyman. Phoebe Pettingell, a student of Hyman's whom he married after Jackson died, notes that they "worked with almost total interdependence. Their effect on each others' writing is too great to be calculated" (xiv). In particular, Hyman depended on Jackson for his many reviews of contemporary novels. In his introduction to an anthology of his reviews, Hyman stated, "[She] winnowed out books for me, discussed each book with me before I reviewed it, corrected each review as I wrote it, and proofread each galley" (*Standards* Acknowledgments). Thus in important respects, they collaborated, each benefiting from the other.

Hyman not only collaborated in Jackson's production, but also manipulated the marketing of that production. At a time when a remarkable media image preserved the moribund career of Ernest Hemingway and pushed Norman Mailer and Truman Capote to the front of the crowd, Hyman saw to it that Jackson was promoted as a witch. He wrote the blurb on the jacket of her debut novel that claimed she practiced witchcraft. Jackson cooperated at first because the story that she believed in witchcraft was important not only for the sale of her writing, but also for the movie deals based on that writing.

While Hyman managed Jackson's literary production, he directed her domestic labor. In short, she did all of it. In addition, Jackson did all of the driving, which meant that she did all of the shopping and transported not only their four children, but also Hyman (Friedman 31). The following anecdote is representative of the way in which he used her. One day he saw her, very pregnant, trudging up the walk with loads of groceries. He rushed out to her, yanked the newspaper from under her arm, and ran back to his easy chair, leaving her to continue struggling with the groceries (which she would soon be preparing not just for him but possibly for one of the many female students he often brought home) (Oppenheimer 115–16). Presumably, two people with their knowledge of psychology understood the manipulation behind such treatment.

For Hyman did not just influence her. He controlled her. From the start, he took the attitude that he was the master and she the apprentice: she would produce according to his specifications. A terse entry in his diary reveals his attitude: "I fixed her story, then she rewrote it."[2] They were not only collaborators but also codependents. At his best he was arrogant and contentious; he was usually malevolent and tyrannical. According to his second wife, Hyman admitted that his talent was "mainly of a destructive order with a highly developed instinct for the jugular" (Pettingell xi). His first book, with the appropriately aggressive title *The Armed Vision,* was a gratuitous ad hominem attack against every critic before William Empson and Kenneth Burke. A reviewer deemed it "one of the least tasteful bits of venom that has appeared in a long time" (xi). Hyman's reviews were as hostile as his criticism. His worst vitriol he directed at homosexuals. For example, he stated that James Purdy "is a terrible writer, and worse than that, a boring writer" (*Standards* 254). And he stated that almost all of the reviews of Purdy except Hyman's were mindless. Similarly, his review of Truman Capote was entitled "Fruitcake at Tiffany's" (148).

As in his professional life, so in his personal life: Hyman was, in a word, hostile. It might be reasonable to posit hostility and domination at the beginning of his relationship with Jackson. Before Hyman met her, he read a story of hers and declared that he would marry her. The story was about a suicidal young woman. He expressed his hostility sexually. One form of his aggression came out in his Don Juanism (an interesting trait in a homophobic Freudian). From the early days of the marriage, Hyman had affairs with numerous women, once at home with Jackson in the next room yelling at them.

In addition to dominating her professionally and abusing her personally, he exploited her financially. She was, in the vernacular of the blues music they both loved, a mule: she did the work and gave him the money. Her labor paid for the vast majority of their consumption. As Hyman put it, "My earnings pay the bar bill and that's it" (Oppenheimer 175). He bought her a dishwasher (with her money) because her labor was worth so much more as a writer. She wrote to her parents, "stanley said he figured it was costing us a couple of thousand dollars a day to have me wash dishes." The effect of this attitude was to make the household income even more of Jackson's responsibility, and she therefore had to spend more time writing, especially her most profitable production, the domestic narratives for slick women's magazines. For Hyman was bent on keeping his wife busy. In 1955 Jackson wrote her parents,

> one of stanley's inspirations was the singing lessons, which i start the first of the year. he has the idea that i must busy myself at interesting things, and not have any time idle to be depressed, so he has about three dozen brand new books lined up for me, all kinds of lists of new things i am to decide about buying, and these darn singing lessons.

Despite his ostensible concern for her—his seeming desire for her to have constructive hobbies such as singing lessons—it must have been obvious to him that the depression of the primary breadwinner and sole housekeeper, cook, and chauffeur was not a result of inactivity. Referring to her family doctor, Oliver Durand, Jackson wrote to her parents, "stanley says he is going to kill oliver for deciding that my jitters were due to overwork, because now i am all calm and collected again i still don't work, and he wants oliver to find something that he can diagnose as underwork." By 1964, after she had had a nervous breakdown, she felt guilty about writing in her diary because she was using time that could be spent making money: "i am oddly self-conscious this morning because stanley is at home and there is literally no telling him what i am doing. i think he would regard me as a criminal waster of time, and self-indulgent besides. i feel i am cheating stanley because i should be writing stories for money."[3]

Apparently Hyman was not only pleased that his wife did all the dirty work and brought in a lot of money, but also jealous that his wife was making much more money than he was. Indeed, his friends chided him about her success. Burke's letters to Hyman often alluded to Jackson's success. For example, in a letter of 9 September 1961, Burke refers to Jackson's royalties, calling them "a check you can cash at your wife's bank."[4] This jibe also alludes to Hyman's book, *The Tangled Bank,* which he had been unable to finish for over a decade (during which time Jackson's writing was at its critical and financial peak). Burke made similar allusions about the biographical investment Jackson made in her fiction. Two of Burke's letters alluded to Jackson's *We Have Always Lived in the Castle:* Burke addressed Hyman as "Castleman" and called the Hyman home "the castle," a veiled reference not only to the true breadwinner in the family, but also to the recurrent theme in Jackson's fiction of patriarchs appropriating the fruits of women's labor.

For Jackson's writings were among the most lucrative of her time. Her novels were best-sellers. There were movie deals on two of those novels, *The Birds' Nest* and *The Haunting of Hill House.* Her short stories and essays were also extremely profitable. Jackson's agent, the powerful Carol Brandt, demanded and got a minimum of one thousand dollars for each short story and essay appearing in a mass-market magazine (SJP Box 4). Her average fee was undoubtedly much more. The editors of the women's magazines knew that Jackson's name on the cover meant higher sales. The advance on her contract with *Good Housekeeping* to supply a few mass-market domestic narratives each year enabled Hyman and Jackson to move to Westport, Connecticut, in 1949—only a few years after she started writing.

These Marxists of the thirties became consumers of the fifties. Their house in Bennington had about nineteen rooms. The house was so big that it had once been divided into four apartments. They amassed their own library, which was bigger than the town library and even bigger than Bennington's college library. Their commodities fetish required ever more goods, and in turn ever more income to pay for them. Like Herman Melville confessing that some of his books were "jobs" done only for money, Jackson was quite honest with herself and her parents about the monetary reasons for writing the mass-market domestic narratives: "they are written simply for money and the reason they sound so bad is that those magazines won't buy good ones, but deliberately seek out bad stuff because they say their audiences want it."

In addition to her commodities fetish, Jackson was dependent on alcohol. Turning down an invitation to a panel discussion on the misfortunes of alcoholism, Jackson wrote to her parents that she was "more in favor of alcoholism than against it." Dr. Durand encouraged her to drink:

> i will just have to get the food down to fewer calories to make room for the cocktails. oliver said definitely plan to include some drinks in each day's count, since the intention was to make me feel better, not worse. . . . oliver said to plan on a couple of cocktails before dinner, just for morale, but if i have two cocktails before dinner now i almost pass out.

After checking into a hospital to give birth, she had Ellison bring her liquor and she drank it to hasten her delivery. Eventually, she could not travel without alcohol. She wrote to her parents in 1963, "tomorrow we leave for michigan. . . . we have a bedroom on the train (i am still not equal to flying) and we get on at nine-thirty with a bottle of bourbon and a bottle of scotch and wake up at six a.m. in detroit. . . . i will be full of wine when we get on board."

She was dependent not only on alcohol but also various drugs. In her early twenties, she took large doses of codeine not only for her toothaches, but also for her migraines (which started after she married Hyman). She depicts the hallucinatory effect of this opiate in two of her stories, "The Tooth" (1950) and "The Bus" (1965). Jackson started out on codeine but soon hit the harder stuff. In her early thirties, a doctor in Westport got them both hooked not only on diet pills but also on amphetamines. Jackson wrote home,

> i got me a real fancy doctor—did i tell you about him? He is what i would call a westport society doctor, and he was highly recommended to me by about the kind of people who *would* recommend such. . . . i am supposed to go back once a week, having eaten all i want, and he will give me an injection which will take it off me. it's sort of diets anonymous. . . . p. s. went to the doctor yesterday and discovered that i had lost seven pounds in a week; he says it will keep up at about that rate.

Later her psychiatrist in Bennington, James Toolan, treated her obesity and food addictions (she ate a pound of butter a day) by prescribing even more amphetamines. Shirley wrote to her parents, "i am on a very lenient diet . . . and taking fancy pills." Jackson and Hyman were so impressed by the system of amphetamines as an energizer and diet aid (and so unaware of the danger of these new drugs they and others confused with vitamins) that they sometimes gave Dexedrine to their children.

By the fifties, she added tranquilizers (such as Miltown, Phenobarbital, and Thorazine) to her regimen of amphetamines, alcohol, and codeine. She wrote to her parents, "my pills also include one of these relaxing dopes, which does take the edge off that jumpy feeling." Jackson wrote to her parents regarding her delirium and high blood pressure, "Toolan gave me a shot that put me out cold." Toolan later denied that he was the source for her tranquilizers.[5]

She became dependent partly as a result of her growing agoraphobia. In the forties, she began to develop a fear of New York City. (This anxiety was probably part of the reason why she and Hyman moved to a small town like Bennington.) Soon she felt threatened by small towns as well, although for different reasons. While her fiction and biography suggest a fear of collapsing buildings in the big city, it was the reactionary small-mindedness of the villagers that frightened her in the small towns. A particular sore point was the locals' racism. She once publicly denounced a Bennington blackface play. She was especially worried that the incubus of provincial racism would infect her children. She made a special point of warning her son and his friends about mistreating Jackson's black housekeeper. Racism and anti-Semitism threatened her personally, not just because she knew many blacks and Jews but because she had married a Jew (and therefore she and her family would have been subject to the Holocaust had they lived in Europe).

Her fear of Bennington was not delusional. Some of these local Vermonters sent her hate mail. Some of them dumped garbage on her lawn. When she walked into the post office to mail her manuscripts, all talking stopped. Her fear of such provincialism emerges, of course, in "The Lottery." But it informs her fiction all the way from the beginning of her career through her last completed book, *We Have Always Lived in the Castle*. She told Nemerov that the townies' harassment of the reclusive sisters in this novel referred to her life in small town New England (SJP Box 10).

But her agoraphobia was a response not just to the built environment of cities and the social environment of villages, but to many kinds of stressful situations. In 1951, she risked accepting an invitation for a job interview at Smith College, but she passed out during the interview and declined the position. By the sixties, she could barely go anywhere without drugs and alcohol.

She was similarly anxious about publicity—about being exposed in the media. Beginning her career before the age of television, she could at first manipulate her public image rather easily. Few knew what she really looked like because she appeared only on radio and released only two photographs of herself, ones that had been taken when she was young and not yet obese. As her books kept coming, the reviews kept running the same photographs of her. Those who met the real Jackson were shocked. By the late fifties she turned down a televised interview with Edward R. Murrow, an opportunity that for others would have meant lucrative publicity. When *Time* published a photograph of what Jackson really looked like in 1962, even her mother was stunned. Anxious almost everywhere but home, Jackson eventually could not stand to be there either because of the pressures of doing all of the domestic duties while producing not only mass-market moneymakers but also serious literature.

Harassment by the locals was not the only reason for her fear of the outside. As a result of all of the *stress* (if that word can cover the ravages of scapegoating plus alcoholism, drug addiction, and abuse by her husband) Jackson developed colitis, which gave her not only nausea and diarrhea, but also caused a precipitous drop in her blood pressure. The attacks were, she wrote to her mother, "exactly like getting kicked in the stomach, and i all but pass out; i get dizzy and sick and staggery and shaking, and of course very scared." These attacks usually occurred in the morning: "i stay home as much as possible in the mornings, and so am making fine progress on my book; there's nothing like being scared to go outside to keep you writing."

Her agoraphobia, however, was not absolute. In an unsent letter to Nemerov, she said that she had a great urge to travel. In the months before her death, she sometimes yielded to the impulse, if only to drive herself thirty miles away to North Adams (maybe to see Edith Wharton's home). Once she even drove alone to New York City. And in June 1965, two months before Jackson's death, she drove Hyman to Georgia so they could meet the mother of the recently deceased Flannery O'Connor. Given the amount of chemicals it took just to get her across town, it must have been a road trip oddly rivaling those of Jack Kerouac and Ken Kesey.

Another reason why Jackson became agoraphobic is that she had long felt controlled not by her will but by forces outside herself. Jackson felt like a subject, not a site of her own agency but the effect of agencies that resided elsewhere—a result, not a cause. Like a Gothic victim, she felt powerless, controlled from without, at the mercy of the Other. In her diary as an adolescent, she wrote of her writing as something that came not from her but from her pen or her typewriter. As an ineffectual adolescent to whom things happened, she marked the days on her calendar as lucky or unlucky according to whether or not she happened to see her secret love (whose name, in a case of life imitating parodic art, was Bud Young) (SJP Box 1).

Apparently she believed that she needed Hyman to control her. While the chemical dependencies were bad enough, they were matched by her psychological dependency on him. She felt dependent on Hyman for what stability she had. In the late forties, she wrote in her diary,

> i know perfectly well that i have no control over what i think or say right now and that whatever comes from me is not made by my mind or the thinking part of me but by the small hysterical part which has taken over the whole system. . . . stanley . . . stopped taking care of me and my one security is gone. . . . will he let them lock me up or will he start taking care of me again when it's too late. . . .

She felt this dependence in spite of his mistreatment of her. Early in the marriage, she wrote in her diary about Hyman's psychological abuse: "We should never have gotten married and I keep thinking that now." And the abuse was not just psychological. In one of the many telling passages not cited in any of the Jackson scholarship—not even in her biography—Jackson wrote that Hyman raped her: "If it's sex I can't do anything about it. He forced me god help me and for so long I didn't dare say anything and only got out of it when I could and now I'm so afraid to have him touch me."

Jackson continued to vacillate between her desire to stay with Hyman and her desire to get away from him. In the late fifties, she again wrote about the marriage ending. In a letter to Hyman that she apparently did not send, she wrote, "there are going to be, eventually, the reasons why our marriage ends." But she blames herself: "you have said positively that our sexual difficulties are entirely my doing; i believe you are right" (SJP Box 1). In her diary in late 1964, after she had broken down and would not live another year, she was still writing to herself that she wanted the marriage to end—over twenty years after the first statement in her diary that she wanted out of the marriage: "i do want the marriage to be broken yes i do because i have no chance to be alone." Thus she felt both isolated and crowded.

It is something of a cliché to find origins of such cyclic, compulsive dependency in the first object relations. Yet Jackson seems to be a textbook illustration of Nancy Chodorow's theory of the pre-Oedipal, for Jackson's compulsions seem undeniably to have begun with her mother. Moreover, her mother appears to have been a perfect example of what Jane Gallop calls "the phallic mother." The first line of her biography, "She was not the daughter her mother wanted," understates the problem, for Geraldine Jackson did not want any children at all. When Jackson was an adolescent, her mother told her that Jackson was the result of a failed abortion (Oppenheimer 14). Her mother felt that her neo-Victorian duties as a mother interfered with her status as a proper bourgeois; she was more interested in her activities as a member of the country club and the Daughters of the American Revolution.

As Hyman would be later, her mother was controlling. She insisted that Shirley conform to the most mundane gender conventions (although her mother resisted the nurturing role). Also like Hyman, her mother insisted that Jackson perform the duties of domesticity. The spectre of an introjected authority figure haunted Jackson. To the end, she was subjected to her mother's manipulative attempts to force her to conform to superficial conventions. Affronted by Jackson's less than anal-retentive grooming and housecleaning, the mother wrote her, "I don't know how you are training your children—with you and your house in such a sad condition." (Note the connection of "you and your house"; in many texts, Jackson makes detailed use of the house as a symbol of the self). When *Time* published the picture showing how unattractive Jackson really looked, her mother wrote, "Why oh why do you allow the magazines to print such awful pictures of you? I am sure your daughters at school are proud to show off your picture and say, 'this is my mother'. . . . Your children love you for your achievements but they also want you to be worth looking at too."[6] And about those achievements, which were altogether too nonrealist for the mother, she wrote her daughter, "We love getting your letters and like them better than your stories." Jackson's mother, then, would rather read of her daughter's own Gothic entrapment in addiction than to read nonrealist fiction. In late 1964 during her nervous breakdown, Jackson wrote in her diary, "Who is looking over my shoulder all the time?" (The schizoid protagonist in *The Haunting of Hill House* asks, "Whose hand was i holding?") Her biographer says it was Jackson's mother who was looking over her shoulder all the time (15), but that puts it too literally; the mother determined the floor plan of her daughter's self, and Jackson's compulsions were constructed on that design and in turn form the basis of the storeys in that design.

In her ambivalence about identifying with her mother, Jackson modeled herself mostly after her father. She got her intelligence and literacy from him. Uprooted as an adolescent from his native England and transplanted to America, he passed on the favor to Jackson by relocating her as an adolescent from San Francisco to Rochester, New York. Leslie Jackson arrived in San Francisco just before the earthquake of 1905. (The scene of architectural collapse will recur in her fiction.) Her speech contained traces of his English pronunciation.[7] For Jackson, her relatively feminized father manifested the mother country, whose former pre-industrial conditions Jackson came to fantasize as a reference point from which the modern world had fallen. She found in the eighteenth-century sentimental novel a kind of golden age, and she found in the Gothic novel figures of the fall into modernity. One of her favorite authors was Samuel Richardson, for he was her emblem of fairness and love.

In addition to the actors, the scene is significant in the playing out of Jackson's pre-oedipalism. Her fall from a tolerable childhood into a pathological adolescence co-occurs with the family's move (in 1933 when Jackson was sixteen)[8] from warm and sunny California to cold and snowy Rochester, New York. As soon as she arrived, she got hay fever for the first time in her life; such stress-related symptoms recurred for the rest of her life. Jackson herself regarded the move as a spatial correlative of the loss of innocence. For Jackson, a friend recalled, California was a "lost paradise" (Oppenheimer 18).[9]

Jackson compulsively returned the rest of her life to this scene of adolescent conflict in which the subject tries to compromise conflicting demands by resisting and yet obeying both Desire and the Symbolic; Jackson struggled with not only becoming but also possessing both her father and mother, each of whom significantly inverted the dominant culture's gender rules, beginning with their androgynous names, Leslie and Geraldine. Jackson resisted socialization based on these two models of adulthood and this scene of maturation by becoming an introvert and social outcast. She simultaneously tried to fit in and yet cultivated her sense of self as Other. She spent most of her time in a room of her own, writing. When her parents insisted that she attend the University of Rochester, she dutifully obeyed and then (passive-aggressively) flunked out. She again withdrew to her room at her parents' home, and she resumed writing, this time for a year. Then she went to the more bohemian and radical Syracuse and took up with other Others: first a libertarian French woman, and then Hyman and his circle of radical Jews from New York City. When he came to visit her in Rochester, he had to hide so that Jackson's parents did not know she was fraternizing with a Jew.

Jackson remained a tangled bank of contradictions. She wrote both domestic narratives and proto-postmodernist short stories and novels that are among the most significant of her time. Despite the domestic narratives that gave her a national reputation as an expert on home-making, she was even more indifferent toward some domestic duties than was her mother. Jackson's children were sometimes so unkempt that a neighbor once washed off one of Jackson's daughters and combed the child's hair. The person who produced expert advice on motherhood had to go to Burke's wife Libby for advice on homemaking (Libby probably missed the irony in her advice to leave Hyman and "go home to mama" [SJP Box 7]). The same Marxist who protested against Bennington's blackface show wrote a letter of complaint saying she would not "enter into explanations with tradespeople" (SJP Box 12). She was such a complex case that Burke arranged to have her studied as a special research project at the Center for Advanced Study in the Behavioral Sciences at Stanford University. Unfortunately, the study was never conducted, because her agoraphobia kept her from returning to her Eden.

Jackson was such a site of conflicts that it seems she was almost, at least at times, a multiple personality. As is well-known, multiple personalities often arise from sexual abuse, and it seems that Jackson might have been so victimized. A childhood friend recalls that she was molested by Jackson's maternal uncle, Clifford Bugbee, and speculates that he probably did the same to Jackson, or worse (Oppenheimer 27). Scenes of molestation occur in Jackson's fiction. A child in her first novel, *The Road Through the Wall,* is probably abused. The teenaged female protagonist of her second novel, *Hangsaman,* is molested by a friend of the family. The female protagonist in her third novel, *The Bird's Nest,* is a multiple personality who was molested by her mother's lover. Similar characters appear in her short stories. But it is inaccurate to describe her as a multiple personality, even during her breakdown. Following Michael Holquist's statement that for Mikhail Bakhtin the self is *dialogic* (19), it would be more accurate to use that term as a metaphor for her personality, not because she literally heard voices, but because her personality consisted of so many traces from the discourse of the social text.[10]

More precisely, the repressed oppositions were not so repressed in her. She was a bit like the multiple personality described in a book by Prince, which Burke had loaned her, and it had such an effect on her that she used it to develop Elizabeth, the protagonist with a multiple personality in *The Bird's Nest.* For Prince, we are all multiple personalities held together by one ideal personality, the others residing more or less in the unconscious. True multiples arise when their ideal personality does not maintain sufficient repression.

Jackson represents the personality (and the productions in which it takes part both as producer and consumer) as liminal, protean, and processual (with the repression of the other identifications incomplete). The conflicts are not always conscious; as with Elizabeth in *The Bird's Nest,* sometimes the ideal self has to sleep so that the other selves would communicate with each other. Sometimes when Jackson awoke, she found disturbing notes that she had written to herself while sleepwalking. One such note read, "Dead dead" (SJP Box 1). She wrote in a long unsent letter to Nemerov, "There is not a he or a she but the demon in the mind, and that demon finds guilts where it can and uses them and runs mad with laughing when it triumphs; it is the demon which is fear and we are afraid of words" (SJP Box 1). Significantly, her agency here was ungendered, played on her guilt, and was intimately connected with language.

Herself an active site of aporias, Jackson spoke of her mind in spatial terms as several selves with no center. She wrote in her diary in the 1930s while at Syracuse, "i am a psychotic case and i am going to go insane. . . . there is an empty space inside my head." In the end, she could not get access to a necessary room in her mind. The last entry in her diary suggests one of those locked chambers: "only way out is writing please god help me please help me and do not show to anyone do not show to anyone someday please god help me do not show to anyone because locked." Her fictions, a reproduction of her structures of conflict, convert the synchrony of her conflicting propensities into the diachronic outpouring of production—the projection of her inward structure into outward arrangements. In her diary in late 1964 she wrote, "i have been thinking of these pages as a refuge, a pleasant hiding place." In those words, her mind creates a model, a trace of itself, and then retreats into itself by going out of itself. Having performed that act of contradiction, she doubles it by stating the opposite; she claims that her writing is *not* a refuge, not a place, but a process, an act: "this is not a refuge, these pages, but a way through, a path not charted; i feel my way, but there *is* a way through. not a refuge yet. on the other side somewhere there is a country, perhaps the glorious country of well-dom, perhaps a country of a story." What she first gives and then takes away she gives back: process turns into place, act into scene. As Hawthorne said of Melville, she keeps going over the same ground, shuttling from one opposition to the other. Like Faulkner's Darl Bundren, in *As I Lay Dying,* she desires to "ravel out," outside of herself, and to penetrate the skin of others and to see inside them (193). For she experienced herself as Other, her in-here as conflicting traces constituted by the out-there.

Writing in this diary that she kept at the end of her life, she wrote about the joy of writing: "i am at home here," which is an ironic metaphor for someone who felt exhausted because of her husband. For the home that this late diary (like all of her writing) returned her to was her first diary, the adolescent diary in which she first expressed the contradictions impressed upon her when she fell out of her childhood in California. In her notes for a lecture on writing, she states, "i personally love writing. it is a logical extension of the adolescent daydream" (SJP Box 10). Among the stories she kept telling as an adult were figurations of the pre-oedipal conflicts that developed during her adolescence and then with Hyman.

## CHAPTER TWO

# The Lottery or,
# The Adventures of James Harris

This collection features the defamiliarization and estrangement that Shirley Jackson will develop throughout her career. Perhaps more than any other volume, this one uses the double in psychological fables of the disunified subject.[1] Moreover, it establishes what will become her recurrent use of architecture as a metaphor for the self. It also begins what will become Jackson's increasingly complex forms of unreliable narration. And it develops what will become her lifelong theme of writing about writing, particularly the role of language in subject formation. Most of these stories appeared in such prestigious venues as the *New Yorker* and *Harper's*. Also noteworthy is that she produced such a large collection of significant fiction in only about five years. And the editors of the *New York Times Book Review* included this anthology on its list of the "Best Fiction of 1949." As proto-postmodernist fiction, it should be ranked with the most significant proto-postmodernist debut anthologies of the 1940s and 1950s.[2]

"Like Mother Used to Make" takes place in two identical apartments down the hall from each other. The setting of twin apartments tropes the doubles who occupy them. As in much of Jackson's fiction, this story uses architecture as a metaphor of the subject, and it uses doubles to disrupt notions of a unified subject. In the case of these doubles, the similarities of the apartments contrast with the differences between the two characters. Each subject is the mirror opposite of the other, but is also the mirror opposite of traditional gendering. The woman, Marcia, is masculine, and the man, David Turner, is feminine.[3] Marcia is "a tall handsome girl with a loud voice, wearing a dirty raincoat." Like a stereotypical bachelor, she leaves her bed unmade and her laundry on the floor. And when she arrives late for a dinner David has made, she sounds like the stereotypical husband: "I didn't forget, Davie, I'm just late as usual. What's for dinner? You're not mad are you?" (33). She is oblivious to the place setting and correct silverware. Marcia is dynamic, eating "enthusiastically," and waving her hand "largely" (34). When Mr. Harris arrives (unannounced—at least not to David) she initiates the handshaking with Mr. Harris. Then like a stereotypical husband, she asks David to cut Mr. Harris a piece of pie.

By contrast, David is domestic. His sparse furnishings, little more than a "neat small table and four careful chairs," indicate his fastidiousness (30). He arranges every detail of his modest home. The floor plan of Marcia's apartment is the same as his, but its decor upsets him. Like a newlywed wife, he tells Marcia that he never made more than two pies before in his entire life. And he shakes hands with Mr. Harris "limply" (39). Also, he serves and cleans while Harris and Marcia talk.

As with many of Jackson's female characters—and like Jackson herself—reading and writing figure David's identity. According to the third-person narrator, the main room of David's studio apartment is "where David read and slept" (30). It features a bookcase and a pen in a holder. While waiting for Marcia, he reads a letter (and it is from his mother). He writes a note to Marcia to remind her of their dinner date. He signs his note to her as "D," which sounds like the androgynous name "Dee." And he lives up to his biblical namesake only by being dwarfed by his counterpart. Rather than slay a giant, David Turner continues his role of turning into a diminished, feminized victim. In addition, the story ends with him picking up her papers.

Mr. Harris fits the era's stereotype of the masculine male. He is big and smokes a cigar. He is empowered in the workplace—probably an owner or manager. His assumption that the woman made the dinner leads him to the deduction that the apartment he has entered is hers.

With Harris as the agent of change, Marcia and David become even more oppositely gendered. Marcia controls David by pretending that the apartment is hers and that she has made the dinner. She manipulates David with the same tone of voice that David had expected to use on Harris. Then David follows her casting of him in an even more feminized role. He wants to be "rid of them both" (37), but rather than kick them out, he says, "Thanks for a simply *wonderful* dinner, Marcia" and passively withdraws to Marcia's apartment (39). As soon as he gets there, he begins to clean it. David's work is never done.

It is not only gender but also class that leads Marcia to exploit David in order to minimize her own exploitation. Mr. Harris is Marcia's empowered superior. Apparently, it is after Marcia sees that Mr. Harris assumes the apartment is hers that she follows his casting of her in the domestic role. But it may be that she knew he was coming and that she would impress him by switching roles with David. At any rate, Harris is further masculinized, Marcia is further feminized in relation to Harris but further masculinized in relation to David, and David is further feminized in relation to both. Marcia is both exploited and exploiter. The gender reversal shows Jackson's Marxist notion that the central factor in this social formation is not sex but class—the power in the literal economy. The dominator and the dominated can be of either sex. Also, Jackson does not gloat over the empowerment of a woman or the feminization of a man.

"Trial by Combat" also uses the setting of twin apartments as a figuration of doubles. The protagonist is a young woman named Emily Johnson. Her counterpart, Mrs. Allen, one of Jackson's many characters with an androgynous name, is also one of Jackson's many sweet little old ladies who, like many of her sweet little children, turn out to be sour. Emily lives one storey above Mrs. Allen in an apartment identical to Mrs. Allen's. Emily has maple furniture, and Mrs. Allen's is the same; Emily's key fits Mrs. Allen's door, and Mrs. Allen's key fits Emily's door; Emily's husband is in the army, and Mrs. Allen's husband was in the army; Emily has no children, and Mrs. Allen has no children; Emily has flowers, and Mrs. Allen has flowers. Emily's older self begins stealing from her younger self. First, Emily is missing "an initial pin"—a signifier of her identity (41). Then she is missing cigarettes, a handkerchief, and earrings. Emily decides that Mrs. Allen must be the culprit, so she plans to sneak into her double's apartment.

A typical Jackson character, Emily writes her way into action. She writes (in this case a letter to her husband) and then goes to sleep (disrupting the plot and subject so that it is undecidable whether or not she may be dreaming or imagining from here on). In the morning, she calls in sick—that is to say, she makes up a story, and that story is about her absence. In case she gets caught, she prepares another story: "If anyone comes I can say I was mistaken about the floor." She enters Mrs. Allen's apartment while the old woman is away. Entering the private space of her counterpart, she has the uncanny experience that the unfamiliar is familiar: "For a minute, after she had opened the door, it seemed as though she *were* in her own room" (45). In this story about an Other's story, she also learns what it must be like not only to be Mrs. Allen, but to be Mrs. Allen in relation to Emily: "She had a sudden sense of unbearable intimacy with Mrs. Allen, and thought, This is the way she must feel in my room" (46). She finds the cigarettes, handkerchief, and earrings, but not the initial pin.

Yet she does find out about herself when Mrs. Allen inadvertently reveals that Emily is more dishonest than Emily's double. When Mrs. Allen catches Emily snooping in her drawers, the young woman changes her story and says she is searching for aspirin. Mrs. Allen says, "I'm glad you felt you knew me well enough" (47). The old lady allows her to have this lie, but not out of altruism, for it permits the old lady to avoid admitting her own guilt. In this psychological fable, each finds herself in the other—the other is not wholly Other. But each is a liar and a thief. The old woman keeps the initial pin because Emily cannot ask for it lest she reveal her true motive for invading the other's space.

"The Villager" also uses architecture to demonstrate the inter-changeability of identity. Miss Clarence, another of Jackson's many female characters with a man's name, resides in Greenwich Village. Now thirty-five, she went there at twenty-three to become a dancer but had to settle for being a stenographer. Following a text by answering an ad, she goes to a Mrs. Roberts's apartment to see about buying used furniture. Mrs. Roberts, another one of Jackson's androgynous charac-ters, is gone but leaves a note telling the protagonist to come in and look around. The protagonist can see from the artifacts that Mrs. Roberts also came to New York to be a dancer but met defeat. Mr. Roberts, an artist, phones and says he is going to Paris; he is evidently a success. Also, he is evidently dumping his wife: Mrs. Roberts is going back to her parents.

Inspired by a book of dance photographs, Miss Clarence tries out a dancing posture, one with which Mrs. Roberts would be familiar. But she finds that her old dancer self is so far gone—as absent as Mrs. Roberts—that the pose hurts. Then a would-be writer looking for furni-ture arrives—another of Jackson's many untrustworthy males named Harris. Whereas Miss Clarence is a failed artist, Mr. Harris is a begin-ning aspirant. He says he also needs a wife to do his cooking, as perhaps Mr. Roberts had needed one to help him get his career started. To Mr. Harris, the protagonist presents herself as Mrs. Roberts, her absent self, implying that she is not a former dancer but an active one. The soreness engendered by the pose lingers—her history stays with her. Although she has quit trying to read it, she carries a copy of *The Charterhouse of Parma* "for effect"—she is still posing (49). But the soreness that her pose caused will stay with her in even more debilitating ways. She is one of many Jackson characters who have failed in their youthful aspira-tions—in a romantic quest plot already ended—and now face a mun-dane, repetitive, entropic life. She is only a secretary who has no prospects and whose actual reading is the *Villager*, the text that con-structs and names her.

As "The Villager" features two sets of doubles, "The Dummy" features not only a ventriloquist and his partner but also two metaphoric dummies, a pair of women in the ventriloquist's audience. Like the dummy, which is literally wooden, Mrs. Wilkins's mouth opens and shuts wordlessly. Similarly Mrs. Straw, as genuine as a scarecrow, "watche[s] blankly" (207). There is essentially no difference between Wilkins and Straw, except that the latter is subservient to the former. For example, when Mrs. Wilkins remarks that the restaurant is clean, Mrs. Straw echoes her. Mrs. Straw also echoes herself. Of the ventriloquist she says, "I haven't seen one since I was a kid" (203) and then a little later, "I haven't seen one of those for years" (205). Similarly, her counterpart in the other pair of doubles, the dummy, repeats himself. Twice he tells the ventriloquist to tell the young woman with them to "shut up." Of course the dummy is really the ventriloquist repeating himself in the role of the dummy. And soon the ventriloquist repeats himself again, telling the young woman twice to "shut up" (206).

The dummy, "a grotesque wooden copy" (203) of the ventriloquist, is the performer's double. As an alcoholic, the ventriloquist is a kind of dummy himself, spoken through by demon rum, or more precisely through the subjects within the subject. As the addictive demons of the ventriloquist's unconscious express themselves through his conscious self, the ventriloquist displaces his anger by projecting it through the dummy. The wooden double calls the ventriloquist's girlfriend "old deadhead" (206). Similarly, the artist uses the dummy as his authorial surrogate by having the dummy add, "She can't make *me* stop"; "*I'm* the one making a fuss" (206). The ventriloquist employs his assistant as a scapegoat—he lets the dummy take the blame and punishment. Mrs. Wilkins is so literal minded that when the act offends her, she slaps the dummy. The setting for this madness is a "well-padded" restaurant (199).

The writerliness of this story obtains not only in the scripted quality of the performance, but also in the audience's response as a ritual. Consisting mostly of regulars, the audience knows the lines that are coming and laughs before the ventriloquist and the dummy finish delivering them. As it often is in Jackson's fiction, writing here is the basis of ritual. Indeed, ventriloquists and dummies evolved from ritual dolls.

"Come Dance with Me in Ireland," one of the *Best American Short Stories, 1944,* uses the double in a different way. Where the doubling of the ventriloquist and dummy allegorizes the subject within a subject by featuring two manifest subjects, "Come Dance with Me in Ireland" allegorizes the subject within a subject by having one character's conduct turn an about-face.

When three women apparently help an old beggar, their apparent selflessness turns out to be selfish. The women reveal that their charity derives not from a desire to help, but from a desire to believe they are helpful. While ostensibly solicitous, no one asks him to take off his coat. And Mrs. Archer does not want the old man to sit in "the good chair" (220). Likewise, her willingness to feed him turns out to derive from her need to do something with the leftovers from lunch. In addition, she puts his dishes not on a place mat but on a paper bag. Similarly, Mrs. Corn does not speak to him directly when she asks about his condition. Rather, she asks the other women, "Does *he* feel better now?" (221) In addition, Kathy has stereotypes about the poor: "They always eat pie" (223). And they assume that an Irish pauper must be an alcoholic. Mrs. Archer reveals her sense of superiority when she complains that living on the bottom floor exposes her to the proletarians who ring her door-bell—she believes she is above their level. She has climbed (or perhaps sunk) to the lower rungs on the middle-class ladder, and identifies with those higher.

At first the old man selling shoelaces door-to-door seems to be merely passive. He says pathetic, self-pitying things, for example, that Mrs. Archer is "the first person on this block who has been decently polite to a poor old man" (219). He appears dependent, but he is a passive-aggressive manipulator playing on the women's sympathy and guilt. For example, he pretends to be weaker than he really is: "The old man started to offer her some shoelaces, but his hands shook and the shoelaces dropped to the floor." But the apparently guileless third-person narration uses the ambiguous qualifier "seemed": The derelict "seemed barely able . . . to stand" (220). By playing on their guilt, he gets a meal from them. Then his true self comes out when he acts superior to them. If the reader shares the women's stereotypes, the reader is as surprised as the women when the old man, having eaten his fill, turns the tables on them by correcting their manners. Acting out a satiric parody of their hypocritical benevolence, he drops shoelaces on their floor and says contemptuously, "for your kindness" (225). Moreover, he says that unlike them he "never served bad sherry" to his guests. He adds, "We are of two different worlds, Madam" (226).

But just as the last laugh may be on Edgar Allen Poe's Montresor in "The Cask of Amontillado" (in the emblem of the snake being ground underfoot, the snake is biting back at the heel, and Montresor may be confessing on his deathbed, about to meet his Maker) the old Irishman is not as intellectually superior as he thinks he is (part of the humor is that he is a fool feeling superior to others for their foolishness). He tries to turn the tables by spouting a William Butler Yeats poem, "I Am of

Ireland." This poem derives from a medieval ballad, just as the haunt-ingly recurrent but varying character of James Harris does. Just as Jack-son will use Harris to figure women's illusions, so here a male character is trapped in his illusion. Thus even though the protagonist seems to have defeated the women, the larger ideology defeats him while he con-tinues to subscribe to it. He attempts to analogize Ireland to America as culture to barbarism only to reveal the extent to which he is imbued with the attitudes that oppresses him. The old man is a victim of ideol-ogy and recycles that ideology. By being hypocritical and unkind him-self, he assures that the next hungry person needing a handout will not get it from any of these women. This fable, then, moralizes about the arrogance of humility on both sides.

The narration seems dependable but really is not. By taking the old man as the point-of-view character and yet keeping the vantage point outside of his head, Jackson dislocates the reader by showing that the reader will identify with the women. As such, Jackson fools the reader, thereby making the reader interchangeable with the hypocritical women. As Poe in "The Cask of Amontillado" puts the reader and Fortunato in the same benighted position of the butt of the joke who receives the clues but does not understand them, so Jackson puts her reader in the same benighted position as the three women who receive clues but do not understand them. Fortunato, these women, and the reader are all unaware of the fact that they are playing the role of the fool and that Montresor and the old man have written their scripts for them. The plot inversion, with the old man being victim then victimizer then victim; the reversal of subject positions, with each character turning out to be the opposite of what he or she appears to be; the deceptiveness of the nar-ration, which withholds information so that the reader enters the story as another fool—all of these techniques make this a proto-postmod-ernist story.

The next three stories move from figurations of the double to figu-rations of the Other. In "The Daemon Lover," the boundary between the third-person narrator and the point-of-view character is ambiguous. The third-person narration looks so thoroughly through the protagonist's perception that the narrator reports on the protagonist's delusions as if they are verifiable. Consequently, the narration creates the same illusion in both the protagonist's mind and in the reader's mind.[4]

The fallibility of the narration begins to emerge with the report that the protagonist drinks a lot of coffee and yet falls asleep. While it is possible to drink coffee and fall asleep, the ambiguity of that report seems to be a result of the narrator's immersion in the protagonist's mind. The unreliability of the narration merges with the unreliability of the point-of-view character's perceptions when the narrator states that the protagonist did not think until the morning of the wedding what dress to wear for the occasion. Similarly, the narrator implies in free indirect discourse that the protagonist does not know much about the man she is to marry: "What sort of person was he actually?" (20). The protagonist cannot remember Jamie's voice or even his face. Likewise, she has never been to his apartment before. Jackson implies that the talking the protagonist hears is in the protagonist's mind. The narrator's report that the protagonist "could hear voices" is not the same as reporting that there actually were voices. And to suggest that the character imagines hearing voices is to suggest delusional perceptions. (Yet it also suggests that the voices could be real and that therefore there could be some reality to the character's paranoia.) Similarly, the report that when an apartment dweller opened his door "the music swept out at her" (16) suggests both that the character's perceptions might be delusions (that the music is aggressive toward her) and that they might not.

On the other hand, as the characterization develops, the unnamed subject appears more clearly schizoid. This repressive splitting appears to be exacerbated by her consumption of a lot of coffee, cigarettes, and aspirin all on an empty stomach, which makes her "dizzy and weak" (13). Her internal splitting begins to appear when she forgets to change the sheets before their wedding night, but then when she does remember to change the sheets, she continues to deny the reason why she is changing them: "They planned to come back here tonight and everything must be correct. With sudden horror she realized that she had forgotten to put clean sheets on the bed, . . . working quickly to avoid thinking consciously of why she was changing the sheets" (10). It is not just the sexual association to the sheets she represses but also the textual. The man she imagines marrying is a writer.[5] This delusion projects her own denied textualizing, as does her giving him what could be a woman's first name. At first she projects Jamie on to the apartment dweller, who is "for a minute resembling Jamie" (17). Despite the story's elusiveness, its fantastic techniques lend themselves to a psychological reading.[6]

The development of the subject proceeds through textuality. In the first paragraph, she awakes from a dream text but only apparently (in Jackson, waking up is not total). After awakening from a dream, she immediately moves metonymically from dreaming to reading and then to writing: "She sat down to read, thought she might write a letter to her sister instead, and began, in her finest handwriting" (9). But as she has just done with the dreaming and the reading, she quickly quits writing. After giving up on the sheets of paper, she remembers the sheets of linen on her "studio bed," where she composes her dream texts (10).

The fictionalizing within is also without. The lines around her eyes tell part of her story, but she writes most of it. She casts herself as a character, and then revises that characterization. In the blue dress, she is familiar: "She had worn it several times with Jamie." So she decides to change to a "print" dress (11). As Jackson had done, she has fictionally misrepresented herself on her marriage license as younger than she is. When she goes to find him at the place where she believes he lives, his name is not on the mailbox. When she returns to her apartment after a trip to the drugstore, the note she left for him on her door is unread (but that report comes from a narration reported through a delusional character—how would she know it is unread?).

The architecture also suggests not just character but the protagonist's writing. She imagines that a building is a person: "The apartment doors lined up, four on the floor, uncommunicative and silent" (16). Similarly, it is while she is sitting at the window that she believes she has fallen asleep. Like a writer sitting down at a sheet of paper that is framed by a margin, the protagonist sits down at a framed window, looks out, and her vision projects a world—a world in which she will no longer be a pink-collar spinster, a world in which she will be married to a writer. Jackson modernizes the Gothic motif of the mirror.[7] Where the mirror in traditional Gothic not only reflects the percipient but also allows the percipient to see through it, the window in Jackson's fiction not only allows the percipient to see through it but also reflects the percipient. The protagonist also frames herself when she stands in a doorway and asks herself of her ostensibly impending wedding, "Is it really *true?*" (12) Neither she nor the narrator answers.

The plot develops according to the reader response of the characters to whom she tells her story. She starts with a two-part description of him: he is a tall, fair writer and often wears a blue suit. Her story grows as her audience gives her more revisions of it. Each of the characters from whom she seeks information about Jamie is preoccupied with textuality and more concerned with self-interest—usually financial—than with helping her.

First she goes to what she believes is Jamie's apartment. She begins by asking the apartment manager which apartment is Jamie's. He says he never heard of him but that Jamie might have sublet the Roysters' unit. Mr. Royster and his wife apparently really think that Jamie might have been the sublessor who damaged their apartment—they fit her fiction into their lives. But how would they not know to whom they sublet it? And even if Jamie used an alias, the Roysters and the protagonist do not ask each other any of the detailed questions that would establish whether or not Jamie was their sublessor. She takes that possibility and fits it back into her fiction—she believes them and suspects that he has moved without telling her. Like all of the men she talks to, Mr. Royster is more involved in his own textual concerns. As he responds to her, Royster talks into his magazine, changing her text as much as processing it.

Next, she inquires at a delicatessen. There the man she speaks with is more interested in reading a newspaper than in helping her. She suspects that the reason for his lack of sympathy is that she's "not buying anything" (19).

Next she goes to a man at a newsstand. Instead of continuing to say that Jamie often wears a blue suit, she now says that Jamie is wearing a blue suit on this particular day. While the Roysters might have been feigning interest, this newsdealer clearly pretends. At first he says there are too many men in blue suits for anyone to stand out; then to get rid of her so he can deal with another customer, he says he saw a man matching Jamie's description. His pretense becomes obvious (though not to her) when he makes a face to another customer. When she asks if he saw him at about ten in the morning, he says yes. When she asks what direction Jamie was heading, the news dealer says uptown. She believes his fiction, adding it to the story that she and her audience are writing together.

This textualization continues when she asks a florist if a tall man in a blue suit came in at about ten in the morning; he looks in his logbook. He says he's sure Jamie was there and bought chrysanthemums, adding that she should buy flowers too. Now she keeps this added detail alive, looking for not only a writer in a blue suit, but someone tall and headed uptown with chrysanthemums.

Continuing her circulation in this literal and textual economy, she sees a shoeshine man (whose customers typically read while being serviced). He tells her that a man matching this extended description walked by. He adds to the fiction by saying the man looked like he was going to see a girl—something he could not have known.

Finally she circles home (figuratively she has not really left). Here there is another hint that Jamie is an imaginary character split off and projected: "For a minute she saw only the empty coffee cup, thought, He has been here waiting, before she recognized it as her own" (25).

This textualization ends when she heads out again (or perhaps imagines that she does) and sees a boy. The lad imagines that she is going to divorce her man and manipulates her for a dollar in exchange for what he knows about Jamie. He directs her to an apartment. No one answers at the first door. The second she finds empty except for discarded paper: "There was a crumpled florist's paper on the floor outside the door, and a knotted paper ribbon, like a clue, like the final clue in the paper-chase" (27). Still the protagonist does not catch on and imagines that Jamie is behind the first door. She comes back daily but no one answers her knock. As her story begins at a window frame and doorframe, it ends at a doorframe. Along the way, she was afraid to talk to the only man she saw who was probably wearing a blue suit: a police officer.

Jamie comes from a ballad called "James Harris, The Daemon Lover," which Jackson probably discussed with Hyman, who was an expert on ballads. In this one, reprinted at the end of this anthology, Harris is a sailor absent for seven years and presumed dead. He returns to his lover, but she has married and borne children. Nonetheless, she yields to temptation and follows him to sea, whereupon he turns out to be the devil. (A recurrent theme in Jackson's fiction is the discovery of the true evil of people in general and of the male love object in particular.)

This story is enabled by another short story by the same title. One of her favorite writers, Elizabeth Bowen, also used this ballad for an undecidable Gothic tale. But in the end, the Bowen version leaves the strong possibility that the demon lover could be supernatural—an actual visitor from the dead. By contrast, the undecidability of Jackson's version results from the ambiguous boundary between narrator and character, between character and setting, and between reader and text. The uncanny quality derives from the protagonist's subject formation and from her circulation based on textuality.

Like many of Jackson's characters (and Jackson herself), the protagonist in "Pillar of Salt" is her own double. Margaret views herself through the eyes of others. For example, she worries about what even strangers in the street will think of her, yet Margaret is in denial about what they must be thinking of her. She is anxious about being revealed, but also worries about being invisible. When the party guests overlook her, she says to herself twice, "I might as well not be here." Her anxious desire to be both anonymous and yet acknowledged leads her to imagine (apparently) that a fire a few buildings away is right next door. She panics and flees the building, but later says that she left to check out the fire and that she "felt trapped" because "they wouldn't listen" (241). At the end, she goes out for a newspaper because she feels claustrophobic, only to have an agoraphobic panic attack. Her anxious movements are so odd that pedestrians now part as this frenzied character passes by, yet she is in denial about their response, still thinking they do not notice her.

As before, Jackson destabilizes the third-person focalization by immersing it in the point-of-view character, Margaret. Moreover, the narration sometimes slides in and out of second person, thereby merging narrator, point-of-view character, and reader. As a result, the reader must hold various possible explanations in mind while receiving more evidence. Also like many of Jackson's protagonists, this one undergoes psychic disintegration in a setting that is also disintegrating. Because the limited omniscient third-person narrator takes the protagonist's point of view, the reader cannot be sure how much the setting's disintegration is Margaret's projection, and how much her disintegration results from the setting. Qualifiers such as "it seemed" (249, 251) "she heard" (240), and "she had begun to notice" (243) condition the narrative reports. For example, "She stopped suddenly when it seemed to her that the windowsill she had just passed had soundlessly crumpled and fallen into fine sand." But the narrator also reports the crumpling as if it is actually happening: "When she looked across the street, the . . . sills [were] dissolving and falling downward" (249).

The image of the built environment disintegrating as a figure of the subject's disintegration begins just before the protagonist enters the city—in the middle landscape between the rural and urban, a place that in American myth is supposed to be a golden mean of stability but here is a figure of dislocation. Next she and Brad mention that an airplane recently hit the Empire State Building. Then she sees a taxi door held on with string, and then the taxi gets a flat tire. Similarly, buses are cracking open. Likewise, "corners of the buildings seemed to be crumbling away" (243). After being in the city for a few days, she takes the train out to the suburbs and again experiences the breakdown of her self and the city as she travels through the liminal edge of town:

> Passing through the outskirts of the city, she thought, It's as though everything were traveling so fast that the solid stuff couldn't stand it and were going to pieces under the strain, cornices blowing off and windows caving in. . . . It was a voluntary neck-breaking speed, a deliberate whirling faster and faster to end in destruction. (244)

As a result of her apocalyptic visions—but also in concert with her recognition of entropy—she concludes that the disintegration begins on the margins: "I suppose it starts to happen first in the suburbs, . . . people starting to come apart" (248). She hates the traffic light for being "a dumb thing, turning back and forth, back and forth, with no purpose and no meaning," yet she becomes like the light, dumb and turning back and forth (252).

That it is Margaret who is disintegrating appears more clearly when she experiences gaps in her memory, suggesting that another personality has taken over. In the next passage, the conscious states called "Margaret" are absent after her body gets in the cab, goes somewhere that is outside of Margaret's (and the narrator's and the reader's) awareness, and then comes back to the cab; similarly, she (and the narrator and the reader) are not sure of everything she does between the moment when she gets on the elevator up to her room and the moment when she gets on it back down: "She stepped into the taxi on one side and stepped out the other side at her home; she pressed the fifth floor button on the elevator and was coming down again, bathed and dressed and ready for dinner with Brad" (244). Despite the fantastic narration, this story is finally resolvable as a psychological fable.

In this story, writing about representation includes various forms of representation. As usual, the characters read. On the train from a small town in New Hampshire (only a few miles from Jackson and Hyman's home in Bennington, Vermont) the husband has a magazine, and he does not look up from it when talking to Margaret. She has a mystery book. She carries a list of plays and things to buy. Pictorial representation emerges when they enter their friend's apartment and recognize it because each of them "carries private pictures" of it in their minds (237). She also carries a picture in her mind of a theatrical production. She visualizes the children of New York acting out "parodies" of adults with toy cash registers, toy mailboxes, small phonographs, and even children's cosmetics (242). In addition, when Margaret was young she knew New York only from movies. Musical representation appears as she regresses to the days when she was fifteen or sixteen hearing a tune in her head from that time. These various forms of representation combine. For example, when the protagonist cannot get the old tune out of her head, she forgets whether it is from a play or a movie. She also remembers not just musical theater but also movie musicals.

Representation also characterizes the setting. Jackson uses forms of the term *arrange* to describe place: outside the apartment, "New York was below, as arranged" (237). Jackson also uses the musical term *arrangements* to depict time: "All arrangements [are] made" (235–36) and the events will follow "the smoothness of unopposed arrangements" (236). Music combines with architecture and text to register the disintegration of both subject and setting. When Margaret scans the building in sync with the tune in her head, she looks across each storey of windows from left to right, stopping at each window in time with each note of the tune, just as one might read sheet music or scan a poem for meter. The building is like a page of music: she reads it from left to right and top to bottom. The tune also takes her back to thoughts of writing. In the recurring fantasy that she uses to escape her alienating existence, she imagines herself on a beach writing love stories. (The beach was the place of Jackson's Edenic childhood, the Eden that she had to trade for upstate New York—from shoveling sand to shoveling snow.) The beach and sand are recurrent scenes in her characters' dreams of escape from domesticity, but also the scene of their fantasy romance with a James Harris, the figure who promises deliverance but who returns them to even worse conditions. Thus Jackson uses music to trace the metonymic chain of desire. According to Jacques Lacan, "All discourse is aligned along the several staves of a score" (Stoltzfus 9).

Representation, then, is a medium for disrupting repression. It facilitates regression into the unconscious. For example, when Margaret is on the train, she has "nothing to do but read and nap" (235). When she is stressed, she repeats to herself, "No sense worrying . . . as though it were a charm against witches" (250). Her chant is a ritual, and as such it is part of ideology's imaginary solution to real problems. Her response to seeing a building crumble is similarly obsessive. She reverts to rituals of domesticity by remaking the bed. But this regression figures not a turn away from the Symbolic, but a return to the realization that all of the Symbolic's representations are arranged like a language. In other words, representation in this story accesses the social text. Critics have mistaken stories like this one as evidence that the anxieties of Jackson and her characters are private. But Jackson's fictions undermine the opposition of private and public. Many introjections as well as dissociations constitute Jackson's subjects. Her subjects are not unified but rather are the sum total of many conflicting and even competing subject and object positions.

In "The Tooth," the subject splits and the new consciousness casts off the old self and follows a new imaginary identity. Through years of a stultifying marriage, Clara Spencer has lost much of her self. As the center of what remains of her after several years of marriage, Clara's aching and rotting tooth figures what remains of her identity after marriage: it is "the only part of her to have any identity." In fact, when the dentist x-rays her tooth, it seems "to have had its picture taken without her" (276). Her husband points out that her tooth started to go bad as soon as they got married. Thus her identity of pain and decay is a displacement of her unmarried, pre-oedipal self. As Clara puts it, "I just feel as if I were all tooth" (266). If pain and decay are her identity, and if her identity is that she is his wife, she can, according to her metonymic associations, be rid of him and her miserable self by getting rid of the tooth. Her "lunatic flight from her home" is a crazy attempt to get rid of husband, current identity, and tooth.

Little wonder that with this psychology fueled by several chemicals, she is disturbed by "fantastic sleep" (270). The plot starts to develop with the protagonist having consumed codeine, whiskey, and a sleeping pill, but nothing to eat. As her bus journey from the small town to the big city continues, she drinks enormous amounts of coffee, yet repeatedly falls asleep readily—entering the unconscious. For Jackson's characters, energy does not move to one pole or the other; rather, it moves to both poles at once. Like the divided subjects in "The Pillar of Salt" and "The Daemon Lover," Clara is her own mirror opposite. She is hyper and hypo, agitated and numb. And furthermore like the protagonist in "The Daemon Lover," she is not so much falling asleep as going into other psychological states, quite possibly another personality. As her oral surgeon's anesthesia takes effect, she imagines herself leaving down a hallway—a transformation that suggests death. When she awakes, she asks the nurse, "Why did you pull me back? . . . I wanted to go on" (281). After she leaves, she throws away the prescription for pain pills—she is so alienated from her old self that she does not feel the pain. In the women's lavatory, she is standing at the sink with several other women. She looks into the mirror in front of them and cannot tell which one she is: "You'd think my own face would know me." She wonders if the mirror, rather than a reflective depiction of herself and the others, is a window onto reality outside the edifice of herself: "Perhaps it's not a mirror, she thought, maybe it's a window and I'm looking straight through at women washing on the other side" (283).

As does the woman in the ballad "James Harris, The Daemon Lover," Clara hears the siren call of temptation. A figure she calls "Jim" bids her to "come along" (271). Later the nurse who leads Clara to the near-death experience says the same words—this after a "grave professional doorman" ushers her into the medical building (286). (Like its title, *Come Along with Me*, the novel she had started just before she died begins by implying that the reader is coming along with the protagonist. But perhaps the protagonist was answering the call of another James Harris.) Like the anonymous protagonist of "The Daemon Lover" splitting off her subject position as a writer, Clara projects her denied masculine in the figure of Jim, who is tall and wearing a blue suit. Like the protagonist in "The Pillar of Salt," she associates romantic love with the beach—the adolescent Eden of Jackson's youth in California before the fall into not only sexual maturation but also the great depression in both senses.

The plot, then, is a satiric parody of the quest for romantic love. The protagonist's transition from the world of marriage to the world of erotic fantasy is a would-be escape. But instead of leaving domesticity behind, she returns to the prison of domesticity by way of the vestibule of romantic love. Following the chimerical Jim, she escapes the domestic dream gone bad by pursuing the romantic myth that impelled her toward dependency in the first place. As such, she goes from the epilogue of the metanarrative of romance back to the prologue. In her end is her beginning. She is an emblem of the antiromantic stories studied by Marianne Hirsch, who says, "The absence of plot and progression locks woman into an endless moment from which she is incapable of emerging; beginning and end, origin and destination are identical" (45). Jackson foreshadows this sad circular history when Clara comes back from her near-death experience saying, "God has given me blood to drink," an allusion to Nathaniel Hawthorne's words for a similar eternal return in *The House of the Seven Gables* (247). So again Jackson's Gothic proto-postmodernism unsettles plot convention.

And again she uses deceptive third-person narration in league with destabilized characterization. As before, she uses the term *seem* or its derivations or synonyms: "There were labyrinths and passages, seeming to lead into the heart of the office building" (279). As before, the third-person narration focuses through a point-of-view character who is disordered. For example, the subject's consciousness merges with the setting. In her semiconsciousness, the bus is "panting" (265) and "groan[ing]" (268) and passing "sleeping houses" (271). And in the subject's mind the two primary elements of the setting—space and time—merge. For example, faces disappear "in the space of a second" (284). As a result of these dislocations, the narrator reports the fact that the bus moved along the road by stating Clara's subjective experience: the "street slipped past" (268). Furthermore, the narration sometimes does not clarify whether Clara is conscious or unconscious because she is often "not aware she ha[s] fallen asleep again" (270). On the other hand, in Jackson's fiction even if a character is in the unconscious the experience is not necessarily delusional. Just because she dreamed it does not necessarily mean it did not happen.

Although, as several critics have shown, women in "The Lottery" are more prone than men to be the victims of the stoning,[8] it is also important that women are more likely to be the victims of the general exploitation ritualized by the lottery. First of all, the lottery encourages childbearing. It derives from a midsummer fertility ritual, the incantation of which is "Lottery in June, corn be heavy soon" (297). And by having two rounds in the lottery, the ritual enforces the mind-set that encourages maximum childbearing: first someone draws for each nuclear family, and then each member in the family draws to determine the loser. So a married woman minimizes her chances of being selected by delivering babies early and often. (A large family also increases the father's chance of survival, and most of their care does not fall to him.) Her financial exploitation precedes her ultimate victimization. Jackson indicated this prior abuse in the way she performed this story. She read the last line as if it is a question: "And *then* they were upon her?" (302).

They were upon her before the stoning, and the referent of the pronoun "they" includes not just men but women, all of whom endorse the dominant culture. Tess sees nothing wrong with the lottery until she is about to die, and then she complains only about the process of selection. Thus she subscribes to legalistic discourse. She tries to circumvent the absurd judgment only by questioning the procedure involved. Moreover Tess tries to save herself by shifting the risk to her daughter. She tries to get her married daughter to draw with Tess's family, even though the rules state that married daughters will draw with their new nuclear families.

The contradictions of myth and ideology, the imaginary solutions to real problems, emerge in the specific rituals that ostensibly endorse the myth and ideology. "The Lottery" exposes time's degradation of the original myth and ritual. Jackson's first version was set on 26 June, the summer solstice. *The New Yorker*'s editors cleverly changed it to 27 June, the day of publication, which makes this story even more a document about the corruption of myth and ritual, for the townsfolk seemingly do not know that they are celebrating on the wrong day. In addition, many of the original accoutrements have been lost. Others have been modified: originally the participants drew wood chips, but they now draw scraps of paper. In addition, "there was a story that the present box had been made with some pieces of the box that had preceded it," but no one remembers that part of their oral tradition (293). Also, the villagers have abandoned parts of the ritual—for example, the recitation of a chant or song. In addition, justifications become circular. This town keeps doing it because other towns keep doing it (and yet other towns have stopped, but this one does not follow their lead). Also, the justifications ignore the obvious. When Mrs. Graves says "All of us took the same chance," she ignores the fact that individuals from larger families have a smaller chance of being victimized (298). Moreover, the officials are the new secular priests: the postmaster, a petty government functionary, and the coal company owner (who is therefore probably one of the richest people in town). What the villagers do remember— what they do conserve—is to be cruel and selfish.

In one of the best analyses of the many written about this story, Peter Kosenko's Marxist reading shows that this ritual endorses not only totalitarianism but also liberal capitalism. The characters observe the ultimate logic of rugged individualism: the isolated individual sacrifices not only other citizens but also his or her family. In that respect, family here is what it was for the nineteenth-century farmer: to get cheap labor, parents are obligated to have as many children as possible. This story thereby exposes the economic base of family values in rural America. And very importantly, Mr. Warner is not only a Jeremiah urging the town to stick with the past, but also the liberal prophet of continued prosperity. He says they will go back to being cavemen if they do not stick to the old ways (which derived from cavemen).

This story also disables both the dominant literary movement and the dominant school of criticism in Jackson's time. "The Lottery" exposes the reactionary tendencies not only of the mythy modernists, but also of the myth and symbol school of literary criticism (and its cohort, the consensus school historians). The origins of myth are in witchcraft. In fact, it is Others' myths and rituals that we call "witchcraft." But of course the modernists reified myth, and the myth and symbol school often valorized that reification by papering over the ideology implicit in myth. For Jackson, premodern cultures have witch doctors, and modernity has critics like Stanley Edgar Hyman, whom she will increasingly undermine in her fiction. As such, this story participates in the decline of modernism, New Criticism, and the myth and symbol school, even though it uses myth and ritual, and even though it does not supersede its prior texts by becoming fully postmodern.

One aspect of the inchoate postmodernism of this tale is its writing about writing. At the beginning of the story, several schoolchildren are talking about schoolbooks. Paper succeeds the original wood chips. Mr. Summers has written the X with a "heavy pencil" mark (301). One of the men overseeing this marking is the postmaster—one who polices the exchange of writing. But the writerliness of this story also lies in the plot's frustration of reader expectation, which results in both recognition and incredulity. As Philip Roth would say thirteen years later, the fiction writer cannot rely on the techniques of realism to delineate either the stupefying absurdity of reality, or the sickening reality of absurdity (224). There is also the subtle dark humor in the names: a female victim named Hutchinson; a Jeremiah named Warner; a deadly summer fertility ritual directed by a Mr. Summers; and a Mr. Graves, who greets Summers "gravely" (297).

A more important aspect of this tale's nascent postmodernism is its theme. Not only is the surface of events random, but even the mythic infrastructure, far from the purportedly stable mythic base of modernism, is an imaginary solution to real problems. What is worse, those myths resist interrogation. In other words, this story's subjects, like Claude Levi-Strauss's pensive savages, cannot read the determinants of their contradictions. Rather than understand that their social formation is absurd, they militantly embody that absurdity.[9] They have no inkling of the logic of their absurdity, the determinants of their social formations. The general pattern is determinate: the victimization will continue, and the victim will more often be female. But the particulars of the absurdity, the imaginary solution, hide the determinacy with a random surface: it is indeterminable who the exact victims will be.

Jackson's next anthology also exhibits such proto-postmodernist forms as third-person unreliable narration, writing about writing, and psychological fables, plus such themes as the disunified subject, the role of language in subject formation, and, as Joan Wylie Hall demonstrates, the strict gender roles of the 1940s and 1950s.

CHAPTER THREE

# Come Along with Me: Part of a Novel, Sixteen Stories, and Three Lectures

The best stories of this posthumous anthology compare with the finest of *The Lottery or, The Adventures of James Harris*. The *New York Times Book Review* included *Come Along with Me* among the "Best Fiction of 1968." Its ability to compete with Jackson's first anthology results from the fact that these stories come from not just a few years' production but rather from her whole career. Since she wrote many of these stories after her first anthology, the second volume features significant developments in her theme of writing about writing, in her psychological fables of the double, and in her manipulation of unreliable narration.

"The Beautiful Stranger" showcases Jackson's technique of slowly and almost imperceptibly moving the limited third-person viewpoint from a somewhat unreliable position outside the point-of-view character, to a very unreliable point of view inside the delusional character's mind, and then back out to a somewhat unreliable position again. Jackson limits the third-person narration and reports thoroughly through the eyes of the protagonist to such a degree that the reader must process the situation in the way the protagonist does. Jackson, then, puts the reader into the story by making the reader read the way the protagonist reads.[1]

The possibility that the reports may be filtered through a delusional subject first appears on the second page. As the protagonist waits at the train station for her husband, the third-person narrator implies that Margaret does not know if she is coming or going. The narrator states that the protagonist "could not for a minute remember clearly whether she was coming home, or whether they were yet standing here to say good-by to him." Next comes another suggestion that the protagonist is disturbed. Before her husband left, she had thought about unifying her subject positions: "While John is gone I can try to get hold of myself again" (59). But her self is not one self but several. For this subject to get hold of herself, she must still hold onto her contraries.

The reader must negotiate the possibility that the narrator's reports are dependable even though they filter through an unsettled point-of-view character. For example, even if Margaret is disturbed she could nonetheless be right when she thinks her returning husband seems taller. Likewise, she could be right in perceiving that he "hesitated noticeably before he spoke" (60). Moreover, Jackson encourages the reader to identify with the protagonist and to regard her as sympathetic by implying that her husband has abused her: "This is not the man who enjoyed seeing me cry" (61).

On the other hand, her ideation seems to get increasingly unreliable. Qualifiers such as "she was aware" or "thought" introduce reports. For example, "She was aware from his smile that he had perceived her doubts" (63) and "She assured herself with the thought that naturally he would have taken some pains to inform himself before coming." She seems to have an incipient delusion of persecution: "There was, she thought, an edge of laughter behind his words" (61). Her belief that this man is not her husband but an imposter in a conspiracy to fool her seems to be even more delusional. When he seems to know minor details about her—for example, how she likes her martini—she rationalizes that the conspirators have helped this "beautiful stranger" to study up on her. When he seems to her not to know or remember certain facts—who their Shakespeare professor was, for example—she believes that he has let her in on the secret: "After he knew that she had recognized him for a stranger, he had never made any attempt to say words like 'coming home'"; in fact, "they laughed at his parody of John" (61–62). Absurdly, then, she believes she is a privileged participant in the plot against her: "When she called him 'John' she did so demurely, knowing that he participated in her secret amusement. . . . They seemed to have agreed soberly that mention of the subject would be in bad taste, might even, in fact, endanger their pleasure."

The impetus for this delusion appears to be her desire for a replacement of her husband. The imposter is attentive, considerate, and solicitous. So the romance is back: "There was an odd illicit excitement in all of it; she was 'entertaining' a man" (61). She even does housework happily. But her happiness depends upon her denial: "She was happy, she was radiant, she had no conscience." As an example of losing her conscience, she is not just committing adultery but in exchange robbing

John of his labor: "She would gladly share with him—indeed, give him outright—all that had been John's" (62). But she gets anxious about her freedom and tries to collect herself by going shopping. When she tries to return to her home (usually the self in Jackson's fiction) she is so dissociated that she cannot find her house.

Thus the theme of the demon lover returns: the protagonist imagines that a knight in shining armor has arrived to take her away from all of this. But "this" is the place her previous knight took her to get away from it all. As the narrator anxiously reports of the stranger, "He had not bothered to master all of the past, then; he had learned enough . . . to get to her" (63–64). The final narrative vantage point is from outside of Margaret, showing her lost in the suburbs. But this demon lover is not the only trickster in Jackson's fiction. She often seduces the reader into regarding as dependable something that clearly emerges as issuing primarily from the subject's Imaginary—and from the reader's as well.

"The Summer People," named one of the *Best American Short Stories, 1951,* again creates ambiguity through manipulation of narrative point of view. This time the third-person limited narration begins outside the point-of-view character, Mrs. Allison. She and her husband are a retired New York couple staying at their summer cottage. Because the narration is sympathetic to her biases from the start, the surface seems to endorse the couple's fears, but the subtext exposes those fears as bourgeois anxiety about the underclass. As such, this story anticipates one of postmodernism's central themes: paranoia.

Even though they still get their heating oil, newspapers, radio programs, and processed food from the big city, the older couple subscribe to the romantic myth that small towns have not been penetrated by urban improvidence: "'Makes you feel good, knowing there are still towns like this,' Mr. Allison said." His wife shares the mind-set that one can have pre-industrial simplicity just upstate from industrial complexity, so she buys some dishes in the little town: "'You know, in New York,' Mrs. Allison said, 'I might have paid a few cents less for these dishes, but there wouldn't have been anything sort of personal in the transaction'" (69). Even the narration speaks in the voice of the bucolic myth: "It was not possible to remain troubled long in the face of the day; the country had never seemed more inviting, and the lake moved quietly below them, among the trees, with the almost incredible softness of a summer picture" (74). The narration thereby encourages the reader not only to sympathize with the couple, but also to rehearse their notions about the innocence of small towners.

However, a note of qualification slips into the heart of the heart of the country, a note of nature's insouciance: "Both times when she looked the sky was clear and serene, smiling indifferently down on the Allison's summer cottage as well as on the rest of the world" (75–76). The narrator reports as objective fact, rather than Mrs. Allison's bias, that the gestures of the locals are irritating. For example, the heating oil delivery man taps his finger "exasperatingly" against the steering wheel (72). Likewise, the old clerk in the hardware store wraps newspaper around plates "maddeningly." (The narrator's bias hides the fact that the locals would not be exasperated or maddened; these are Mrs. Allison's observations.) Then the narrator subverts the bucolic myth of the good country people. Their resistance to newness reveals them as old-fashioned. The ostensibly objective narrator editorializes, "The country people, with their instinctive distrust of anything that did not look as permanent as trees and rocks and sky, had only recently begun to experiment in aluminum baking dishes instead of ironware, and had, apparently within the memory of local inhabitants, discarded stoneware in favor of iron" (68). The older couple from the big city informs the natives that these urbanites will be staying on at their cabin past Labor Day, which is longer than they or any other city visitor has ever done before. The locals seem inscrutably taken aback. Through gossip, seemingly everybody in town soon knows the old couple is staying on, which the Allisons take as vaguely threatening.

A string of coincidental occurrences leaves the city folk suspicious, projecting their feelings of superiority, which are implicit in their patronizing valorization of rustics. When one of the dishes they buy from Charley at the country store has a chip in it, the narrator reports this incident ironically, slanting it toward the way in which the protagonists and the urbane reader see it: "In his innocence Charley Walpole had neglected to notice the chip in the edge of one " (70). (As with "The Renegade" in *The Lottery,* a seemingly innocuous character has the ominous name of Walpole.) When the heating oil supplier tells them he has none left to sell them, they start to suspect there is a conspiracy. Like the nineteenth-century descendants (Nathaniel Hawthorne, Herman Melville, Henry Adams, etc.) of the first families of New England believing that declension had hit their relatives and neighbors, the old woman believes that these people (the grocer looks to her like Daniel Webster) have declined: "It was horrible to think into what old New England Yankee stock had degenerated" (68). Next the old woman thinks her son Jerry's letter does not sound like him, as if his letter is a hoax as part of the townies' conspiracy to run them off so they can perform some Hawthornian devilment. She draws that conclusion and then looks for evidence to support it but finds none: "It was impossible to find any sentence, any word, even, that did not sound like Jerry's regular letters. Perhaps it was only that the letter was so late, or the unusual number of dirty fingerprints on the envelope" (77). Next the old man thinks that the reason why his car will not start is that someone has meddled with it; he draws that conclusion even though he evidently has little mechanical knowledge: "The car had been tampered with, you know. Even I could see that." He cannot fix the car, apparently because he does not know how. Next the slanted narrative point of view seems to endorse the characters' belief that the reason why the telephone is out of order is that someone severed the wires: "Mrs. Allison hesitated a minute and then said very softly, 'I suppose the phone wires were cut.' 'I imagine so,' Mr. Allison said." But neither of them has checked. Mr. Allison implies that he detected a plot almost twenty-four hours ago. One of the locals had told Mr. Allison that the Halls, who supply the Allisons with butter and eggs, are traveling. For Mr. Allison, the fact that there was a light on at the Halls' house means there is a conspiracy: "'I knew when I saw the light down at the Hall place last night,' Mr. Allison said" (78).

The story ends ominously with the protagonists waiting for whatever is going to befall them. The point of view is so sympathetic to the Allisons that their anxiety seems to be well founded, not paranoid. But the events that perturb them are all frustrations of their attempts to live in an industrial age with a pre-industrial ideology. These frustrations arise because the goods and services they desire are unavailable to anyone out at the lake after Labor Day—no heating oil, no grocery deliveries, and so forth. The object of their paranoia is misplaced. Rather than fear urbanites who have more control over and more benefits from the economy, they direct their animosity toward the rural underclass and petty burghers. Mrs. Allison says, "You could not expect to overrule a country employee as you could a city worker" (72). They identify with the privileged, maybe because they are apparently privileged. Since he is sixty and she is fifty-eight, they have retired early, which is likely the result of having surplus wealth. This story, then, is ultimately unsympathetic to the Allisons' hypocritical devaluing of the locals for their lack of urbanity.

Jackson dedicated "A Visit" to Dylan Thomas (with whom she claimed to have had sex on her back porch while Hyman entertained guests). This story is one of Jackson's most Gothic. In *American Gothic Tales* (1996), edited by Joyce Carol Oates, this story once again appears as it did when it was first published: without the dedication to Thomas and under the title, "The Lovely House." Both titles are indicative of the story's concerns. The first title pertains to the visit by another demon lover; the second title pertains to the house as a trope of the subject.

In this story, the house recalls a Richardsonian landed gentry's (pre-bourgeois) estate.² At the outset of "A Visit," Jackson uses not only personification but also the pathetic fallacy to trope the house as the protagonist's self. The narrator describes the house as a "long-boned structure . . . resting back against the hills." Aspects of the house appear to be living. For example, as the protagonist approaches the threshold to enter the home for the first time, the statuary feels alive: she touches "the warm head of a stone faun" (91). Even the table setting has lifelike qualities: "The dinner service was white china with veins of gold running through it" (95). Carla introduces the protagonist, Margaret, to the gallery of family portraits by describing the room as the place where the portraits "live." Moreover, the ancestors in these portraits lean down "to stare at Margaret and Carla" (94). The house also features tapestries of family ancestors (an artistic endeavor continued by Carla's mother but not by Carla herself, who prefers sketching). Margaret thinks of the tapestries and house "as a complete body of story together, all joined and in sequence" (92).

That body of story links the metaphor of the house as self to the metaphor of the house as representation. In addition to the many portraits and tapestries of ancestors, there are tapestries and mosaics of the house. Some of the tapestries show how the house looks reflected in the lake—a representation of a representation. In addition, there is a floor mosaic depicting not only the house but also its counterpart, a young woman with the same name as the protagonist. As the narrator of Poe's "The House of Usher" does, and as one can actually do at Edith Wharton's estate (which is near Bennington) Margaret looks into the lake and sees a reflection of the house. Like Narcissus, she imagines going into this depiction: "They stood by the lake, and Margaret looked at the pure reflection of the house and said, 'It almost seems as though we could open a door and go in'" (98). The house as Margaret's self and as artifice appears in a hall of mirrors: "They passed then into a room where everything grew smaller as they looked at it: the mirrors on both sides of the room showed the door opening and Margaret and Carla coming through, and then, reflected, a smaller door opening and a small Margaret and a smaller Carla coming through, and then, reflected again, a still smaller door and Margaret and Carla, and so on, endlessly" (93). As in the house in general, so in the mirrors in particular: the protagonist loses her unified, isolated subjectivity in reflections of various subject positions. As Larry McCafferey says in a similar context, "If one plane in cubism can intrude on another, then a fantasy of one person can intrude on another's fantasy" (78). When Carla's mother makes tapestries of the house and family, she uses as models the many depictions and reflections already on the walls and floors around her. As a result of her concentration on these reproductions from and of the past, the mother is so absorbed by domestic ideology that she is alienated from the real people in her family. The narrator states, "She had of course learned the faces of the house better than the faces of her children" (99).

In stories like this one, Jackson approximates postmodernism's concern with representing representation. Inger Christensen contends that "metafiction does not concern itself with its ability *per se* to imitate reality. It focuses on the difference between art and reality and displays its consciousness of this distance" (22). But Jackson does not observe such an opposition. In stories like this one, reality and art merge.

In the mother's reproductions, the house never changes; it remains eternally what it was when her ancestors depicted it. Like the house in the mother's tapestries, Margaret in the mirrors lasts forever unchanged (but reduced). Matching this image of infinity is another one from the tapestries and from other furnishings:

> a carved wooden bowl holding within it another carved wooden bowl, and another within that, and another within that one. The tapestries in this room were of the house reflected in the lake, and the tapestries themselves were reflected, in and out, among the mirrors on the wall, with the house in the tapestries reflected in the lake.
>
> This room frightened Margaret rather, because it was so difficult for her to tell what was in it and what was not. (93–94)

This theme of infinity, of metaphoric deathlessness, appears in the mother's reading of the mosaic of the older Margaret: "Isn't she enchanting? . . . I've always loved her" (97). Paul remarks similarly, "'The house is the same as ever,' he said. 'It does not change'" (110). Similarly, an old lady tells Paul he'll never age (107). This old lady is Margaret's double; the mosaic shows the elder Margaret when she was young, and the elder Margaret reveals what the younger Margaret will become.

Yet this image of Margaret as a mosaic eternally belonging to this eternal house is ambiguous. "We were so young," the old lady tells Paul. "I can hardly remember" (108). Since Paul is many decades younger than she, he apparently has not fallen into time. Moreover, the inscription under the mosaic says that the elder Margaret is dead: "Here was Margaret," it said, "who died for love" (97). Her everlasting life now appears to be a death in life, as if the old Margaret is the ghost of the one who lies buried here, and the young Margaret is the latest displacement in the cyclic return of domestic imprisonment.

The story's motif of everlasting life continues to crack and unravel. The captain points out that there is a statue broken, a tapestry abraded, and a sofa worn. The nature of this eternality is that the past cannot be changed but only added to. Paul says that nothing in the house can be replaced: "All *we* can do is add to it" (111). The timelessness of this tale emerges as the iron trap of history. The characters can only do what they have always done. This theme emerges when Margaret and the captain appear to be characters in a play (rather than in a story) who have forgotten their lines:

> "I forget what I am supposed to say now," she told him.
> "You're supposed to say," he told her seriously, "And do you really leave us so soon?"
> "And do you really leave us so soon?' said Margaret obediently.
> (107–8)

When the madwoman in the attic appears as Margaret's double, the theme of Margaret trapped in the history of her disunity as a subject emerges. When Margaret asks Paul about the ancestor locked away in the tower, he responds incredulously, "Did you think we kept a political prisoner locked away?" Of course, that is what the old lady is. She is a captive of the rest of the family's attempt to defeat time through artifice. Paul says she willingly withdrew to the tower and stays there "because she says she cannot *endure* the sight of tapestry." As a rebel against a life of cycling through timeless reproductions of domesticity, the old lady seems to him to be a witch. He says, "She has filled the tower with books, and a huge old cat, and she may practice alchemy there" (101). Up in the tower, the elder Margaret avoids the frames of portraits, tapestries, and mirrors, preferring the window frame that opens onto reality. She waves at the tower windows and says, "My tapestries" (103). She has no glass or shutters on these windows. She lets the sun and rain and wind come in. Margaret decides that she will climb the tower and meet the old woman named Margaret, "feeling somehow that there might be a thin thread of reason tangling the old lady and the cat and the tower and the rain, and even, with abrupt clarity, defining Margaret herself and the strange hesitation which had caught at her here in the tower" (105). The suggestion that the younger Margaret's reason is hanging by a thread appears again: "The small thread of days and sunlight, then, that bound Margaret to the house, was woven here as she watched" (99).

The possibility that the younger Margaret is delusional emerges clearly only at the end when the narrator reveals that Paul and the elder Margaret exist only in the younger Margaret's imagination. Through manipulation of narrative point of view and emplotment, Jackson reveals hints that those two characters are delusions, but she also camouflages those hints. For example, after dramatizing a scene in which the younger Margaret opens the tower door and climbs the stairs, Carla's mother remarks, "I saw you one day try the door of the ruined tower" (112). The discrepancy is explainable. Carla might have tried the door on one occasion and opened it on another. But the narrator makes other reports that are not easily explainable. For example, the narrator dramatizes a scene in which the younger Margaret leaves the group to go on a walk with Paul, whereupon Carla tells Margaret that Margaret is always walking off alone. Similarly, the narrator dramatizes a scene in which Paul and both Margarets are talking when the captain comes up and says he will capitalize on the fact that she is alone by asking her to dance. On first reading, the captain appears to be making an odd joke at the expense of Paul and the elder Margaret. But further reading shows Jackson tricking her readers by making them the butts of the joke—in effect including her readers within the scene's frame and the point-of-view character's consciousness.

The trick she plays is possible only with the deceptive narration of the fantastic. For example, on stage the following scene would have to reveal that the captain is the brother and Paul a delusion because the father, mother, and daughter would not only have to look at their son while greeting him but also shake hands with him or embrace him: "Mrs. Rhodes said 'We've missed you so,' and Mr. Rhodes said 'Glad to have you back, m'boy,' and Carla said 'We shall have such times'" (97). Likewise, it is only through wily narration that Jackson can hide the protagonist's delusions. Otherwise the audience and the characters would see Margaret not only talking to, but also dancing with, air. Thus like postmodern fiction, this story does not, because it cannot, replay anything mimetically. Despite its referential power, the narrative sleight of hand undoes the whole foundation of the story just as it undoes the protagonist as a unified subject. Contrary to Lenemaja Friedman's literal-minded conclusion that Paul and the older Margaret are "charming ghosts," the possibility of the marvelous is balanced by the protagonist's bewilderment (52). This story, then, is another of Jackson's fantastic fables that are referential not despite their ambiguity but because of it. As Malcolm Bradbury notes, "Fantasy is not an outright escape from reality, rather a mode for interrogating the real, dispersing and displacing its forms, creating its expectations only to displace them" (159).

"The Rock" uses intimations of prison to figure the subject as inescapably bound by her victimizer. The protagonist and point-of-view character, Paula (another female character with an androgynous name) and her brother and his wife take a ferry to an Atlantic island for a brief vacation. The destination is unexpectedly estranging. This maid's Tartarus, the hostelry, seems to be carved out of the island's ubiquitous black rock. It is further estranging when the sun reflects off of the water and on to Paula's ceiling, and when the Hawthornian firelight on the rock walls is "caught and pursued by reflections of sunlight" (120). The wife says that the island looks like a "pirate stronghold" or "prison" (113). As a native of greater San Francisco, Jackson would have known Alcatraz as the "the rock" and seen it many times. The prison here turns out to be the sense of entrapment the protagonist feels when, apparently, she and the hotelier see a piratical devil figure come for her but her brother and his wife do not see it. The journey becomes a one-way trip to the under-world. While it is unknown what will happen to the vacationers, especially Paula, that something horrible will befall her is certain. This is one of Jackson's starkest examples of how she, like other fiction writers, uses Gothic and the fantastic to undermine romance. As in many of her stories, the protagonist does not win but rather is held in a netherworld.[3]

The estrangement continues when Paula meets the only other guest on the island: "She felt an immediate shock of recognition, as though this were someone she had known all her life, and then realized that she had never seen him before" (121). When she asks him his name, he dissembles: "'Ah—Johnson,' said the little man. 'Yes, Johnson.'" Later Mrs. Carter says the man's name is Mr. Arnold. When Paula introduces herself to him, his response reveals that it was her sister on whom he had designs:

> "I'm Paula Ellison, Mr. Johnson."
> "Yes, of course. It was Virginia Ellison I was—yes, of course."
> (124)

There is some ambiguity about who will become his victim. That his victim will be one of the women, and he prefers the wife, is certain. But he has to take whichever woman steps onto the island first, which is Paula. He says, "It had to be one or the other of you, you see; I told you I was waiting for your sister-in-law, but you *would* come first." So the agent of evil is controlled by other necessities. Exactly who his victim will be is indeterminate; that he will victimize is determinate. So there is a logic underlying this absurdity. The tormenter tries to obscure the origins of persecution by blaming the victim. He says that she determined that she would be the victim: "It was your decision, you know; I would have been satisfied with either" (129). The victimizer thereby deploys a con-struction that for Marxists exemplifies the contradictory capitalist ide-ology of choice—victims deserve their fate (predetermined necessity) because they choose to lose (free will). Of course the victimizer does not apply the belief in free will to himself; if he can choose freely, he can choose not to victimize. But his choice is limited too, though not by his victim but by the agencies that determine that he will victimize.

Further estrangement occurs when Mrs. Carter, the hotelier, appears to offer Paula protection. Mrs. Carter tells her, "Try to hide behind me" (129). But of course Mrs. Carter might just be an accomplice with more trickery for Paula. She could be the agent determining Johnson, or an effect of that agent, or an effect of Johnson as agent. At any rate, Mrs. Carter must have known about Johnson and therefore might have been able to prevent this danger, but her self-interest is not to turn away tourists. When finally Paula's perception is that both she and the hotelier can see "Johnson" but that her brother and his wife cannot, she is unable to tell if she is delusional.

Nor can the reader tell if Paula is delusional, because the narration is so thoroughly filtered through her point-of-view character. As in other stories where the focus hardly exists outside the point-of-view character, the narrator (and therefore the reader) perceive from within the story's frame. This manipulation of narrative optics is typical of Jackson's technique of using the elements of modernism and the fantastic that remain in postmodernism.

As in much of Jackson's fiction, the unresolved ending also anticipates postmodernism. As Stacey Olster says, "Post-modern authors deliberately leave the conclusions of their works open, . . . choosing, like Oedipa Maas, to accept a doubtful place in the 'excluded middle'" (143). However, this protagonist does not choose the excluded middle; rather she is excluded from the either/or. The specifics of what will come next are unsure, but the fact that she faces a tortuous end is assured. Thus her undecidability is determinate; her absurdity has a logic. This recurring juxtaposition of undecidability and determinacy in Jackson's fiction also points to the nature of representation. As such, this story is another Jackson text notable for a proto-postmodern characteristic: its self-reflexiveness. Even more than modernism, postmodernism is self-conscious about its form.

This fable's signifying practice is a dialogic use of the Gothic setting and fantastic focalization to limn another divided subject allegorically. This story features an oedipal protagonist who splits herself into several others. When Paula arrives, she is at a later stage of the oedipal situation. Having given up her father for her brother, she is jealous of the sister-in-law. Johnson uses this trait to make Paula anxious. He tells her several times how close the brother is to Paula's sister-in-law and how they do not need Paula. She responds by rushing to her brother and trying to come between him and his wife. Johnson, the hidden power in this home away from home, is the father figure. Both he and Paula's brother are, like several of Jackson's male characters, feminized weaklings. The gruff Mrs. Carter, who runs the unaccommodating inn, is the phallic mother. A large portion of the shock at the end is that she has apparently done the father figure's bidding. Claire Kahane says that the object of the female Gothic plot is the girl's search for her lost mother ("Mirror" 334–40). The ambiguity of the mother's complicity registers Paula's anxiety about both the feminized mother and the phallic mother. If, as Adrienne Rich says, matrophobia is "a womanly splitting of the self" for fear of being oppressed like the mother, it is also the fear of being oppressive like the mother, which is as true in Jackson's fiction as in her life (236).[4]

"A Day in the Jungle" features another increasingly disarranged subject. The protagonist, Elsa, grows more disunified as she pursues the belief in the self-fashioning, unified subject. She is one of Jackson's few point-of-view characters who are unsympathetic despite being left to deteriorate as a result of domesticity. Like many of Jackson's wives, Elsa will be unable to flee the tender trap. She will seek refuge by returning to her husband. As Eugenia C. DeLamotte says of similar protagonists, "The happy bounded world of home, the heroine's compensation for the loss of full selfhood, is the same prison from which she [seeks] escape" (188).

This story also uses writing about writing to advance the plot, which begins with the protagonist rehearsing the script she has in her head for the scene of her leaving her husband. She writes several drafts of a note telling him she is running away from home. She leaves for a particular hotel because it appears often in the gossip columns. Once there, she relaxes not by doing anything new that she could not do at home but rather by doing just as she often did at home, reading a mystery story and napping—entering the dream text. She likes the thought of having "her own book on the arm of the chair." She thinks smugly of the cleaning woman having to read the newspaper. When her husband calls, she says, "You should have read my note," ignoring the obvious fact that he must have read it (137).

The protagonist is an *alazon,* a comic fool. She is a privileged bourgeois who wants not only more privilege for herself but less for others. She gloats that her husband will be strapped with supporting her so she will not have to work: "Don must simply find a way of providing them both with money, . . . now that her interests no longer participated in his." She has late capital's version of the American dream: "A new world for her" (132). (But not for the cleaning woman.) The protagonist manipulates a man to pay for her lunch. She fantasizes about commodities: "I want to wear pretty clothes all day long, she was thinking, . . . I want to be beautiful and free and luxurious" (137). She regresses to the exploitive and dependent Imaginary, thinking of freedom as involving wealth for herself but labor for others. She wants to play out the master narrative of romantic love. She thinks it is "possible for some vaguely glimpsed stranger to be telephoning right now to ask her to dine, to dance, to go off to Italy" (137). Her spatial flight masks her loyalty to the narrative that ensnared her originally. On her own for only several hours, she has a panic attack. She has become so split that she looks at herself from outside of herself: "She saw herself turning and going back to her hotel" (140). Her panic is a sign that the return of the repressed is eroding her illusory unity. But she projects this disorder on the built environment. She imagines signs falling down, and then buildings collapsing, and cars running onto the sidewalk and over her. She regresses to her central narrative of domestic dependency; she is desperate to reinscribe herself into the social text of her husband's ostensible protection—back into the subject position that encouraged this breakdown. This allegorical tale is one of Jackson's most moralistic.[5] For Jackson's characters as for herself, to break out was to break down. Jackson did not write about women successfully breaking out until after she had what was probably her most serious breakdown, which occurred in the early 1960s. Before that, stories such as this one seem to be cautionary tales against her own impulses.

The mobile viewpoint sometimes merges sympathetically with the point-of-view character's feelings, but at other times is outside and satiric. This next sentence starts with external focalization then shifts to internal in midstream: "She told the waiter that she would like an old-fashioned, please" (134). In this next example, by stating not that the signs are insecure but that the protagonist sees them as such, the narrator's report implies that she is projecting—it is the subject that is disintegrating, not the signs: "She turned once and saw with sinking horror the precarious rocking of the signs overhead" (140). So although Elsa is the protagonist and point-of-view character, the narration is often ironic.

Jackson uses that irony to undermine the belief in choice, free will, and self-fashioning by making them the notions of this character: "For the first time she moved knowingly and of choice through a free world, that of all her life this alone was the day when she had followed a path she made alone." Again she thinks of freedom while nonetheless acknowledging that the doorman in his labor has none: "Free and at peace, she thought as the doorman held the door open for her and she passed out onto the street with dignity and a half-smile for the doorman's enforced kindness; free and at peace and alone and no one to worry me." The illusion of self-fashioning dissipates when the heretofore denied anxiety at the root of her frantic desertion surfaces: "She had not gone ten steps from the doorway when the nagging small feeling which she knew clearly now as fear and which had been following her cautiously for hours, perhaps for weeks and years, stepped up suddenly as though it had been waiting outside the door for her, and walked along beside her" (139). She fears being swallowed up by the earth. But according to the ideology that has conditioned her into thinking she has not been conditioned, this anxiety cannot be: "This is madness; this is idiotic; I am not supposed to be *afraid* of anything; I am a free person, and the path I have chosen for myself does not include fear" (140). The repressed anxiety over randomness in general and violence against the wealthy returns:

> An enemy, hidden in a second-floor room, peering out through the half-open window, could shoot her easily; . . . not even an enemy, but a stranger, mistaking her for someone else. . . . Or, even worse, a mad-man, chuckling and raising the gun and estimating, telling himself he would shoot the tenth person, or the first woman who walked by wear-ing a fur coat. (141)

When she imagines her enemy's sex, it is male. Perhaps the cleaning woman imagines at least some of her enemies as female.[6]

Winner of the Edgar Allen Poe Award, "Louisa, Please Come Home" delineates a subject (another one with an androgynous name) who gets lost in her own misrepresentation of herself. After the nineteen-year-old protagonist, Louisa, runs away from home, her family and law officials search for her, and journalists discuss her case. She becomes fas-cinated with narratives about herself on the radio and in the newspaper. Finding a job in a stationery store (appropriately enough), she refashions herself as a different character with a new background. Like the charac-ter in "The Daemon Lover," her self-fashioning snowballs as she incor-porates what others tell her about herself. Even Louisa's new landlady prattles on about her. Inspired by newspaper coverage, the landlady inserts Louisa into narratives of rape, gangsters, and gun molls. The landlady lives in her own reinscription so deeply that she sees no like-ness between the woman in front of her and the picture of Louisa in the newspaper in front of her.

When a friend from Louisa's hometown discovers her, Louisa agrees to go home. But when she gets there her parents do not believe that Louisa is really their daughter. They are entrapped in their revised mem-ories of her. They like their reinscription not only as parents with a lost child but also as the would-be victims of con artists seeking the reward for Louisa's return. It surfaces that the man who found her has twice before brought girls back presenting them as Louisa. The story thereby grows even more estranging because the man could have been not only dishonest the first two times, but also deluded the third time: Louisa may indeed not be Louisa. And she, too, could be either dishonest or deluded.[7] Louisa decides not to prove her identity with fingerprints ostensibly because even if she did her family still would not welcome her back: "Could the law make my mother look into my face and recognize me?" (169). Her true reason may be that the fingerprints would reveal her as a fraud or a psychopath. She goes back to her self of not being herself, listening to the radio to hear her mother's appeals for her to come home.

Jackson's technique for unsettling the reader lies, of course, in her deceptive narration. As in "A Visit" or in an M. C. Escher drawing, each detail makes sense in realistic terms, and yet the whole depiction dissolves into absurdity. Unlike the other stories, this is one of Jackson's few notable stories with a first-person narrator. However, it is ambiguous whether Louisa is either dishonest or delusional. She may not be either while all of the others around her are. Or she could be both while the others are not. Or they could all be. In addition, since the reader is almost always prompted to sympathize with a character who is narrating (more than the reader would be if another character were narrating) the reader sympathizes and empathizes with a character who shatters, regardless of whether she is dishonest or insane. In the end, her family casts her out. As a result, she must go back to being who she is not: "I behaved just like everyone else, and dressed just like everyone else, and even *thought* just like everyone else" (161). She had intended to be indistinguishable from the crowd, faceless and unnoticeable—"to fade into some background" (156). And now she will be there permanently. This story, then, is one of Jackson's most unsettling.

In "The Bus" (1965), an old lady, Miss Harper, visits the house of the self. Like Louisa, this protagonist cannot go home again, in part because she has never left it. She has never completely left the Imaginary, and finds out that she is not a unity but rather contending propensities. And like the protagonist of "The Tooth," she begins a journey on the bus and on drugs—this time sleeping medication. Her destination is her home, but in midjourney that destination becomes not her home as an adult but her home as a child.

After the old woman falls asleep, the first hint of her regression to the Imaginary surfaces when she believes she hears a young female runaway speaking. This ostensible runaway suggests the protagonist's childhood self. The driver awakens the old woman and tells her this is her stop. His extreme rudeness and repetitive speech seem to be exaggerations on her dream screen. After she gets out, she realizes (or believes) that the driver has dropped her off at a crossroads (where, myth has it, the devil lurks) on the edge of the wrong village, for she does not recognize the little one-bar town. She flags down two men in a truck. They, too, speak repetitively, saying five times that she is "wet"—like a new-born (184–85). The men drive her to the inn. Formerly a mansion, it is now a tawdry roadhouse carved up into rooms for rent. (Jackson's house in Bennington had at one time been partitioned into four apartments.) The innkeeper also speaks repetitively, saying three times, "the hell you say" (187–88).

The stairs and Miss Harper's room seem like those of her childhood, but they too are altered, aging, and sagging. Regressing to the nexus of a childhood trauma, she anxiously regards the bed as a place of illicit sex: "Miss Harper was frightened at the faint smell of dark couplings and a remote echo in the springs." As the protagonist in *Hangsaman* does after she is sexually assaulted, Miss Harper repeats that she will suppress her associations with the bed: "I will not think about such things, Miss Harper thought, I will not let myself dwell on any such thing; this might be the room where I slept as a girl" (189). She immediately displaces her anxiety onto a phallic object. As in Ambrose Bierce's "The Man and the Snake,"[8] the protagonist believes she sees a live snake in the closet. It is one of her childhood toys come to life, and the toys deride her and tell her to go away. The uncanniness in her shock of recognition is not just that this event is so new and strange but also because it is so old and familiar. (As Sigmund Freud defines the uncanny, it is "nothing new or alien, but something which is familiar and old—established in the mind and which has become alienated from it only through the process of repression") (241). Panicked, she flees the room—running away like the runaway she hears on the bus.

At that point, the bus driver again awakens the old woman, and the reader feels cheated that this ending is of the it-was-all-a-dream variety. It appears to the reader that the illusory narration clearly begins when the old woman falls asleep and ends the second time that the driver awakens her. But then the bus driver drops her off at the same cross-roads that she dreamed about—either the point-of-view character and therefore the reader is still in the dream, left detached from reality, or the dream was prophetic, which also distances the reader from normal reality. Not resolvable as mimetic or marvelous, this is a fantastic fable of being trapped in cyclic history, in an eternal return of the Imaginary.

And because the narration is sympathetic to the viewpoint character, the reader is trapped not knowing what events, if any, are dreams or delusions. The third-person point of view moves from rather trustworthy and outside the character to very untrustworthy. At first, the events do not appear to be dreams or illusions. But when the narrator concludes so ambiguously, even the opening reports will seem to be in retrospect untrustworthy. As before, the narration qualifies its reports by revealing that they are the point-of-view character's perceptions. For example, "She was aware that the bus had started." In addition, the narrator is mobile, in and out of the character. For example, the narrator reports on what Miss Harper cannot see: "Around her other people slept, or spoke softly, or stared blankly" (181). The dislocation of such reports also arises from their diction. If "around" were "in front of" or even "near," she could know, but "around" implies not just in front of her but also behind, so the dependability of that report depends on hair-splitting precision.

By contrast, other reports do not provide the decidable diction necessary for accuracy. For example, "Miss Harper was not awake, but she opened her eyes a little and looked up to the ceiling of the bus" (181–82). One can open one's eyes when asleep, but can one look at something when asleep? And in each case, what does it mean to say that the agent of the action is "she"? If "she" denotes the locus of consciousness, then the subject cannot be asleep. But if "she" refers to the body, then the subject can be asleep. Further undermining the veracity, the mind that the narrator often enters is both in and out of consciousness at the same time. The character remains conscious of some elements of her environment even when she is asleep: "The feeling of rattling and throbbing beneath the soles of her shoes stayed with her even when she slept at last" (181).

This story, then, is one of Jackson's greatest achievements in manipulating the instability of subject and narration. As before, with narration this unstable, the story becomes less a mimesis of reality than writing about writing. Yet the story is nonetheless referential. While the surface as a whole cannot stand, the story's parts comprise a fragmented fable of the disunity of the subject—the one in the story, the one reading it, the one narrating it, and the one writing it.

In all of these stories, there is the proto-postmodern tendency to dispense with epiphany. As Philip Stevick says, postmodernism minimizes epiphany because epiphany privileges the subject's ability to understand (38). Thus the reader understands more about the characters than the characters do about their interpellation. Also, dislocation in these stories results from the tendency in Jackson's psychological fables to disrupt the continuity of plot by making it contiguous. Moreover, she compounds the dislocation by using allegory, which, Robert Scholes asserts, uses metaphor as its "animating force" (145). Dialogically, then, Jackson achieves a juxtaposition of metaphor and metonymy.

## CHAPTER FOUR

# Just an Ordinary Day

Edited by two of Shirley Jackson's children, *Just an Ordinary Day* (1996) is an anthology of stories that were either previously uncollected or previously unpublished. As Joyce Carol Oates points out, a few of these pieces are on par with Jackson's best (Rev. of *Just an Ordinary Day* 9). Containing more selections than her other two compilations combined, this volume features as many noteworthy stories as the second anthology. And because the second and third anthologies were drawn from a lifetime of work, their forms and themes are similar: unstable characters developed through unstable narration, and heteroglossic writing about writing. However, there are more examples here of psyches and plots whose discontinuity emerges from metonymic contiguity. Character traits do not cohere. And plot events do not grow out of each other but rather succeed each other. Unfortunately, this collection appeared after Joan Wylie Hall's study of Jackson's short stories.

"The Smoking Room" leads off the anthology's first half, which consists of the previously unpublished items. Except that this story's humor is darker and more satiric, this story prefigures the kind of parody that another writer would soon be publishing regularly in the *New Yorker*: Woody Allen. Where Allen's pieces parody such narratives as the execution of Socrates as well as the arrival of death in a human form, this story parodies narratives of the devil. This story satirizes the mystifying operations of the literalization and trivialization of evil implicit in sanitized mass-market versions of myth, religion and witchcraft. Plotted like magical realism, it begins with the absurd premise of the devil appearing in a women's dormitory but then develops formally (though not thematically) according to the laws of realism: literalizing the absurd narratives of the devil, this story features what would follow if the motifs of devil narratives were valid. His appearance is true to form: he has horns and cloven hooves. Since he is infernal, he lights cigarettes by simply touching them. So the title "The Smoking Room" is apropos not only of the room for smoking but also the room that smokes. It is fitting when the dormitory's housemother says he is a fire hazard. He gets young women to sign their names and sell their souls. In liberal capitalism, the rewards for selling one's soul are trivial. The narrator asks the devil for an A in chemistry and a date with the captain of the football team.

This parody, then, is not only a satire on the trivialization of evil but also a satire on the conventions of realism inasmuch as the story does not question its assumptions but rather develops them. If one grants that evil is representable by reducing it to one incompetent fool, this is the character that would result. He would no longer be the *eiron* of cosmic dark humor, but a feminized *alazon* from a mass culture eager to mystify evil designs even to the extent of denying that they exist by categorically dismissing theories of conspiracy and exploitation at home but projecting them abroad. The devil in this story does not signify evil; he signifies the mystification of evil, and that mystification is the evil to which this story refers.

It would also follow, in a dominant culture marked until recently by hysterical optimism, that the narrator would defeat this Goliath, and do so by wits. First the protagonist cons the devil into thinking that she is helping him. She says that his crude, old-fashioned method of signing up converts would leave "a thousand loopholes for a smart lawyer" (4). The traditional signing of the devil's book will not do. She types up a modern contract with a carbon copy. She uses this contract to turn the tables on the devil, who cannot understand the legal language. By signing in his place and fooling him to sign in hers, she has him sign away his soul to her.

But she does not defeat evil as much as she displaces it. She is a trickster, and there is no indication that she will use her power for anything good. The witness to the signing, Bobbie, wants "a couple of hundred thousand dollars" (7). The magical transfer of property mystifies the fact that it comes from labor and natural resources. The narrator and Bobbie are gaining privilege not just at the devil's expense. Like many of Jackson's characters who would defeat evil, they are secret sharers, reinscribing that which they would erase.

Jackson also satirizes the ideology of self-reliance. Here the self-reliant individual defeats evil with legal forms—by working through the system. But her victory is specious because the devil has supernatural power (e.g., he can set things on fire just by touching them, and heal burns instantly). In this fable, evil is discoverable—susceptible of demystification—but readily controlling it is absurd.

"Nightmare" is another story with a dissociated character pursued by herself. A secretary named Tony Morgan (another character with an androgynous name) apparently is being chased as she runs an errand for her employer. Here, as in much of her fiction, Jackson anticipates the postmodern theme of paranoia.[1] In this case, Jackson's protagonist is so overwhelmed that she responds to her persecutor by telling herself that she wants to give in to him. Like the characters in "The Lottery," she not only acquiesces in her own exploitation but also is unaware of her exploitation.

As she travels by foot, bus, and taxi across town to deliver a package for her employer, the loudspeaker of a truck advertises a contest; the winner needs only to find Miss X, who the voice over the loudspeaker describes in terms that fit the protagonist exactly: wearing a red and gray topcoat, blue hat, blue suit, blue gloves, and blue shoes, and carrying a large package. When she asks the driver why he is following her, he claims to be on a predetermined route. The driver, then, implies that his following her is just a random coincidence. But events seem to be not random but predetermined. A parade advertising the contest comes by with a marching band that has a large X on each drumhead, and posters advertising the Miss X contest hang on walls and telephone poles. Moreover, after she disguises herself by buying a different hat, putting on her coat, taking off her gloves, and carrying an additional package, the contest participants reflect those changes. The voice says, "Miss X is now wearing her coat buttoned up so you can't see her blue suit, and she's taken off her gloves" (40); "Miss X has changed her clothes now, but she is still walking alone through the streets of the city. . . . Miss X is now wearing a gray and red hat, and is carrying *two* packages" (42). It now appears not that these events are random but that they change as she changes—that she is cause and they are effect.

However, some of the changes around her would take so much time that they would have to be started before she herself changed, in which case agents outside of her would have to have known what she was going to do before she did it. For example, "Then came a line of twelve girls, arm in arm, each one dressed as Miss X, with a red and gray hat, a red and gray tweed topcoat, and blue shoes. They were followed by twelve men each carrying two packages, the large brown package Miss Morgan was carrying, and the hatbox" (45). Likewise, all of the posters and flyers register her change in appearance. In fact, the behavior of others might even cause the moves she makes. Perhaps they determined that she would make these particular modifications, in which case she did not choose—she did not have free will.

At the same time that she seems to be determined by a preexisting logic, the surface events grow increasingly more absurd. For example, the list of commodities the winner will receive starts with necessities (e.g., a refrigerator) but soon includes luxuries (e.g., a mink coat, a lifetime membership on the stock exchange, and a bulletproof car). The protagonist's errand is to deliver Mr. Lang's package to a Mr. Shax, a name Jackson uses in several stories to suggest a demon, witch, or the devil. The inside joke is that Shax was also the name of Jackson's cat.

Finally a resolution to the protagonist's struggle begins when a man in a blue suit, a demon lover figure, walks up to her and says, "This town's no good. No one spotted you. . . . We'll have to do it again tomorrow in Chicago." She seems to acquiesce in this seduction, to naturalize it as if it is her choice: "That night, falling asleep in the big hotel, Miss Morgan thought briefly of Mr. Lang and the undelivered package she had left, along with her hatbox, in the shoe repair shop. Smiling, she pulled the satin quilt up to her chin and fell asleep" (46). Apparently lying in the demon lover's bed, she tries to reconcile the fact that this morning she was a secretary at the job she has held for six years yet this evening she has disappeared with the boss's property. The protagonist, then, is another of Jackson's disconcerted workers, broken up by her position as a part of late capital's machine.

The fallibility of the narrative reports arises somewhat from focusing through a perplexed character. The narrator makes some reports not as if they are facts but rather as Miss Morgan's perceptions. For example, "She saw a young man with a microphone" (39). Any further report about that man depends on the veracity of the previous report. Thus when the narrator goes on to state that the young man jeers at Miss Morgan, that report is undecidable. On the other hand, like the use of free indirect discourse, the use of qualified reports is minimal—just enough to make the narration somewhat unreliable without immersing the narrator in Miss Morgan's consciousness. Most of the narrative statements come from outside the point-of-view character. Thus the narration is illusory less because of the point-of-view character than the events themselves. In other words, the narration resists verifiability because the events as a whole are fantastic in the Todorovian sense: they cannot be resolved either naturalistically (the character is crazy) or supernaturally (the impossible is happening).

Added to the absurd setting, disconnected protagonist, and fantastic narration is the fabulous plot. The ambiguous plot allows the fabulation to surface. Taken one by one, contiguously rather than continuously, the events constitute a fable of alienated circulation in the commodities fetishizing economy. First of all, the contest refers to Tony not by her name but as Miss X (with no irony, the advertisements of Jackson's era named inferior products as Brand X, a practice that later became a staple of parody). Withholding any account of her height, weight, age, coloring, and so forth, the descriptions of her exclude her body. Instead, they concentrate on the commodities covering her up— her clothes. She fears she could be arrested for impersonating Miss X— for pretending to be herself. And no one recognizes her until she disguises herself by taking the feather out of her cap (an emblem of Holden Caulfield's identity) and by removing her red topcoat. In the course of the story, she becomes so alienated from herself that it does not even occur to her to present herself and claim the prize money.

Similarly, in an estranging displacement, the truck driver is separate from his voice; it seems that the loudspeaker is doing the talking—that it is in fact a loud speaker. This disembodied voice is the perfect picture, or rather sound, of alienated labor. In the end, Miss X goes away with a man in a blue suit—another James Harris figure. The plot resolution, or rather the lack thereof, leaves the specifics of her mental state and social position uncertain, but the conditions of her existence are clear— she is a peripatetic effect of some agency outside of herself.

Similarly, "Lovers Meeting" features an anxious woman who leaves her apartment and is followed. After trying to escape her pursuer, she returns to her apartment apparently to meet her pursuer and acquiesces in his poisoning of her. The plot is contiguous. As in the language of the unconscious, events do not grow out of each other; they displace each other. The four men she sees each have the same function, to help her flee. The journey has no purpose until after it begins—she discovers her goal (or maybe invents it) after setting out. First she recalls a song. Then she leaves her apartment. Next, without planning to take a taxi, she goes to one. Then without planning to, she happens to see the footman at a building's entrance. Without planning to go inside, she happens to talk to an usher. Without planning to flee immediately, she does because he tells her to. Without planning to catch a bus, she does.

True to fable form, Phyllis does not act out of choice but out of obligation. In this case, the obligations are the logic of her unconscious. There is no logical reason for her to leave the apartment when she hears the song; there is only her underlying psycho-logic. She associates the music with a demon lover. But denying and repressing the (immediate) origin of the demon lover in her psyche, she projects an image of him and goes in pursuit of him. Her confusion of origin and destination—that her destination originated at home, that in her end is her beginning—emerges when she asks herself, "Am I walking toward something I should be running away from?" (143). What she is running away from, the sound of steps behind her, is what she will find in front of her when she gets home. That she leaves the lights on suggests that she is unconsciously preparing for the arrival of the man and her return. The men who ostensibly help her on her journey—a taxi driver, a footman, and a bus driver—are father figures who act to prevent her union with the demon lover.

Adding to the bewilderment, the unreliable narration develops in three ways. First, the reports come through a disconnected character. For example, the fact that the narrator reports not that there were steps but that the protagonist heard them cancels out the ostensible surety that there are actual steps behind her: "She heard the sound of steps behind her, coming as surely along the street as herself" (142) and she "saw" the taxi driver hailing her (143). What she senses may not be there, and what she does not sense may be there.

On the other hand, what dependability there is increasingly diminishes until the narrator sees from outside of the point-of-view character and yet does not provide information that would be noted in a reliable report. For example, the narrator does not report that Phyllis mistakes the taxi driver for her father but rather dramatizes the scene indeterminately. Apparently she starts to call him "father" and stops: "Yes, fa—" (143). Likewise, in the objective position (outside of the point-of-view character) the third-person narrator does not clarify whether the steps Phyllis hears behind her are echoes of her own footsteps: "If she heard the footsteps when she left the apartment, she did not notice them particularly, or perhaps they merged perfectly with the sharp sound of her own high-heeled shoes going down the corridor" (142).

Appropriately, free indirect discourse also dislocates the narration. Coming from an imaginary position halfway between a fully objective point and a point within Phyllis's consciousness, the narrator's report sounds like the character trying to make up her mind: "These sounds meant, why they meant there was someone who would say, 'Hello, Phyllis, hello'" (143). Similarly, the narration sometimes starts with free indirect discourse's focalization midway between the narrator and character, then moves to a point distant from her, and then back to the midway point: "Did the footsteps still follow? She almost ran down the dark street toward home, but stopped suddenly; was that one last footstep, unable to stop as soon as she?" Similarly, introjected free indirect discourse is further dislocating: "She ran up (was that a footstep on the marble of the stairs behind her?) past the landing" (145).

This tale is also one of Jackson's allusive stories. Phyllis roams like the protagonist in Ralph Ellison's *Invisible Man*, who is sent from one place to another with a sealed letter (which he cannot see) that tells each recipient to send the invisible man on to the next recipient. Another allusion emerges in the song that also appears in *The Haunting of Hill House*, which she was writing at about the same time: "What's to come is still unsure, in delay there lies no plenty" (142). As in the novel, this protagonist hears these words at the beginning of her journey and at the end when she acquiesces in another agency's desire that she die. Here the protagonist takes a "vial" from the ominous man waiting for her in her apartment: "'Such a tiny glass,' she said. 'No, plenty,' he answered. 'There lies their lies.' The music swelled. 'Drink. In delay there lies no plenty . . . In delay there lies repentance . . . What's to come is sweet and sure . . .'" (ellipses in original 145). In addition, the protagonist's disunity emerges in her dialogic thoughts. Both threatening and reassuring, the language in her mind is double-voiced: "The words clashed in her against those other words" (143).

"The Story We Used to Tell" features one of the very few first-person narrators in Jackson's serious fiction. Like this one, almost all of these appear very late in her career. Prior to that, her first-person narrators are almost always the ones in her domestic narratives. When she assumes the voice of "I" in the domestic narratives, she is at her most alienated but not at her most dissociated—she knows what she is doing. But in her serious fiction, the first-person narrators are, like this one, schizoid. As is frequent in Jackson's fiction, the language of this anxious character is repetitive. This protagonist is anxious about maintaining certain constructions. The italics indicate a word or phrase that the narrator repeats in these few lines:

> This is the story that Y and *I used to tell, used to tell* in *the quiet of the night,* in the hours of *the quiet of the night, and the moonlight* would come, *moving* forward, *moving* close, used to whisper to each other in *the night . . .*
>
> And *I, Y would say, had to go first,* with *the moonlight* making white patterns in her hair, *she would* shake her head and *say:* I *had to go first. Remember, she would say.* In this very house. That *night. Remember?* And the picture, *and the moonlight,* and the way we laughed." (italics added, ellipses in original 179)

These characters, like many in Jackson's fiction, do what characters in postmodern fables do: they act out predetermined allegorical roles that do not mimetically represent but still refer to actual people. As in fables, this narrator is another subject who does not make things happen; rather, things make her happen. Nonetheless, if fables by definition contain the allegorical, and if allegory, as Therese M. Kelley contends, "makes unexpected alliances with historical and realist particulars," then this fantastic fable refers to the historical (3).

One of the agents that make her and other things happen is the traditional Gothic motif of the family estate. The story is set in a big old house that was remodeled by Y's grandfather. And the agent of events in this house is the ostensibly dead grandfather. He remodeled the house, adding (Freudianly enough) the plumbing. The house contains its own representation, a painting of it from the innocent days before it fell into the age of the grandfather's renovations. The other important change made after the painting was done is a new wing on the house; after her husband's death, Y closed off much of the house where she had lived with him and moved into this wing. The painting hangs at the foot of Y's bed (place of both sexuality and nightly transgressions on the dream screen of the unconscious). Chris Baldick notes that "typically a Gothic tale will invoke the tyranny of the past . . . within the dead-end of physical incarceration (the dungeon, the locked room, or simply the confinements of a family house closing in upon itself)" (xix). In Jackson's proto-postmodern turn on that Gothic motif, the protagonist will get trapped in a reproduction of the house that reproduces history.[2]

But just as the painting reproduces the house, the house reproduces the self. Y has walled off part of herself in an attempt to repress it. And in this metonymic chain of the painting representing the house and the house in turn representing the self, to look at the picture of the house is to look at Y's portrait. So when Y and the narrator look at the painting as it hangs at the foot of Y's bed, they imagine it turning into an avalanche of no longer containable subject matter:

> We looked at the picture of the old house . . . with the windows of this very room shining faintly through the trees, and the steep winding road coming through the gates and down to the very edge of the picture.
> "I'm glad the glass is there," I said, giggling. "I'd hate to have a landslide start on that mountain and come down into our laps!"
> "Into my bed, you mean," Y said. (180)

The last term in the metonymic allegory is that Y is a projection of the narrator's; Y is the narrator's double. As with some of Jackson's other fragmented characters, Y comes and goes with indeterminate cycles of waking and sleeping. Y disappears when the narrator says the narrator awakes. And after the narrator says that Y "might come back tonight," Y reappears not just when the narrator awakes but when the narrator awakes while sleeping on Y's bed (181). However, Y comes back not just in a dream—the narrator's depiction of her—but in the painting. The narrator sees that Y is trapped inside the glass of the painting (just as the narrator is inside the window shown in the painting). When the narrator tries to free Y by breaking the glass, the narrator gets sucked into the painting as well.

Now both of them are inside the house before it had plumbing and the new wing. The bizarre grandfather makes them dance with him every evening, and he abuses his old female accomplice:

> "Not so pretty nowadays, are you, old hag!" he screamed suddenly, and ran over to the old woman to give her a shove that sent her rocking back and forth, giggling wildly and nodding her head.
>
> "Has she been here long?" Y asked timidly, but the old man skipped back and forth, pirouetting with exaggerated grace. "No questions, young ladies, no questions. Pretty heads should be empty, you know!" (183)

Thus they are trapped by the "malevolence of the old house" (181). But that old house, the agent of the malevolence, is the narrator: as a phallic woman, the narrator has the grandfather (and his phallic grandmother-accomplice) living in her. The narrator and Y use that masculinity to get free (exactly how they get free is undecidable due to the beguiling narration) by apparently smothering him and perhaps also hanging him, but at least tying him up in the forest along with his female counterpart. John, a friend of the dead husband's, kicks the glass and lets Y and the narrator out.

But as in "The Bus" (in *Come Along with Me*) and in most of Jackson's other fictions of women escaping, this apparent quest erases that last note of triumph by returning the narrator to the trap she only apparently escaped: "John runs constantly about the house, screaming and beating the walls. For I have no partner, now in the evenings, and Y and John do not like to dance alone" (185). She has to be Y and John—they have to exist in her—because if either one exists outside of her, that one is not alone.

"Lord of the Castle" is another fable of psychic division. Like "Devil of a Tale," it resembles the fables that Howard Nemerov wrote. Narrated not only in first person but also by a male, perhaps because of Nemerov, it is a rarity in Jackson's oeuvre. The narrator begins by condemning the ignorant belief in witchcraft that led to his father's execution. Although he denies that his father was a wizard, he inadvertently lends credence to the accusations by revealing that the father had a large collection of satanic texts. Moreover, to exact revenge, the narrator reads the satanic texts, practicing their rituals, and is thereby "bound by that very devil lore that had killed" his father (162). As in "The Smoking Room," Jackson satirizes the literalization of witchcraft. (When the protagonist in "The Smoking Room" calls on the devil, he says, *"In nomino lutheris"*) (italics in original 166).

But ultimately the humor is much darker and corrosive as the protagonist undoes himself. The son's double appears in the person of his half brother, whom the protagonist's father sired by an illicit relationship with a commoner. Of course, the half brother is really the protagonist's projection of his unconscious. The narrator asks this evil double his name, but the half brother does not ask the protagonist's name in return, presumably because the double, as one who has resided in the basement of the protagonist's consciousness, already knows. Similarly, when the half brother reveals that he knows their father was hanged, the host asks the guest if he was there at the execution. The double replies, "I saw it." Creating his brother by projection, he regards the half brother as delusional: "He told me strange tales of . . . places that existed, I was certain, in no country but that of his moving mind" (163).

Once this repressed content comes forth, it brings more with it. The half brother summons the temptress, his mother in disguise. The protagonist yields not just to the desire to avenge his father, but also to the temptation aroused by the temptress. Unaware that he is immersed in desire for power and lust, he does not realize until it is too late that his half brother and the temptress have successfully conspired to have the narrator overstep his bounds. In his fury, he accidentally burns down the castle and gets himself executed for witchcraft, while the double goes free. With evil succeeding, this story exemplifies "Lewisite or masculine Gothic," in which, as Kate Ferguson Ellis notes, "the home is destroyed utterly and the destroyer continues to wander upon the face of the earth" (44–45).[3]

In several of the heretofore unpublished stories, there is a lot of homicide between husbands and wives. That this theme occurs in stories that did not find a publisher suggests that she had trouble with explicitly fictionalizing her conflicts with Hyman. In the two versions of "The Honeymoon of Mrs. Smith," the groom is attentive and loving, but in the end he apparently is planning to kill his wife. In "Mrs. Anderson," the story ends with the suggestion that she kills her husband. In "What a Thought," a woman suddenly has the urge after ten years of marriage to kill her devoted husband for no reason at all—or rather for no reason she can think of. She picks up a heavy ashtray and strikes him over the head. The story ends there so that whether or not he dies is unclear. In "Before Autumn," the wife plans to manipulate the teenaged neighbor boy into killing her husband.

☙

Of the twenty-three previously published but not collected selections, several are as noteworthy as Jackson's most significant stories. For example, "One Ordinary Day, with Peanuts" was included in *Best*

*American Short Stories, 1956.* The first-person narrator of "The Order of Charlotte's Going" has no money and no home, so she moves in with her older cousin Charlotte, who has "all the money in the family" (288). After fourteen years with the protagonist, Charlotte becomes terminally ill. Right after she is diagnosed, a double-voiced communication arrives in the mail: "Best Wishes on Your Plighted Troth" (289). Her plight continues with another double-voiced note, ostensibly of birth and arrival on earth—"Love to the New Arrival"—but really of death and arrival in the hereafter (290). Someone starts sending candy, a treat Charlotte cannot resist even though it is very bad for her precarious health. Soon candy and cigarettes lie hidden about the house. Likewise, the mailings grow more threatening. After Charlotte almost dies of fright from opening a letter with two live spiders in it, the narrator confiscates all subsequent mailings before Charlotte can see them. Finally Charlotte does die of fright when a snake crosses her path.

The narrator tricks Charlotte and the reader into thinking that the young cousin's devoted care is just that. In the end, the narrator reveals that she was the one who had sent all of the mailings. Moreover, she had passively encouraged Charlotte's overeating. And it was not so much the snake that scared Charlotte to death as the narrator's studied overreaction to it. With hindsight, the reader can see that the narrator was jealous of Charlotte's privilege when they were young, and jealous of the attention Charlotte received when she was sick. But the more the reader expects two female cousins—two metaphoric sisters—to care for each other, the more unprepared the reader is for Jackson's exposure of the ideology of female nurturance.[4]

A similar uncovering of sisterhood obtains in "The Friends." The protagonist, an upper-middle-class homemaker named Ellen, has known her counterpart, Marjorie Acton, since their school days twenty-two years ago. These doubles are mirror opposites. Ellen has always been much less attractive than Marjorie and felt inferior because of it. On the other hand, Ellen's husband is much more successful than Marjorie's, and Ellen is condescending because of it. When Ellen discovers Marjorie in flagrante delicto with John the banker, Ellen feels superior to her fallen friend. But Marjorie Acton does not act inferior. Instead, she uses Ellen to cover for her when she is meeting John. When the friends are playing bridge with their husbands, Marjorie talks as if she went out to lunch with Ellen that day. Put on the spot, Ellen feels obligated to converse as if she had, indeed, gone to lunch with Marjorie. Thus an accessory after the fact, Ellen feels shameful, no longer superior to Marjorie. Ellen says to herself, "It's as though *I* were doing it; *I* feel guilty" (276). Similarly, she says to Marjorie, "Don't try to drag *me* down with *you*" (279).

The next time the couples meet, Ellen turns the table by performing a similar manipulation of Marjorie. Ellen turns to her husband and says, "Marjorie has offered to take the boys this weekend so we can go skiing" (276). Ellen thereby blackmails Marjorie, who cannot reveal the truth lest Ellen divulge Marjorie's secret affair. Other such incidents follow. For example, Ellen obliges Marjorie to do Ellen's work at a flower show. When Marjorie balks, Ellen does not need to threaten her explicitly. Instead, she refers to their lunch hoax and gives Marjorie no opportunity to respond: "'Shall we discuss it today at lunch?' Ellen said, and hung up" (277).

So begins the double-voiced process through which they hide Marjorie's affair and Ellen's complicity. They speak in code:

> She and Marjorie had developed a private language where comparatively harmless words substituted for the disagreeable ones the rest of the world was required to use: "Cloakroom," for instance, was a word of such threatening import to Marjorie that it might easily have meant "exposure" or "scandal," and even such a trivial phrase as "lunch in town" had come to mean something close to "liar" or "hypocrite." (278)

They can use this private code in public, casting their husbands and others as comic butts left out of the irony:

> "How are you this morning?" Marjorie asked, and the words had a special weight, as though they should be translated ("I suppose you told Arthur?") before they could be entirely understood.
>
> "Very well. And you?" ("No, of course not; how could I tell anyone?") (275)

They also use the code to avoid talking about the affair, Ellen's complicity in it, and their mutual exploitation of each other. Ellen says, "Poor Marjorie, you *do* look worn out. I'm really tempted to speak to Charles about you—you're doing too much. I'm going to tell that husband of yours that he has to keep more of an eye on you" (278). Ellen uses a gesture that some of Jackson's other dishonest and disloyal women use when mistreating other women. She tenderly touches Marjorie's cheek while being cruel: "'After all,' she added, touching Marjorie' s cheek gently with one finger, 'We've always been pretty honest, you and I'" (279).

When Marjorie breaks off the affair, Ellen does not stop. She blackmails the banker into covering her overdrawn account. And she uses the same code language to do so: "'Is it part of the business of a banker,' she asked, almost flirtatiously, 'to take his clients out to lunch? I've been waiting for you to ask me'" (280). Marjorie does not drag Ellen down with her; Ellen drags herself down with Marjorie and trades positions—exchanges identities—with her double.

The first-person narrator of "The Very Strange House Next Door" resembles those in Truman Capote's story "My Side of the Matter" and Eudora Welty's story "Why I Live at the PO." Like their narrators, Jackson's has no knowledge of what a comic fool she is. Addie Spinner, the village's addled spinner of rumor and innuendo, starts her story by saying, "I don't gossip" and then does nothing but. When she sees a family from the city move in next-door, she spies on them. As Jackson did with her audience, the family's maid sports with the old busybody by claiming to be a witch. Addie states that "there isn't any such thing and never has been" (328) but then is mesmerized by the maid's tales of witchcraft. She believes that the maid's evil cat, like a familiar doing the devil's work, is responsible for her own cat's impregnation. Addie becomes a modern day witch when she bands together with the village's coven of other xenophobes and runs the sinful city folk out of town. Addie, then, is another one of Jackson's discordant characters who project their own evil. And the style is again like that of a fable, with the narrator's hypocrisy too extreme to be mimetic. She is, instead, an allegorical character in a fable that refers to, rather than represents, the kind of small town mindlessness common to Jackson's fiction.

Like "Nightmare," several more of Jackson's most proto-postmodern stories show subjects circulating in an absurd economy. The order of the plots is always arbitrary.

In "The Omen," a kindly grandmother makes a list of gifts to get for her daughter's family and herself. The daughter wants a brand of perfume called Carnation, the son-in-law wants a brand of cigars called El Signo, the granddaughter wants a blue stuffed kitty, the grandson wants a walkie-talkie, and the grandmother wants a ring. She makes a list of these: *"Carnation. The sign. Blue cat. Telephone. Ring"* (italics in original 320). After the grandmother loses her list on the bus, a young woman, Edith Webster, finds the list. Edith is looking for a sign to tell her if she should get married or not: "If only somebody, something, somehow, would show me the way, make up my mind for me, give me an omen" (319). Distracted, she does not "look up in time to see the sign on the front of the bus" and gets on the wrong one, where she finds the list. She takes this discovery as an omen that she should get the items on the list. But the bus drops her in a strange part of town where there is "not even a sign" of where she is. Of course, she takes this lack of a sign as a sign. She goes about getting the items on the list in their order of appearance, but she is frustrated when a man mistakes her for the woman sought in a contest similar to the one ensnaring Miss X in "Nightmare." But the man has a carnation in his buttonhole. Since the first item on her newfound list is a carnation, she takes his carnation as another sign that the list is indeed a sign, especially since the next item on the list is "the sign" (320). Then, looking for a blue cat, she sees a "dingy sign" that reads "KITTY'S LUNCH" (324). Inside the diner there is a telephone, so she takes that as a sign that she should call her boyfriend and accept his marriage proposal.

Meanwhile, the grandmother cannot remember the signifiers or signifieds on the list that she lost, so she gets substitute gifts. The children eagerly await the unwrapping of their gifts: "The grandchildren signified hysterically that they were all ready" (326). The children are just as happy with these shifted signifieds—their Imaginaries have not passed through the Symbolic sufficiently. Accordingly the adults are dissatisfied with their gifts. The displacements more readily satisfy the children's desire than the parents'.

The happy resolution of happy children seems to be matched by the happy resolution of the impending marriage, but as usual Jackson inconveniences such a decidable ending. The Eden that Edith expects to enter after leaving her mother and marrying has fallen to selfishness: "She'll have to take care of herself,' Edith said. 'I need someone to take care of me'" (325). The dark humor here is that she wants to trade places with her mother. Her expectations of marriage are as invalid as her belief in signs. When the narrator states that Edith is looking for an omen, the narrator calls that "a most dangerous way of thinking" (319).

In "The Possibility of Evil," the protagonist does not circulate. Rather, her letters circulate for her. The protagonist sends letters anonymously. She is one of Jackson's many Hawthornian moralists who project their evil on to others and then attack it: "As long as evil existed unchecked in the world, it was Miss Strangeworth's duty to keep her town alert to it" (382). For old Miss Strangeworth, just the possibility of evil means there is in fact evil: "Miss Strangeworth never concerned herself with facts; her letters all dealt with the more negotiable stuff of suspicion" (381). Obsessively rooting out imperfections in her manicured garden is not enough. So she sends letters that purport to expose people; however, her victims not only do not know their accuser, but also do not know that they are accused. For example, assuming that a teenage boy and girl are involved sexually, Miss Strangeworth sends an anonymous note to that effect to the girl's father. The father then forbids the girl from seeing the boy. Later, when Miss Strangeworth drops her letters into a mailbox, one falls out on the ground unbeknownst to her. She has addressed it to a friend of the teenager who sees Miss Strangeworth drop it. This teenager takes it to the addressee, who discovers that it is Miss Strangeworth who has been sending the anonymous secret indictments. As in "The Omen," then, the signifiers slip their signifieds; Miss Strangeworth did not expect to be fingered by her own letters. To punish her, the victims leave an anonymous note under her door that reads, *"Look out at what used to be your roses"* (italics in original). She cannot know who did it because she does not know that she dropped a letter, and she cannot surmise who would want revenge because she has sent so many letters—there would be a town full of suspects. But the punishing of the sinner will only extend the cycle, because now Miss Strangeworth believes that there is even more of an acute problem of "wickedness" in the world (385).

In "IOU," the note that circulates is an IOU. When a retired school-teacher finds a boy tramping through her garden, she punishes him by making him write an IOU that says he owes her two hours of labor. Soon other people in the town are buying and paying with IOUs for services such as baby-sitting, cleaning, and cooking. These IOUs are negotiable; that is, the holders can pay debts with them. For example, the schoolteacher pays for her groceries by giving the IOU to the grocer. As a result, the boy's labor circulates; it can be exchanged, so he can be exchanged. Like exploited workers who think they are changing jobs by choice, the laborers are actually exchanged by the owners. As this form of labor catches on, the compensation for work decreases. A laborer can contract to do a particular job but then have his labor traded so that he has to do something more arduous. And like the grocer, some of those controlling the trading of labor can accumulate wealth. The grocer can get a dollar's worth of labor in exchange for seventy-five cents worth of groceries that cost him fifty cents. Some can also accumulate labor (and thereby accumulate wealth). For example, the schoolteacher accrues so much more labor than she needs to maintain her garden that she is thinking of having them build a cottage. This story, then, is one of the best examples of Marxism's influence on Jackson's writing.

The protagonist and his wife in "One Ordinary Day with Peanuts" also circulate. The husband walks around town doing good deeds—being nice to children, helping old people, giving away peanuts. But his charity is only peanuts. When he gets home, his wife has just returned from a day of walking around town causing trouble—falsely accusing a woman of shoplifting, trying to get a bus driver fired by filing an unfounded complaint, and so forth. They agree to swap roles the following day. The misleading narrator mystifies the self-interest of their ostensible selflessness by withholding their secret until the end. For example, instead of saying that the protagonist starts his days genuinely feeling that all is well, the narrator says that the protagonist starts out "with a feeling that all was well" (296). Thus the protagonist is just playing the role of a philanthropic optimist; he goes around with that feeling the way an actor does. The protagonist knows that he does not really feel it, but the narrator obscures that fact.

So good and evil appear purely arbitrary and capricious. But the logic beneath their absurd wandering is that the economy gives them nothing better to do with their labor, and no definition of right and wrong besides the libertarian one that whatever one "chooses" is justified. Their absurd repetitiveness is implicit in the man's name, John Johnson. Their forms and themes are similar: unstable characters developed through unstable narration, and heteroglossic writing about writing. However, there are more examples here of psyches and plots whose discontinuity emerges from metonymic contiguity. Character traits do not cohere. And plot events do not grow out of each other but rather succeed each other.

Like *Come Along with Me,* this anthology draws from Jackson's entire career. But because *Just an Ordinary Day* contains so many selections, it features even more variations on such proto-postmodernist themes as class, gender, and the unstable subject, and even more variations on such proto-postmodernist forms as fable, parody, allegory, discontinuous plots, fragmented characters, and absurd settings. But variation and proto-postmodernism do not characterize Jackson's first novel, which is less antirealist than the rest.

## CHAPTER FIVE

# The Road Through the Wall

*The Road Through the Wall,* Shirley Jackson's first novel, appeared early in 1948 before the *New Yorker* published "The Lottery" and a year before her first anthology, *The Lottery or, The Adventures of James Harris.* Of all of her novels, this one comes closest to expressing her political themes about gender, ethnicity, and class explicitly. And its form owes more to modernist realism than do her others. Its episodic plot makes it a composite novel—it reads a little like a short story cycle. This discontinuous quality arises not only from the episodic plot but also from the dizzying array of characters, none of whom is readily identifiable as the protagonist. And the matching array of family households creates a setting that frustrates spatial orientation. As such, this debut volume is solidly modernist and does not give strong hints of the complex forms to come. Nonetheless, this novel evinces concern with language in subject formation and interpellation, destabilizes narrative reliability a little, and lacks clear plot resolution.

The characters most relevant to this study are the protagonist, Harriet Merriam, and her friend Marilyn Perlman. At thirteen, Marilyn is a bookish loner. However, she does not withdraw; rather, she is shunned. She is the object of anti-Semitism. Marilyn is not just the only moral exemplar in this novel but the only moral exemplar in any of Jackson's novels. She is both forgiving and yet the only character to defend not only herself but others. When one of Marilyn's tormentors, Harriet, later befriends her because Harriet cannot get any other friends, Marilyn forgives her. But when Harriet again rejects her for being Jewish, Marilyn calls her a "big fat slob" (221). Similarly, Marilyn sticks up for Frederica when the children harass the new proletarian in the neighborhood.

As with Jackson, Harriet Merriam's quandary is her attachment to her father. Both Jackson and Harriet are traces of Cathy, but they have no Nelly to help them. James H. Kavanagh describes the Brontean situation from which Jackson and Harriet arise:

> Nelly . . . enacts a "progressive" quasi-analytic project of tearing Cathy out of the Imaginary—that is, out of an attachment to the desiring Father (itself . . . a transference of the attachment to the enveloping Mother). This incestuous obsession with the Father *is* in the realm of morbidity, closure and self-absorption/consumption, the realm of the pre-oedipal and the pre-linguistic, of the womb and the tomb. (48–49)

Similar to Cathy and Jackson, Harriet is also enveloped by her mother. When the neighborhood girls write childish love letters to the neighborhood boys, Mrs. Merriam takes it upon herself to prevent Harriet and the neighborhood girls from writing any more "filthy" letters (207). Mrs. Merriam makes Harriet destroy not only her letters but everything else she has written, not just her diaries but her notebooks: "She and her mother stood religiously by the furnace and put Harriet's diaries and letters and notebooks into the fire one by one" (42).[1] Their sadomasochism—and their denial of it—surfaces when the mother follows this cruelty with lavish forgiveness and Harriet responds with gratitude: "Warmly Harriet smiled at her mother, and thought how pleasant it always was after these scenes . . ." (44).

Yet Mrs. Merriam (her first name is Josephine; Jackson's mother was named Geraldine, perhaps the origin of the many androgynous names that Jackson gives her many phallic women) does not want her daughter to cease writing. In fact, Mrs. Merriam requires her daughter to write for two hours every day. Mrs. Merriam just wants her to write so innocently and childishly that her daughter's only production could be a pale, sanitized parody of the most pale and sanitized genre, sentimental literature, with even the implications of romantic love expunged. And Harriet agrees to show her textual reproduction to her mother. Mrs. Merriam will also read and write with her, but in conjunction with the proper domestic activity of teaching her how to cook. Mrs. Merriam's aggressive insistence on neutered domesticity emerges in her opinion that her husband, the picture of feminization, is nonetheless not feminized enough. She accuses him of "coarseness" and tells her daughter, "Never marry a man who is *inelegant*, Harriet; I can tell you it brings nothing but sorrow" (76). Part of her sorrow is that she endorses so much of the Law that she imagines herself resisting.

Harriet is victimized not only *by* her mother but also *as* her mother; that is, she fears becoming like her. Pat Macpherson believes that matrophobia is a central issue for women of Jackson's era: "Encountering the fear of becoming one's mother is the central experience of female adolescence, in my book, and denying-while-projecting the fear and hatred of mothers the central experience of the American middle class in the 1950s" (59).[2] The difficulty for Harriet lies in object relations. As Nancy Chodorow has argued, oedipal males can separate from the mother more easily than girls can because the separation will reward the males with a substitute, another female. But for oedipal girls, the separation is more difficult because it is more threatening: they must displace the original object of their desire and replace it with a displacement of the father.[3] The response to the oedipal situation by adopting a gendered position necessarily interpellates the subject, including Harriet. The displacement of the imaginary maternal object exemplifies the Marxist dictum that ideology arises from an imaginary relation to the real conditions of existence.

Alienated by her feminized father and masculine mother, Harriet becomes somewhat dissociative. She wants to accept a Chinese man's invitation for her and her friend Virginia Donald to come to tea, but her interpellation leaves her anxious about such an encounter with the Other. Ambivalent, she and Virginia accept the invitation, but then they do not keep it. When they happen to run into him again, he invites them again, and this time they go. He is supremely polite; they are supremely condescending. When they find out that the luxurious apartment he has taken them to is not his own, that he is only a servant, they leave contemptuously. Later, Harriet keeps secret the scandalous fact that she visited a Chinese man, but tells Marilyn (an ethnic minority) that Virginia "goes around with Chinks" (137). When Harriet remembers how she had taken part with a group of girls who harassed Marilyn Perlman, she thinks not of the victim's suffering but of her own image as "dirty and fat and overbearing" (24). And when she awakes the morning after learning of three-year-old Caroline Desmond's murder, she again thinks not of the victim but of Lillian telling her that she is fat and ugly. As with some of Jackson's other victims, Harriet is not improved by her suffering. As such, she is one of the least admirable of the many antiheroes of the era—another divided subject alienated from both self and others.[4] In the end, Harriet neither marries nor moves out on her own. After her mother dies, she stays single and lives with her father. As such, she can neither conform nor individuate.

But the quest for the self misstates the matter. Although Lenemaja Friedman asserts that Jackson's characters are bent on "establishing their own identity" (158) the fact is that in Jackson's characterization, the self does not constitute the self. Rather, history does. Jackson's characters do not try to formulate a self as much as they try to cope with the self that history gives them. Her fiction represents not self-creating individuals but rather the constituting of subjects. It might even be accurate to say that in many instances, a Jackson character is not just a subject but several subjects. For example, history has made Harriet by turns a friend of Marilyn's and an anti-Semite, attached to, and alienated from, her mother, attached to, and alienated from, her father, narcissistic and alienated from herself. In other words her mind has a mind of its own—or rather several. Harriet does not make her mind up; history makes her mind up. The ability of her mind(s) to do anything is always already conditioned. Her mind is more of an effect than a cause. Her behavior is more a response than a choice. As Patricia Waugh puts it, "Our confidence that we are the source of our beliefs and values is an illusion" (55).

This dissociativeness also describes Jackson's male characters. As a more pathological adolescent than Holden Caulfield, Tod Donald is largely dissociated from simple logic and basic ethics. For example, after snooping through the Desmonds' home, he sees Marilyn Perlman in a vacant rental—all the privacy of it gone—and asks as supercilliously as Mrs. Merriam, "What are *you* doing in other people's houses?" (87). He does not choose; he just acts with little or no thinking in his stunted consciousness:

> Tod Donald rarely did anything voluntarily, or with planning, or even with intent acknowledged to himself; he found himself doing one thing, and then he found himself doing another, and that, as he saw it, was the way one lived along, never deciding, never helping. When he found himself one afternoon walking down Pepper Street nearly at the Desmond driveway, . . . it never occurred to him to slip into the Desmond yard; and once there, . . . his mind did not encompass the notion of stepping into the Desmond house, nor did it suggest to him, once in, that he had no right to be there. (89–90)[5]

In this field of changing matrices of subject positions, Jackson figures her ensemble cast as refractions of each other through doubling. Doubling appears in the arrangement of the houses. Starting at the east end of Pepper Street, doubles line up across the street from each other: the two vacant lots; the Roberts and Donald households with a boy named James in each one; the Byrnes' barely middle-class rental and the house that is perpetually changing impoverished renters, that itself will house two single mothers, each with two daughters, and that is doubled again by being next door to the Donalds' rental; the two old spinsters, Mrs. Mack and Mrs. Fielding; the two wealthiest families, the Desmonds and the Merriams, the latter of whom share a lot with the Martins; and the two houses that face Cortez Road, the Desmonds' and the Martins'.

Names are also paired. Like the two boys named James, two girls have similar names: Marilyn and Mary. Two boys have androgynous names: James Roberts is called Jamie, and Patrick Byrne is called Pat. And the Terrel girls each have an androgynous name, Frederica and Beverley.

Doubles occur in many other ways. There are two houses where poor families live, the Martins and the Williamses. Mr. Desmond and Mrs. Byrne each read a mystery story. Mrs. Roberts and Harriet Merriam are both obese. There are two old spinsters, Mrs. Fielding and Mrs. Mack. That pair is doubled by another aged female double, the two grandmothers, both of them poor, one Williams and one Martin. Lillian twice calls Mrs. Roberts "coarse" (237) and Mrs. Merriam complains of her husband's "coarseness" (76). Two boys appear older and more mature than they really are, Patrick Byrne and James Donald. Patrick Byrne and Artie Roberts agree on descriptors that classify their fathers as twins of insufferableness. These same two boys exploit Tod by feigning friendship to get him to buy them things. Two girls, Virginia Donald and Hallie Martin, do the same to Beverley. Harriet's bosom buddy is Virginia, but then they become enemies; Harriet's best friend is Marilyn, but then they too become enemies.

Scapegoating also comes in twos. The neighbors discriminate against four pairs: the two ethnic minorities, the Chinese servant and the Perlmans; the two religious minorities, the Jewish Perlmans and the Catholic Byrnes (the Chinese man's religion does not surface); the two waitresses, Mrs. Williams and Mrs. Martin; and the two teenage temptresses, Helen Williams and Hester (who of course is a double of Hester Prynne); and the two spinsters, Mrs. Fielding and Mrs. Mack. Two boys, Tod and Artie, are hated by their fathers. Two die, Tod and Caroline; he is scapegoated, and in turn does the same to her. She appears while he studies his reflection; she is his mirror opposite—a female TODdler pampered by DOTing parents.[6] The formation of these subjects through metonymic interpellation necessarily involves language. Harriet's mother tries to forestall Harriet's contact with the "filthy" Other (temptress girls like Helen and tempting boys like James Donald) by controlling her writing. But this intervention requires Harriet to dissociate herself from herself. It also requires that the mother and daughter to both deny that dissociation. Harriet not only has to burn the love letters, but also diaries and even notebooks labeled "Moods," "Poems," "Daydreams," and "Me" (18–19). The importance of writing in her identity surfaces when she tells her father, "Mostly I'm a writer" (128). Like Jackson, the most important activity to her was reading and writing alone in her room. Harriet Merriam even bears the last name of a dictionary.

Also like Jackson, Harriet's favorite reading—the narratives that inserted her into the social text, or failed to—was sentimental fiction. She says her favorite novels are Louisa May Alcott's *Little Women* and *Jo's Boys*. When the Williamses have moved out, she hopes that the new renters will be like something out of Alcott: "Perhaps one of the new girls who would live in the house—they would be like in *Little Women,* and Harriet's friend would be Jo (or just possibly Beth, and they could die together, patiently)—would love and esteem Harriet, and some day their friendship would be a literary legend . . ." (134–35). Later, when Marilyn Perlman introduces her to the notion of reincarnation, Harriet thinks she might be Jo March (152). When she and Marilyn write down what each thinks she will be when she grows up, Harriet writes that she will be a famous writer who is desired by many men but never marries. She is half right. Becoming a spinster living with her widower father, she fits the matrix of her mother's discourse control: she is gendered a feminine heterosexual but is limited in her ability to affirm that identity by virtue of being bound to her father's apron strings.

Marilyn's written vision of herself is that she will be powerful and that everyone will obey her. Oppressed in the discursive matrix of ethnic and religious discrimination, her desire is to compensate for the threat not only to her autonomy, but also, in 1936, to the threat to her survival. Marilyn likes *Vanity Fair* and *Pendennis* and says she remembers Pantaloon, Rhodomont, Scaramouche, Pierrot, and Harlequin from a previous life. Like Harriet and Jackson, then, she has been decentered from her safe reference point in the pre-industrial past.

Mr. Desmond hopes to interpellate his son through the canon. He says he wants his son to read Homer and Chaucer to him someday. Similarly, he imagines extending a discursive helping hand to the neighborhood children through sanctioned texts. He plans to enlist them in a new model army of thespians in a production of Shakespeare, preferably *Romeo and Juliet,* starring his son, of course. But the plan fizzles when Mrs. Desmond (who snubs Mrs. Perlman) says they would have to exclude Marilyn so as to avoid embarrassing her with the anti-Semitic passages. Likewise, she says they would have to exclude the proletarian Martins because Hallie is too young, and so it would be discriminatory to invite any other Martins. Moreover, they would exclude the servant, Hester, because she is not from the neighborhood. After excluding these Others, they are left with too few players, so they scrap the idea rather than sully their home and the texts. Besides, the official texts are not the real texts. While Mr. Desmond arranges his reading list of classics for his son, Mr. Desmond reads a mystery and his son reads a comic book.

Texts also interpellate other characters. When the neighborhood is looking for Tod to question him about the murder, Tod's brother James hears the sacrificial lamb and exclaims, "Christ!" (261). Tod also recalls other victims from other enabling texts. After Caroline is killed, Tod apparently falls asleep nearby with his head against the wall, recalling Bartleby's very literal subject position at the end of Herman Melville's parable of walls and Pierre's death with his head against the wall. Prior textual interpellations facilitate Tod's persecution and suicide. The police officer questioning him is intimidating because the interrogator's display of writing makes the police officer a metonymic displacement of prior threatening authority figures, not just the school superintendent (who would write down notes about Tod's mental incapacities) but other vicious officials like the dentist and doctor (who would write down notes about his physical faults). The narrator states twice that the police officer questions Tod while referring to information on a "piece of paper" (262). Even the interrogator's wielding of his pencil threatens Tod (perhaps reminding him of a medical or dental instrument): "He leaned forward and pointed his pencil toward Tod. . . ." When the inquisitor gathers all of his papers together with finality, Tod responds by regressing to prior textual anxiety: "Tod gasped; once he had been caught copying from his book in an exam." When the cop finds him hanging, he does not try to revive him; rather, he just scrutinizes him while "flipping his thumbnail across the edge of the papers he still held in his hand" (263).

Other neighbors also attempt to use text as power. When six-year-old Mildred Williams moves, nine-year-old Hallie Martin loses the only girl in the neighborhood between three and twelve. To stop time from eroding their friendship, she does what even many adults do. She tries to solve the problem by writing letters. Twice Hallie says, "Write to me" (85). Mildred's mother also desires to defeat time, in her case by losing track of it. When she moves, she leaves the calendar hanging on the wall. Tod's father also uses text to facilitate denial, but whereas Mrs. Williams's calendar is an absence of something necessary, Mr. Donald's is a presence of something unnecessary. While the neighborhood is crawling with people looking for his son to arrest him for rape and murder, Mr. Donald sits in his easy chair reading. Hester resists her marginality by inserting two others into cartoons. She names Harriet "Crazy Cat" and Artie "Popeye" (140). For the retarded Beverley, the function of text is the relief of boredom. When Frederica tells her about the murder, Beverley says twice, "Tell it again" (270). It is fitting that this textually rendered setting is Pepper Street, a name that is almost a homonym of "paper."

As the textuality is decentered, so the narrative point of view is destabilized. The third-person narrator is seemingly reliable and consistent. But three traits qualify that reliability and consistency. First, the limited omniscience necessarily qualifies the reliability. By staying outside of most characters' interiors most of the time, the narrator does not know all of the characters' thoughts and so, of course, cannot report them. Usually these absences are relatively unimportant. For example, when the narrator reports that Mrs. Fielding sold the furniture of the previous occupant of her house, the narrator does not know who that resident was: "Miss Fielding had gradually sold . . . most of the furniture she had been encumbered with at the death of whoever had preceded Miss Fielding in this quiet life . . ." (166). Similarly, the narrator does not know what thoughts Helen might have about her harassment of Marilyn and can only speculate what, if any, those thoughts might be: "Perhaps Helen Williams, if she thought of it, remembered *her*self as friendly and teasing" (24–25).

But sometimes the narrator's claim of ignorance seems feigned. For example, by implication the narrator claims not to know if anyone other than the children has ever explored the woods bordering the neighborhood: "A heavily wooded section [was] probably unexplored except by the Pepper Street children . . ." (10). Yet all of this land has necessarily been surveyed and plotted by and for property owners and public officials. Elsewhere narratorial authority is clearly ironic. For example, the narrator says that when Mrs. Desmond snubbed Mrs. Perlman on the street, she did so "almost certainly not intentionally" (24). But context clues show that Mrs. Desmond was, indeed, acting intentionally.

Sometimes the unreliable focalization works with the destabilizing of character. For example, Tod's guilt or innocence would be decidable if the narrator focalized more thoroughly on Tod's thoughts. In the limited views of his interior, no thoughts of having killed her appear, not even indirectly.

If the destabilizing narrative point of view enables the decentered characterization, then that destabilizing of the focalization's authority also serves the plot resolution's indeterminacy. By speculating unauthoritatively that after the estate was broken into parcels "perhaps small boys with stones" intruded, the narrator foreshadows Caroline's death but does not suggest its agent (185). There are many such foreshadowings that implicate Tod, but do so undecidably. First, of course, is that his name in German means "dead." Next he throws stones at a group of girls. Then at the Desmonds home, he crushes a yellow blossom. When he eavesdrops on Hester and his brother, just before she rejects

Tod, he is leaning against a stone: "Tod . . . felt the cold rough stone of the porch against his shoulder" (130). Right after Caroline disappears, he anxiously tries to sell his bicycle. And when he is lurking behind the brick wall, he twice fears that a brick will fall on him. And there is the possibility he might have fallen asleep with his head against the wall. All of these foreshadowings create the expectation that the plot will continue to be unified through a decidable resolution.

But after his suicide, doubts appear. Mr. Perlman says that Tod was too small to lift the murder weapon. But when Mr. Perlman says that Tod would not have come home, Mr. Perlman applies notions about the unified subject to a fragmented one. Mr. Merriam says that Tod had no blood on his clothes. But he could have changed, and the narrator might not know that or might know and not report it. On the other hand, to say that Tod would have changed his clothes is again to expect behavior of a less destabilized subject. Pat Byrne thinks Caroline's death was accidental, that she fell and Tod panicked. Even so, the implication of sexual assault remains. Mrs. Merriam no doubt expresses the feeling of many of the characters that the absence of a confession or suicide note does not really frustrate their reader expectation. She says that his suicide is "as good as a confession" (267). Others blame outside agitators. At any rate, there is no decidable end.

Thus Jackson undermines traditional plot. She has written a detective story that exposes the detective story; she frustrates the genre that relies most on the expectation of rational explanation. And what is more proto-postmodern, there is no epiphany. This plot is not a continuous one of the successful quest into the outside world and retrieval of a boon. Rather it is a contiguous, metonymic plot of the struggle in the inner world resulting in dissolution and fragmentation. Marianne Hirsch explains, "The plot of inner development traces a discontinuous, circular path which, rather than moving forward, culminates in a return to origins, thereby distinguishing itself from the traditional plot outlines of the *Bildungsroman*" (26). Indeed, the plot makes this composite novel seem more like a short story cycle because the proliferation of characters fragments the plot, making it hard to identify the main characters. There is not one protagonist but several. Although Harriet is on stage a little more than Tod Donald and Marilyn Perlman, her struggles are no more significant than theirs (or even those of the Terrels, the Williamses, Hester, or Artie Roberts, all of whom are misfits for sometimes differing and sometimes comparable reasons). As a result, the subplots are not readily distinguishable from the main plot. Thus Jackson's ending, or the lack thereof, undermines the realist definition of plot and the realist definition of reality. As Fredric Jameson says, "our satisfaction with the completeness of plot is . . . a kind of satisfaction with society as well" (1: 9). Many reviewers objected to Jackson's use of nonrealist form to pursue social criticism. But unlike traditional Marxists of the time, who insisted on social realism, she anticipates recent Marxism because she critiques the dominant culture's social formations by departing somewhat from the dominant culture's reigning forms of representation.

Yet in Jackson's proto-postmodern representations, the phenomenal world as a profusion of confusion still points to an underlying system that is determinate. In other words, her sense is that the absurd plethora of signification nonetheless lies on a largely (though not totally) decidable foundation. Whereas some poststructuralists would later claim that there is nothing outside the text, for Jackson there is a whole lot outside the text. For Jackson, just because she is decentered does not mean the universe is. Indeed, her aporias as well as the world's reveal not just more contiguity but continuity. The destruction of the wall (which restrains the middle class from aping the aristocracy by encroaching on the estate) repeats the recurring moment in the disruptive spread of the middle class. When the narrator says "Once the wall was broken into, the fields of the estate, the sacred enclosed place which harbored the main house, the garages, the tennis courts and the terraced gardens as well as Mr. Martin's greenhouses, would be exposed to intrusions from the outside world," the "would" suggests a future predictably repeating the past (185). Similarly the narrator implies an inevitability to the decay of the neighborhood: "Eventually, of course, it was more and more degraded . . ." (181).

The determinacy surfaces more clearly: "Their lives were quietly *governed* for them by a mysterious faraway force" (italics added). The neighborhood originated in the financial power plays of that "force": "Its very paving had been laid down by men now far away, planned by someone in an office building . . ." (178). Those decisions from the past recur in the three occurrences (in 151 words) of the root word "govern," underscoring the economic base of politics. According to Jackson, the "unseen *governors*" are "the prices in a distant town, regulated by minds and hungers in a town even farther away, all the possessions which depended on someone in another place, someone who controlled words and paper and ink, who could by the changing of a word on paper influence the very texture of the ground" (italics added 178–79). As ever in Jackson, she explicitly textualizes power.

Characteristically for Jackson's fiction, the specifics of production emerge:

> The very chair on which Mr. Desmond sat in the evenings belonged to
> him only on sufferance; it had belonged first to someone who made it,

in turn *governed* by someone who planned it, and Mr. Desmond, although he did not know it, had chosen it because it had been presented to him as completely choosable. (italics added 179)

With illusions of individualism and self-determination, the residents of Pepper Street think they are exercising choice by registering their behavior in words: "They possessed it with statements like 'good place to live,' and 'when I decide to move.' Consequently any change on Pepper Street was beyond their control." The change that comes, the suburbanization of the estate that brings down the wall, issues from an anonymous businessperson and elderly female landowner who "from the depths of their private unowned lives, made a decision with the words and paper . . ." (180). The successful WASPs experience their predetermined status as their just reward for their own efforts, not as a result of their privileged position at the start of the game. But the ethnic minorities should not be blind to the predetermining limits on their status: the narrator says that John Desmond, Bradley Ransom-Jones, Michael Roberts, and Susannah Fielding "thought of their invulnerability as justice; Mr. Myron Perlman and possibly Mr. William Byrne . . . would have been optimistic if they thought of it as anything less than fate" (3).

Jackson deflates the either/or of cyclic versus linear history. She affirms both in a dialectical synthesis: the circular and the linear combine like the spiral that binds a notebook. The cycles are repetition of moral failure. The abstract line pointing straight as a pencil consists of those cycles. In the prison house of history, Jackson subscribes to the Gothic's historicism, in which the past interpenetrates the present. The interpenetration that keeps Tod's past in his present and that will keep Harriet's past in her present is the eternal return of the repressed that is structured metonymically. William Patrick Day is right when he says that in Gothic, "the past is the place from which all evil and corruption flows . . ." (96).

But he is not entirely right. For in the long run, the Gothic is a trace of the middle class' eventual desire to appropriate for itself what it originally abjured in the upper class: unnecessary affluence. The middle class will ultimately preserve the goal of excess in part by preserving one of the means: affirming family connections. One of Gothic's recurrent anxieties, as Chris Baldick notes, is "the decline and extinction of the old family line" (xviii).[7] Most of the families in this novel want to displace the pre-industrial estate by appropriating it (by breaking through the wall and appropriating the estate). In so doing, they affirm the values of the past. In this process of conservative revolution, the home becomes a place for revitalizing the cult of domesticity (and for Jackson, a place for exposing it). This location of women's interpellation, the sphere of domesticity, is ostensibly separate from the marketplace. Never discussing what they do for a living, the male characters maintain the opposition of domesticity and power. Even if Harriet married, exchanging one home for another and one man for another, she would still be harried. The Gothic exposes the home as a repressive location for the policing of gender roles. The separation of public and private spheres restrains women from escaping domesticity. However, this separation also mystifies the fact that to leave the home for the marketplace is not necessarily to repudiate capitalism but also to endorse it somewhat. The domestic sphere is always already interpellated into the marketplace. The victimized, the subjugated, and the feminized are not necessarily purified, are not a new saving remnant innocent of history.

The walls of the home are doubled at the end of Pepper Street by the wall that encloses the estate. When the matriarch owning the estate sells off part of it for a new housing development, the destruction of part of the wall to let Pepper Street extend farther west initiates a breakdown in the neighborhood rules. The first thing that happens after workers begin destroying the wall is that Mrs. Perlman has the temerity to undermine anti-Semitism by paying a friendly visit to Mrs. Merriam. When Mrs. Merriam learns that her daughter is friends with a Jew, she not only forbids Harriet to play with her anymore but also insists that Harriet tell Marilyn Perlman that they must end their friendship because Marilyn is a Jew. Harriet does so willingly, seeing nothing wrong in her mother's policing of the ethnicity line. Next Mr. Roberts and Mrs. Martin go through the hole in the wall apparently for a romantic encounter. Ultimately, Caroline's body is found there. This decline appears to be fated: "Once the wall was broken into, the . . . estate . . . would be exposed to intrusions from the outside world . . ." (185). The demolition of the wall signals the repressive desublimation of Eros and Thanatos. Sigmund Freud's metaphor for repression was the building of a wall. Evil breaks out of the home and out of the subject simultaneously.

In the best analysis of *The Road Through the Wall,* Joan Wylie Hall shows that this novel figures California as a lost Eden ("Fallen"). Indeed, the estate that the Pepper Streeters violate is a lost Eden. That friend of Jackson's who said that California "was her Eden," her "lost paradise," was right (Oppenheimer 18). Living in a house designed by her grandfather, Jackson grew up, like Harriet, close to a large estate appropriately named "Newcastle." For her, Samuel Richardson's texts figure the illusory innocence she lost when she moved as an adolescent to the East at the start of the Great Depression. David Daiches says that for Richardson, Eden "is no garden but an estate" (15).

Yet for the mature, fallen Jackson, the American Eden is consonant with what David W. Noble calls "the eternal Adam in the new world garden." For Jackson as for Noble, Adam is in fact forever postlapsarian and the new world garden a type of the old world garden. According to Kate Ferguson Ellis,

> The Gothic fall leaves Satan in control of a walled Eden, where he can stay as long as its walls conceal the crime that allows him to be there. The fall in the Gothic world, then, in line with the tradition of the spotless regainer of paradise set in motion by Richardson, happens to a virginal place, not to a virginal person. The Gothic landscape is in this respect very much like the world through whose manifold dangers Pamela and Evelina make their way; only a heroine who does not fall can emerge from her trial-filled journey to make herself a home. By having the villain violate the Garden rather than the heroine, we can have an "angel" for the "house" in the process of reconstitution, and at the same time provide her with some real evil over which to triumph. (44)

But for Jackson, all subjects are fallen, and evil violates not only the garden but everything in it. There is no saving remnant, and no place of grace. In fact, it is the very quest for paradise that exacerbates human depravity. What Tony Tanner says about John Hawkes is also true of Jackson: "Evil is in part summoned up by the dreams of innocence . . ." (213).

If Jackson treats America's sacred myths as, in Lauren Berlant's terms, *national fantasy*, she also treats America's rituals as witchcraft. For her close friend, Kenneth Burke, and her husband, who were both leading scholars in ritual and myth criticism, ritual gives the master narrative its structure. For Burke, the structure underlying literature derives from ritual, in this case the breaking of a hymen. The neighborhood ritualizes the breaking of the wall with a suburban version of carnival, with normally staid adults getting drunk, flirting with minors, and becoming aggressive. Michael Holquist says that for Bakhtin, "carnival, like the novel, is a *means for displaying otherness*" (89). During this repressive desublimation (such as it is) Tod Donald and Caroline Desmond disappear. As the neighbors search for them, pondering what has happened and fearing the worst, they wonder if the carnival has been comic or tragic: "Either it was a great climactic festival over nothing, . . . or else it was . . . a tragedy." These decentered subjects, with all of their denial and projection and displacement, have arranged an ostensibly purposive celebration of the wall's demolition, yet this celebration might be a "festival over nothing" (253). They unconsciously intend to ritualize nothingness. For Burke (and for Jackson) this aporia between conscious intent and unconscious intent—that the mind is of two minds about everything—is normative. Burke's understanding of literature and ritual assumes that the bicameral mind is normative. For Burke (and for Jackson) ritual is comic because it totalizes (and does so through self-interest), but also tragic because it sacrifices.

One kind of sacrifice is the scapegoat. The old, the poor, the minority, and the female are classic examples of scapegoats, Others on whom the dominant culture projects its Otherness. Originally, ritualized sacrificial scapegoating ostensibly resulted in rebirth, as it ostensibly does in "The Lottery." But increasingly in proto-postmodernism, the redemptive results are at best qualified. Scapegoating also serves what David W. Noble calls the central myth of America as a new Eden: "timelessness" *(Eternal)*. In such rituals as human sacrifice, time stops. A scapegoat like Tod (or whoever the killer is) can project his Otherness and scapegoat to someone else, and can do so to a love object—can combine Eros and Thanatos. Love can be perverted into ritual sacrifice because to stop time is to preserve the love object. A recurring theme in Jackson is that scapegoating surfaces in children almost as soon as they enter the Symbolic. But it seems to be innocent, even comic, because it emerges in games. For example, the children's game on Pepper Street called "tin-tin" contains an early step in scapegoating, the pleasurable play of victimization: "The first resisting victim in each game became the next 'It'" (139). And in a foreshadowing of the murder and pursuit, the children play tag and hide-and-seek according to "some ancient ritual of capture and pursuit" (38). But the rituals quickly become hollow. Like the ritual in "The Lottery," some of the ritual has been lost: "The entire introductory ritual had lost its meaning and probably its accompanying dance" (138). Similarly, Marilyn and Harriet ritualize their friendship by each writing down her respective future and then hiding the paper in a pit and, finally, shaking hands over it: "'Rest here, all my hopes and dreams,' Marilyn said, and Harriet, a little embarrassed, said, 'A curse be on whoever touches these papers'" (155). Just as the adults do not know if their carnival is comic or tragic, these girls do not know their friendship from a hole in the ground: "The hole in the ground was so special a symbol of their new and enduring friendship" (150), a friendship that will not last the summer when Harriet conveys her anti-Semitic marching orders. A more lasting ceremony is the purification ritual that sacrifices Harriet's voice by burning her writings.

For Jackson, the dominant culture's rituals and myths were, as Richard Slotkin would later call them, "regeneration through violence." With figurations of witchcraft, she subverts the privileging of the dominant culture and collapses the opposition between its mythology and those of Others. Her brother said that for her, witchcraft was a field of study. As the logical extension of Burke and Hyman's interrogations, she studied demonology and represented demonizing in scapegoat rituals. But she also knew that demonizing was an increasingly Western ritual. In Greek, Hebrew, and Norse myth, demons could be either good or evil. As Angus Fletcher states, "Ancient myth and religion recognized many mild and beneficent daemons, the *eudaimoniai*" (39–40). She did not take demons or witchcraft literally any more than she did recent myths of a new Eden. Rather she used a broader definition of myth—included its Other—to subvert it. As Guy Davenport says, Jackson enables "motifs and fables as ancient as our civilization itself to show through" ("Dark" 4). Her poses as a witch were playful and calculating.

To defamiliarize her readers from their myths, she does what Fredric Jameson notes about one of the seminal figures in mythology; she exposes contradictions in social formation: "For Levi-Strauss, myth is a narrative process whereby tribal society seeks an imaginary solution, a resolution by way of figural thinking, to a real social contradiction . . ." (2:77). She thereby figures ritual myth as fantasy and witchcraft to develop what she said is her recurring theme: "an insistence on the uncontrolled, unobserved wickedness of human behavior" (Oppenheimer 125).

For Jackson, then, the metanarrative of the dominant culture is not the modernist metanarrative of society resting on a base of mythic veracity. In that regard, she uses Burke, Malamud, and Hyman against themselves, undermining the myth of myth by showing it as witchcraft. As such, she anticipates such postmodernists as Barth, Vonnegut, and Pynchon, who figure myth as delusion. For Jackson, myth is not the base; it is still on the epiphenomenal level. Moreover, myth does not encode truth. It encodes ideology. Apologists for myth are interpellated into it. Although necessarily containing contradictions of her own, Jackson uses Gothic and witchcraft not to invent formal solutions to social contradictions but as subversive fictional strategies to expose them. Class, the home, the subject, and the mind—all of these conflict with each other. She reinserts myths of American innocence into sentimental literature, even if she likes Richardson, because her mind has a mind of its own.

CHAPTER SIX

# *Hangsaman*

---

*Hangsaman*, Shirley Jackson's second novel, appeared in 1951. While it is less overtly concerned with class than its predecessor, it makes noteworthy advances in proto-postmodern form. In particular, Jackson augments her delineation of metonymy's role in structuring the pre-oedipal Imaginary. And the narrative point of view features a sustained focalization through a delusional protagonist.[1] More than any other of Jackson's works, this one calls attention to the third-person narrator's language. However, this reflexivity is still far from qualifying as postmodernist.

Reminiscent of her fiction of the 1940s is this novel's use of doubling. Each room in the college dormitory of the protagonist, Natalie Waite, contains a pair of conformists.[2] Natalie's door is like a no-way mirror, neither a window nor a one-way mirror, but a panel that hides the double who is knocking on the other side. Natalie's fair-weather friends, Vicki and Anne, who always appear together, have their dormitory rooms next to each other, and they have changed the furniture to make one room a study (with two desks and two bookcases) and the other a bedroom (with two chests). This arrangement suggests that they sleep together in the same bed; it seems there is one bed in the bedroom while the other serves as a couch in the living room. Anne is also a double of Natalie: Anne apparently has trysts with Arthur, the English professor with whom Natalie is infatuated.

Natalie's brother, Bud, is also a double of Natalie. As one might expect, he looks like her. Her nickname, "Nat," is also a boy's name. And their first names both suggest youth. Moreover, Natalie is a double of Jackson when she was a teenager, and Bud is a double of Jackson's first love, Bud Young, whose surname compounds the doubling. This doubleness appears in each character; everyone seems to contain his or her opposite. The narrator says that Natalie learns one thing about drinking: "When people were sober they repudiated everything they had done when they were drunk, and when they were drunk they repudiated everything they had done when they were sober" (171).

In psychoanalytics, the primary double for almost everyone is the maternal object. Natalie can separate from the maternal, but she cannot identify with it. At seventeen, she imagines what she might be like in seventeen more years: "She would be thirty-four, and old. Married, probably. Perhaps—and the thought was nauseating—senselessly afflicted with children of her own. Worn, and tired" (11). As she fears entering an adulthood in which she changes places with her mother, so she has anxiety about leaving for college and becoming an adult. Yet at the same time she is afraid to stay home. So she suffers from "the recurring thought that she might always give up college if she chose, and simply stay at home with her mother and father" and views this prospect as "horrible" (5). Thus despite her conflicting desire to be both like and unlike her mother, she is like her mother in that she has not only incipient agoraphobia but also what might be called "domestiphobia." Natalie feels trapped by her mother's behavior, which makes the kitchen like a trap for only them. She tells her father, "She makes the kitchen like a room with a sign saying 'Ladies' on the door."

Natalie is not yet able to see that her mother accepts the trap partly because it is the only spot where she and the daughter can separate from the males. For Mrs. Waite, the kitchen is the location for "some sort of mother-daughter relationship that might communicate womanly knowledge from one to the other, that might, by means of small female catchwords and feminine innuendoes, separate, at least for a time, the family into women against men" (20). Sunday in the kitchen is the time and place that Mrs. Waite uses for her "weekly chant" of her concerns and her "refrain of reminiscence and complaint." In spite of herself, Natalie values this time alone with her mother: "Natalie admired her mother at these times, and, although she would go to any length to avoid even the slightest conversation with her mother in the living room, she enjoyed and profited by the kitchen conversations more than even Mrs. Waite suspected" (21). The reason is that this is the only time when the mother squares with the daughter about the war between the sexes in general, and the nature of Natalie's father in particular. Natalie's mother, Charity, tells Natalie that stepping into the mother's position to avoid being under the thumb of the father usually just exchanges the father for a husband: "I guess all young girls . . . get to hate where they're living because they think a husband will be better. What happens is that a husband's the same, usually" (24). She tells her daughter that wives are "tricked" into marrying and staying married; she uses the word *tricked* (suggesting prostitution) six times in 106 words (44–45). She realizes that the result for wives is psychological death: "All these years your father has been trying to get rid of me" (45–46). Despite these perceptions, the mother can offer her daughter no alternative accept to acquiesce and pretend: "See that your marriage is happy, child. Don't ever let your husband know what you're thinking or doing, that's the way" (22). In other words, the mother keeps the trick going.

Thus Natalie has been absorbed into a system in which she, like her mother, denies her own voice and refrains from saying what she wants to say. For example, when Natalie comes home from college for a visit, the mother and daughter can achieve no intimacy: "Her mother had almost said, 'Natalie, are you happy?' and Natalie had almost said, 'No'; her mother had almost said, 'Everything seems somehow to go badly,' and Natalie had almost said, 'I know it and I can't help it'; her mother had almost said, 'Let me help you,' and Natalie had almost said, 'What can *you* do?'" (208–9).

The mother is quite right when she says that the father's "pretensions" (21) and his desire to have no one "equal to him" (46) show that he is "paranoid" (she repeats "paranoid" three times in nineteen words) (21). In his first scene in the novel, he tells his family, in what he thinks is a joke because he is an atheist, "*I* am God" (4). And like a god, he demands obeisance. He tells his daughter, "If you abandon me, you lose yourself" (152). He even determines what his daughter will read, even after she has gone off to college. She says, "My father chooses my books" (115). Not only that, he has even selected her college for her. And he did so on the basis of snob appeal. He says, "I chose this college for you because I knew that it was a fairly exclusive, expensive place and, while I pretend to no less snobbishness than any man, it seemed to me additionally valuable in that you *will*, snobbishness or not, find intelligence and culture accompanying persons of a certain social class" (151). (Unlike her first novel, this passage is one of this novel's few references to class.) His concern for himself overshadows his concern for her. He erases her by projecting his own image over hers. He ignores her problems by talking of his own youthful "foolishness" and "melodrama." When he says she just needs a change in "viewpoint," he again projects his own problem: he can see only from his own limited viewpoint. His goal for her is not for her to be happy on her own terms but for her to "become a profitable member of society" (204). When he hears of her unhappiness, he admits that he had wanted it that way—as if it were part of God's plan: "It was part of my plan for you to be unhappy for a while" (151) and "Your despair is part of my plan" (152). He laughs off her cry for help: "I should hate to deprive you prematurely of the glories of the suicidal frame of mind" (205). After erasing her with himself he says proudly, "I think we understand one another" (206).[3]

The autocracy of this benevolent despot is insidious, as the workings of ideology usually are. He does not consciously intend to banish his wife to the scullery on Sunday. Rather, he gives the maid the day off, the effect of which is that his wife cannot party with the guests because she is stuck in the kitchen. If the kitchen is "the only place in the house that Mrs. Waite possessed utterly," it is because the kitchen is the only place he has abandoned utterly (20). The professor who is capable of telling his daughter "You are of course completely free to write whatever you please about me" (15) is the same one who belittles her when she does. As the defender of the Symbolic, Arnold uses language in his role as the guardian of the gate. To cajole the family into silence, he needs only to mention the book he is writing: "At the mention of the book, his family glanced at him briefly, in chorus, and then away, back to the less choleric plates and cups on the table" (7). At parties, he will skewer them with repartee: "Not even his family were at that time safe from practiced witticisms" (42). Natalie is right when she states that he tends to "substitute words for action" (16). She says he "might leave many things undone but never a word unsaid" (198).

On the other hand, Arnold is sincere in trying to communicate with his daughter: "I was trying to say something very real." But he does not know how. So he tries to impress. In one of his letters to her he says, "Do you get any other letters with footnotes?" (150). He naturalizes the estrangement between himself and his children by saying that their rebellion is, of course, only "natural" (he uses that word twice, thereby naturalizing what he has instigated) (17). He inserts Natalie into a narrative of necessity so that he is not to blame: "A basic sex antagonism . . . separates us" (18). Sometimes he is so concerned with wit, irony, and complexity that he leaves his daughter confused as to whether or not he means what he says: "Natalie was uncertain whether or not to laugh at her father's statements. It was difficult, usually, to tell if his remark was a joke" (11).

When Natalie tells him about her English professor, he reacts to the oedipal challenge with paranoia and projection: "This sort of person is not trustworthy; he will expect more of your compliance than you should be ready to give" (150–51). Arnold is actually the one who expects too much compliance. But more importantly, he is the one who has eroticized his relationship with Natalie. He writes to her joking that he is a knight asking his princess to return to the castle. She responds by asking if it was he who had been "caroling lustily" under her window (177). Before she leaves for college, they meet every Sunday morning ostensibly to discuss her writing. But they are really engaging in platonic trysts:

> It was a fiction of theirs that these little meetings began the day for both of them, although before meeting in the study they usually breakfasted together, and pursued privately their personal morning occupations; Natalie watching the morning from her bedroom window and making hasty notes about it on her desk pad, combing her hair so that it fell carelessly along her shoulders, putting on the secret little locket she always wore. (10–11)

Thus their writing registers their erotic preoccupations. During the Sunday party, he flirts with a woman (perhaps one of his students) who is like his daughter, very young and dark, but unlike her in an important respect: the object of his flirtation is attractive. When Natalie comes around offering a plate of crackers, he introduces his daughter to her ambiguously, as if he is introducing his daughter to his girlfriend: "'This is my little daughter, my Natalie. Don't you think she'll grow up to be a beauty?' He and the pretty girl both laughed, and Mr. Waite, laughing, refused a cracker from the plate" (42). He refuses to break bread with his daughter because he has a prettier version of her.

Arnold, then, is Jackson's most obvious double of Stanley Edgar Hyman—self-centered, tyrannical, overbearing, insensitive, cruel, pretentious, and paranoid. Arnold's napkin holder, consisting of two snakes obscenely intertwined, is reminiscent of Hyman chasing a young girl with his cane made of a snake because she had punched his young son. Like Hyman at the time of this novel's publication, Arnold has published only one book and dawdles with the next, holding it over his family like the proverbial Damocles' sword. (It would take Hyman thirteen years to publish his second book. Reviewed harshly by Howard Nemerov for its viciousness, Hyman's first book, *The Armed Vision*, appeared in 1948, the year of Shirley's first novel. His next book was *Poetry and Criticism*, which appeared in 1961, and then he published two books in 1962: *The Tangled Bank*, which is a monograph, *Nathanael West*, which is a long essay, and *The Promised End*, which is an anthology of essays, came out in 1963. An anthology of essays and reviews, *Standards*, appeared in 1966. Thus his publishing was in eclipse while Jackson sustained hers, and then his flood of production came as she finished her last novel and then lapsed into a mental breakdown.) At any rate, this character is Jackson's most unvarnished parodic satire of Hyman's irrationally lopsided rationalism. Arnold is a grotesque exaggeration of a grotesque exaggeration.

Arnold has another double—one that Natalie imagines. When she is near her father, especially in his study, she imagines that a detective is accusing her of murder. The detective is a double of her father the inquisitor. While Arnold asks her questions about her writing, the detective interrogates her paternalistically: "Do you think that you alone can stand against the force of the police, the might and *weight* of duly constituted authority, against *me?*" (first italics added; 9). More specifically, his interrogation, like Arnold's, centers on her textual production: "What becomes of your story now?" (10). Her situation is like that of another martyr: she imagines that the detective comes for her in the garden, and in this case Judas is the housekeeper—the maternal figure—who puts her at the scene of the murder. And the scene of the murder is like something from not only a murder mystery but also her life: the killing occurred in the study. Moreover, the victim is her lover. The context implies whose study it is and who the lover is. And the erotics are further implied by the fact that the origin of the blood is not specified: "She would be unable to account for the blood on her hands, on the front of her dress, on her shoes, the blood soaking through the carpet at her feet, the blood under her hand on the desk, leaving a smeared mark on the papers there" (14–15). (Similarly, Jackson will link menstrual blood and writing in *The Haunting of Hill House*.) The detective's interrogation resembles a sexual assault: "He would not stop until he had from her what he wanted" (47).

Perhaps because Natalie is already the victim of her father, it is easy for her to become the victim of another of his doubles, a man her father invited to the party. Like Arnold, he notes that she is a writer, and he seems motivated by a desire to destroy her self-confidence. He is inflamed when she makes her only self-affirming statement in their conversation. He asks what she is thinking and she says, "About how wonderful I am" (which is the opposite of what she really feels). Incredulous, he says, "About how wonderful she is" twice (51). When he takes her by the arm and leads her into the trees, she does not object, although she dislikes him: "Natalie was afraid to speak, not trusting her voice." Her father has implicitly stifled the oral voice and explicitly truncated the written voice she might use. As the man leads her away, she associates him with her fantasy detective. She imagines being unable to explain the blood: "'And the blood?' the detective said fiercely. 'What about the blood, Miss Waite? *How* do you account for the blood?'" (52). Arnold becomes an accomplice of his double when she appears before Arnold the next day with a bruised face and he says nothing.

Another double of Arnold's is Arthur. In addition to the similarity in names, each is an English professor with an eye for students and a cock-pecked wife. Each reads the other's "stuff" (108). Like Arnold, he unwittingly reveals himself. When he and his wife, Elizabeth, enter Anne's dorm room, his unconscious gives away the secret that he has been there before: "'You've changed things around,' Arthur said to Anne, thus committing with a grand unconsciousness his first magnificent blunder of the afternoon" (157). Thus like Arnold (and Hyman) Arthur courts a young paramour even when his wife is present. At this cocktail party, Natalie serves crackers as she did at her father's cocktail party. Like Arnold, Arthur is pretentious and arrogant. The narrator calls him "Mr. Almighty Langdon" (129). Like Arnold giving his daughter's writing short shrift, attending to it not to help her but only to gain some benefit for himself, Arthur pretends not to notice her waiting at his office door. After he dodges her concerns the way Arnold does, she says, "My father discusses my work with me very much as you do" (131). When Arthur exhibits the same passive aggressiveness, the narrator says, "It was precisely as Natalie's father would have rebuked her" (132). His in-class behavior is also similar to Arnold's. Natalie tells him, "You reminded me of my father this morning in class" (106).

Elizabeth and Charity are doubles. Each has a husband who passively but effectively enables his wife's alcoholism. Like Charity, Elizabeth resents being limited to the task of housekeeping. When Anne says to her, "I sometimes think . . . that housework must be really the *most* satisfying work of all," Elizabeth responds, "I suppose you've never scrubbed a floor?" (158–59) For that reason, Natalie thinks that Elizabeth ought to meet Charity.

But Elizabeth is also Natalie's double. Elizabeth was a student of Arthur's. Elizabeth is also as self-destructive as Natalie. Whereas Natalie imagines herself "being burned alive" (12), Elizabeth says that on three occasions she has almost burned herself up accidentally. And Elizabeth teaches her how to mix cocktails and how to drink too many of them. When Natalie tries to walk the drunken, semiconscious Elizabeth to Elizabeth's home, they form a *tableau vivant* representing the double relationship with Elizabeth as Natalie's unconscious weighing her down. For Natalie, it seems that the demon of her unconscious has attached itself for no reason: "How dreadful and horrifying it is to have no choice at all about the swinging arms and legs that enwrap you, how sickening to be aware and to know that [in] the unconscious one does not even see that it is you she is embracing" (169). Natalie, then, feels that the unconscious can impinge on the conscious. She also knows that her conscious mind can permeate boundaries normally impermeable. She thinks, "I suppose that any mind like mine, which is so close, actually, to the irrational and so tempted by it, is able easily to pass the dividing line between rational and irrational and communicate with someone drunk, or insane, or asleep" (167).

Nonetheless it is really Natalie who is unaware of the nature of her double within, unaware of the influence her unconscious will have. Unbeknownst to Natalie's conscious mind, the reason why she thinks of trees while embracing Elizabeth is that Natalie associates trees with her sexual assault: "As they went through the doorway out onto the campus Natalie was thinking, for some reason she never knew, of the trees ahead, of how she and Elizabeth could go from tree to tree across the campus, holding onto each one until they recovered themselves" (171). Likewise unbeknownst to Natalie's conscious mind, the reason why she notices the darkness the whole time she is with Elizabeth is that it was dark when she was sexually assaulted. Nor does she understand that because she cannot participate in the family as either her mother or father or Elizabeth, the easiest person to identify with is Arthur as he seduces Elizabeth:

> Suppose I were Arthur, she thought unwillingly, and suppose I *wanted* to do this . . .
> "Dark," Elizabeth said.
> And suppose she were one of my students and I wanted badly to marry her, and suppose we were walking in the dark just like this and I thought *now, now,* and suppose just the touch of her shoulder under my arm, so strong and firm across the weak flesh, suppose just that touch and that feeling, and suppose in the darkness she turned slightly toward me so that . . .
> "Natalie?" said Elizabeth. "Are we nearly in bed?"
> "Nearly," Natalie said. "Only a little way now."
> And suppose, suppose, only suppose, that in the darkness and in the night and all alone and under the trees, suppose that here, together, without anyone ever to know, without even so much as a warning, suppose in the darkness under the trees . . ." (ellipses in original 172–73)

Natalie thereby identifies with the assaulter, a not uncommon response by victims of sexual abuse. She moves out of her position as seducer yet is still erotically charged when Elizabeth gets into bed: "'Good night,' Elizabeth said, and held up her face for Natalie to kiss her. Hesitantly, Natalie moved around the foot of Arthur Langdon's bed and to the side of his wife's bed and femininely kissed Elizabeth on the forehead" (173–74). Moreover, Elizabeth and Natalie each say "Good night, darling" (174).

Natalie can identify with different people and then break that identification because she has ill-formed identity boundaries; she can easily shift her identifications and associations because she is fragmented: She

lived in an odd corner of a world of sound and sight past the daily
voices of her father and mother. . . . For the past two years . . . she had
lived completely by herself, allowing not even her father access to the
farther places of her mind. She visited strange countries, and the voices
of their inhabitants were constantly in her ear; when her father spoke
he was accompanied by a sound of distant laughter, unheard probably
by anyone except his daughter. (4)

Her disaffection with her oedipal situation enables her to imagine not
only that she is the Other (Arthur and Elizabeth) but also to imagine
that she is an Other who is imagining Natalie as an Other. For example,
she projects herself a thousand years into the future and imagines that
she is an archaeologist discovering Natalie Waite's bones. She identifies
with the sexist archaeologist who looks at her skull and says, "Male, I
should say, from the frontal development" (27). She thereby also distances herself from her own intellectuality, which she has been conditioned into regarding as male. She imagines that she is "an old woman,
perhaps, with a year or so to live, or a child having its tonsils removed,
or a woman with twelve children having a charity operation, or a man"
(193) and that Natalie Waite is an imaginary character in their fantasies.
Similarly, she is estranged from herself in her journal; she begins a sentence in the position outside herself but finishes it inside herself: "Perhaps . . . Natalie . . . thinks sometimes about a certain long ago bad thing
that she promised me never to think about again" (135).[4]

These disconnections are from not only herself but also from the
annihilation of herself, especially when she thinks of male love objects.
From her experiences with the dominating adult males, she says twice
that for her to love a man he must be "superior." Displacing Arnold and
Arthur, she imagines that her male love object is a psychoanalyst. And
she displaces her slavish rewriting of herself, Arnold and Arthur's erasing of her, by recasting her relationship with them as close. She imagines
of her male psychoanalyst that their "minds go along together" and that
their "minds were running exactly together, coinciding" (137). She concludes by cooperating in her own erasure by imagining these conditions
for her fulfillment: "He would have to have enough left over after he
had taken all my mind, so that he could keep on thinking by himself,
after I was nothing" (138).

It is not just with her mother that she cannot say what she is really
thinking. On her visit home from college when her father resumes his
critique of her and her writing, she is compliant in spite of herself: "She
wanted to pound on the desk before him and shout, 'What do you
know?' walk wildly up and down the room, pulling words from the very
air to tell him about herself, and she wanted to shout, and to stamp, and

to cry" (206). Similarly, when she is in Arthur's office having her writing critiqued she is compliant but almost unable to contain her resistance: "Natalie heard the back of her mind gibbering obscenities, and thought for a mad moment that she might be saying them aloud and not realizing" (129–30). She pretends to agree with him but she is thinking, "Oh, the fool" (131). This passivity prevents her from resisting her assaulter. As he leads her away, she feels "provoked" by him but is polite to him "as her mother would have been" (49). For Natalie, being polite excludes her from politely resisting when she still has a chance—while there is still a crowd around.

Her repression and denial worsen when the sexual assault obliges her to force the memory of it out of her consciousness. She tells herself that she will not think about it until the next day. Then when she awakes, she tells herself five times that "nothing happened," and she also tells herself three times that she "won't think about" the thing that did not happen (55–56). This contradiction appears again when she tells herself, "I don't remember, . . . nothing that I remember happened." Unable to repress successfully the memory and the contradiction that she does not remember what she remembers, she tries another contradiction. She tells herself four times that "it doesn't matter" (55) even though she repeatedly hears herself telling the man, "please, please, please" (57). No wonder she becomes the kind of personality that desires to "sink away into that lovely nothing-space" (137). The only distortion she succeeds in telling herself is that she was responsible for the attack. Like many victims of sexual assault, she regards it not as what the assaulter did but as what she did. Referring to her mother (whom she will not tell about the attack), she asks herself, "What would she know if she did what I did?" (57).

Natalie's most important fantasy figure is Tony. As Natalie does with the others, she confuses herself with Tony. For Natalie, their identities are not easily distinguishable. When they are downtown at a drugstore fountain, Natalie has trouble even telling their visages apart (because she both wants Tony's power yet cannot integrate it): "They sat together at the counter, looking at each other and at themselves in the mirror facing them. Natalie, on the right (the one on the right *was* Natalie?) looked very thin and fragile in the black sweater; Tony (on the left?) seemed dark and saturnine in blue" (239). Tony is the latest erotic object in the metonymic chain that begins with her father and continues through the assaulter, then Arthur, then Elizabeth, then Rosalind, who at first befriends Natalie but who later turns on her. When Rosalind wakes Natalie and guides her down the dark hall to witness some sexual shenanigans in a dorm room, it appears that this event is imaginary and then projected onto a "dark" and "unidentifiable" fantasy figure who also wakes Natalie and takes her to a room (179). But this time Natalie imagines that her guide is nude and leading her to hear small children, maybe elves, who are either inside or behind the walls. After the fantasy figure develops a face and the name "Tony," their relationship grows increasingly erotic. When dining out, they pass "bits of food to one another" (242). They comb each other's hair. In addition, they go secretly into the dormitory shower room: "They bathed together, washing one another's backs and trying to splash without sound" (232). Moreover they sleep together. But there is no explicit adult sex; this fantasy is pre-adolescent. When they go on an outing to the beach in winter, the bus driver double-voicedly points both to the fact that they resemble two teenage lovers at the carnival and yet points to the absurdity of it: "Carnival spirit? . . . Big night on the beach? See the lights, take a swim, look at the girls, win a kewpie doll, take a chance?" (265).

Tony's dominant trait is power. Natalie's anxiety over her masculine friend with an androgynous name appears when she repeatedly calls her the "girl Tony" (190–91). When other women in the dorm eavesdrop on the pair, giggling outside the door as if they are the children with whom the nude figure invited Natalie to play, Tony's power to dispel them is fantastic: "Tony again went almost silently to the door, opened it, and with a large and menacing gesture drove away the girls outside" (230). Unable to feel empowered, Natalie imagines a figure common in the empowerment fantasies of the unempowered: she imagines that Tony is magical. Natalie wants to be empowered, but imagines Tony as the phallic one with the knowledge of magic. For example, Tony knows the Tarot: "Of all the suits, Tony most favored swords, and the card named Page of Swords was always her particular card; Natalie liked the card named the Magician, and thought the face on the card resembled her own" (228).

When Natalie first imagines Tony, this chimera of power has only a nascent hint of the dominating character she will become. Tony complains that the Tarot will not work for playing solitaire, implying that she wants Natalie as another player. But soon Tony appropriates Natalie's money. When they go on their outing, it is Natalie who has money. Yet Tony says, "We have *plenty* of money" (242). In front of the theater they see a poster advertising a movie; the poster features an amorphous machine-like monster. Tony says it is like "one of those hidden personalities." Natalie says, "It's got hold of some girl" (246). Next, Tony is gratuitously hostile to a one-armed man, and Natalie does not understand why. Nor is she aware of the double entendres when Tony responds to Natalie's attempts at self-empowerment:

"I have talents for resistance they don't even suspect."

"Perhaps," said Tony dryly, "they have antagonists you have not yet encountered."

Trying to imagine the thoughts of those she thinks are conspiring against her and Tony, Natalie believes she and Tony see the conspiracy clearly:

Suppose I wanted to destroy the people who saw it clearly, and refused to join up with all my dull ordinary folk, the ones who plod blindly along. What I would do is not set them against numbers of dull people, but I would invent for each one a single antagonist, who was calculated to be strong in exactly the right points.

Natalie does not catch onto Tony's retort: "You invent someone smart enough to destroy your enemies, you invent them so smart you've got a new enemy" (261). Natalie is similarly obtuse and Tony similarly blunt when Natalie shows that she does not know that Tony is her enemy: "'Only one antagonist . . . only one enemy,' Natalie said. 'That's very true,' Tony said" (ellipses in original 273).

Tony starts showing signs of paranoia: "'The question is,' Tony said . . . 'whether we can still escape, or whether they will have us after all. . . . They want to pull us back, and start us all over again just like them and doing the things they want to do and acting the way they want to act and saying and thinking and wanting all the things they live with every day" (254–55). She makes similar statements. But Tony is projecting: the question becomes whether or not Tony will have Natalie after all—whether Tony will sexually dominate Natalie. At the park, Tony leads Natalie by the arm into the trees just as Natalie's assaulter did: "Tony took her arm and said, 'This way'" (266). Also like the rapist, Tony's vision is exploitive and selfish; she says of her vision of life, it includes "nothing in all time except me and what I want" (267). Tony sounds like a male seducer steeling himself:

Tony put her hand on Natalie's arm, almost casually, and held her.

"Wait a while," Tony said. "I'm almost ready." "I'm almost ready," she repeated reassuringly. "It won't take long. What are you afraid of?" When Natalie, suddenly helpless, did not answer, she patted Natalie's arm lightly and said, "Don't be afraid."

Natalie sees that Tony has become a seducer, a demon lover, but as before she cannot express her thoughts: "Wanting to say, Have there been others? Are you experienced? Am I the first? What did they say? Do? Were they afraid? Did it happen here? Why does it happen at all? Who put you up to it? May I please go home?" (274). Finally Natalie refuses the seduction: "'I will *not*,' said Natalie, and ripped herself away. She *wants* me, Natalie thought with incredulity, and said again, aloud, "I will *not*" (275). (In *The Haunting of Hill House*, Eleanor dreams of resisting her molester after metonymically displacing herself onto a child.)

Natalie does not understand that the figure of the one-armed man is a metonym for Tony as this imaginary double regresses back into her origins as a seducer: "Natalie did not know what Tony had thought of the one-armed man, nor did she know why Tony had spoken to him as she did" (254). Tony speaks harshly to him because he is about to supplant her. At first Natalie, under Tony's influence, believes that the one-armed man is part of the conspiracy. Visualizing through Natalie, the third-person narrator says, "And the one-armed man, then, had been sent to spring the trap as the circle grew closer and closer" (259). Even the sign pointing to the lake is the one-armed man personified, "pointing with one imperative arm at the lake; 'Paradise Park,' it announced" (264). The one-armed man, mediating in a succession of substitutions between Arnold and Tony, is a figure of castration, as is Tony with her lack. But an even more obvious figure of displaced castration is the eponymous figure Tony introduces to Natalie: Hangsaman. Natalie imagines vengeance by using an instrument that protected her assaulter: a tree.

Tony's elusiveness arises not only from her imaginary status but also from the narrative point of view. While Tony is somewhat mimetic, especially in her regression, she is also a fantasy character. As such, she is somewhat like a mimetic character in psychological realism, yet she is like a supernatural character in the marvelous. As usual, readers have missed the necessity of this complex and ambiguous focalization. Nolan Miller wrote in *The Antioch Review*, "We need preserved a consistent point of view; . . . Miss Jackson doesn't play fair" (239). But the real problem is that Miller did not know what he was talking about. For as Rosemary Jackson points out, the fantastic resolves Tzvetan Todorov's supposedly unresolvable tension into the uncanny. A case in point, Tony refers to the psychology of the subject in which she resides. This multivocality with which Jackson constructs her derives in part from seeing her through the dissonant Natalie. Before the advent of Tony, the third-person narration seems to be guileless, but even from the outset of the novel the narration is not fully omniscient even with a vantage point outside of Natalie (who is the novel's only point-of-view character). For example, as the novel begins, the narrator does not know if others besides Natalie hear laughter when Arnold speaks: "When her father spoke he was accompanied by a sound of distant laughter, unheard probably by anyone except his daughter" (4).

As Natalie grows increasingly divided, the narrator grows increasingly fallible. First the narrator implies the unlikely development that after an early lunch the sun is going down: "When they came out of the cafeteria it was unusually dark for early afternoon" (253). The narrator implies that the darkness is not due to clouds, smog, a solar eclipse, and so forth, but due to time. For the day to be this short in fall, the scene would have to be above the arctic circle. Soon Jackson reveals that the narrator, because the visualization is through Natalie, is unaware of things an omniscient narrator would know. For example, the narration here begins like a trustworthy report but moves further into Natalie's consciousness, resulting in a third-person narrator who, like Natalie, does not know if the trees are whispering: "Over their heads the trees leaned toward one another, nodding and perhaps whispering ahead that they had come" (267). The effect of the narrator's fallibility at the end undermines the assertions of the trees' leaning and nodding. Jackson can have it both ways, underwriting the image and yet not endorsing it. Similarly, the narrator is unsure whether Tony is nearby: "And since this was only a clump of trees, after all, the path must go forward out of it and very probably Tony was right now standing just ahead" (271). Similarly, the narrator does not know if Natalie has spoken aloud because Natalie herself does not know, cannot tell if her voice is only internal: "Natalie put her head down on her knees and thought, I wish I could go home, and perhaps said it aloud" (273).

Another way Jackson achieves this double-voicedness is to have the narrator lay out the image with seeming dependability and then in effect to erase it by showing that the image originates in Natalie. For example, the narrator states that Natalie, regarding the trees, felt "that they leaned forward to watch her" (270). Again the narrator separates the image into a relative clause that takes attention away from the fact that this image is happening in Natalie's mind: "It then occurred to her that she was expected here" (272). The ambiguity is enhanced by the fact that some things that occur to her could be verifiable. These ambiguities of point of view undermine the ostensibly successful return of the questing heroine from the psychic underworld to the self-fashioning bourgeois world. The narrator's last utterance that Natalie is now "alone, and grown-up, and powerful, and not at all afraid" only seems to be infallible; the other voice undermining it is that this statement is another of the narrator's mergers with the character's delusions (280). And Jackson destabilizes the affirmation by revealing its individualist underpinnings: Natalie is alone. Her victory at overcoming Tony is only something she thinks is true: "She thought theatrically, I will never see Tony any more; she is gone, and knew that, theatrical or not, it was true. She had defeated her own enemy, she thought, and she would never be required to fight again" (276). The fact that on the last page she resists the temptation to kill herself is only a sop for readers wanting a happy ending. Arthur M. Saltzman writes that a character can imagine an epiphany (9). So can readers.

That she wants to kill herself by jumping off the bridge leading back to campus is less a resolution to the plot than the beginning of a new one: suicidal tendencies are surfacing in a schizoid personality. Natalie has not overcome Tony; Natalie has only lost track of her. Natalie is so fissured that one personality loses touch with the other. The deceptive plot arises from the same technique as the amorphous characterization: indeterminate focalization. Ironically, the ambiguous narration serves not only to make the resolution irresolute but also to unify the plot until that resolution.

One technique that disrupts the reliability is personification. It is not just that the narrator is unaware of whether the garden enjoyed the morning but that the garden could enjoy the morning: "It was a beautiful morning, and the garden seemed to be enjoying it. The grass had exerted itself, . . . the sky was blue and serene, as though it had never known a tear" (9). Such personification foreshadows Natalie's confrontation with sisterhood. Believing the mountains are extending themselves to her, she says twice, "Sister, sister." This scene even foreshadows the sequence that will lead from the assaulter taking her arm, to the one-armed man, to the one-armed sign, to Tony taking her arm. Natalie regards the mountains "with her cheek on her arm" (30). Another image that foreshadows her development along a contiguity of displacements and her regression back to its origins is that of the trees. When Natalie leaves Langdon's party and walks out to a porch, she sees Tony: "One tree demonstrated that it was not rooted and perhaps not completely indifferent by disengaging itself from the others and coming toward Natalie" (190). And in the end when Tony leads her into the park, the narrator says, "They had come, then, to the trees where Natalie had once encountered knights in armor" (53).

Her refuge was the stand of trees in the garden, where she played at games such as pirate. The subtext of pirate stories is that they take not only property but also propriety, leaving female victims inappropriate for the cult of true womanhood.[5] After she is assaulted in these trees, the trees that appear later do so only to foreshadow the arrival of figures in the metonymic contiguity after her assault: Arthur, Elizabeth, and Tony. (And the hangsaman card features a tree.) Similarly, darkness almost without exception appears only when one of the metonyms for abuse appears. The indeterminacy of Tony, achieved by ambiguous focalization, finally emerges more clearly as imagined in the end of the plot. Tony's imaginary nature appears when she says, "Imagine, being people" (260).

She has to imagine what it would be like to be a real person. Natalie is also of two minds about her situation. She says she imagines it, but she does not take her statement literally: "'If *I* were inventing this world,' she said, '—and I may have, at that—I would gauge my opponents more accurately'" (261). But she is imagining, and she has not gauged Tony accurately. Her utterance, like this novel's characterization, point of view, and resolution, is double voiced. Jackson thereby hints to the reader who has read mimetically until the last few pages that the plot, characterization, and optics have all been double voiced.

The setting, too, is double voiced. Her garden's idyllic status in her childhood foreshadows violence: "She had delighted in playing pirate and cowboy and knight in armor among the trees." Another Jackson technique, which appears in her short fiction and that will appear in the rest of her novels, is to merge the character and the setting. Because Natalie dissociates and projects (registered in the personification of the trees), the garden is "a functioning part of her personality" (28). But the garden is a place chosen for her by her father: "She did not really prefer the garden to several other spots in the world, . . . but the garden was closest, and it pleased her father to see her wandering morning-wise among the roses" (8–9). Nature is not an innocent refuge; her notions of it are historically conditioned. Like Americans in Annette Kolodny's *The Lay of the Land*, Natalie femaleizes nature:

> The mountains, full-bosomed and rich, extended themselves to her in a surge of emotion, turning silently as she came, receiving her, and Natalie, her mouth against the grass and her eyes tearful from looking into the sun, took the mountains to herself and whispered, "Sister, sister. . . . Sister, sister," she said, and the mountains stirred, and answered. (30)

The female nature is already the territory of rape and killing—for pirates, knights, aristocrats, industrialists, cowboys, and so forth. Her landscape is always already the fenced preserve of the patriarchal Symbolic. She rehearses her insertion into the Symbolic by circling the campus, imagining herself a landed aristocrat surveying his land. As such, she reinscribes her father, who overlooks his party (where she will be assaulted) "with the satisfaction of a country squire surveying his horses and his dogs and his shooting preserve" (32).

Another fantastic and Gothic technique Jackson uses is the merging of character not just into nature but also into architecture. Just as her parents are displaced by later adults and Tony, her childhood home is displaced into her dormitory. Her childhood home is supposed to be her sanctuary, but she is alienated from her home for at least two years before the plot begins. As a result, even before she leaves her childhood home she takes refuge in a "home of a mind" (88). As befits not only a typical Jackson heroine but also one inserted into the Symbolic by Arnold as a quasi-aristocrat, an eighteenth-century design informs Natalie's dormitory. The exterior looks like an "eighteenth-century town house"; the interior has an "eighteenth-century entrance hall," an "eighteenth-century foyer," and "eighteenth-century wallpaper" (216–17). By contrast, her oppositional fantasy character lives in a dormitory whose design celebrates the carnival that the bourgeois Symbolic would have her repress: "This house was rococo where her own was classic" (226). Natalie's ostensible escape from the dormitory into nature with Tony turns out to be a regression back along the chain of surrogates to her childhood home. As Tony, like the adults and their surrogates in Natalie's life, turns into a monstrous seducer like James Harris, Tony becomes not only a siren urging Natalie's regression but also a seducer trying to hypnotize her into acquiescence: "You can remember it all if you try, and all you have to do is lie back against a comforting hand and close your heavy eyes and say, 'I am here, I am where I belong, I have come home'" (269). The inflection at the end of the next sentence suggests that Tony does not have to keep Natalie in the park because keeping her in the prison of home is accomplished by keeping her in the desire to go home: "If you want to run home, nobody's going to keep you *here*" (275).

Even the college is a metonym for her father's home. She does the same thing at college as she does at home: friendless, loveless, she holes up in her room, the proverbial madwoman in the attic, and attempts the writing cure. And in both places she writes while gazing out the window and daydreaming. At home she looks out at the trees between her and the femaleized mountains; at college she looks out her window at the trees that mediate between her and Tony. As with some of Jackson's other characters, she uses the window as a dream screen. She moves the bed so that it (and her sleeping head) will lie under the window. The undecidable line between consciousness and fantasy is similar to the undecidable line between waking and sleeping: "She sat on the bed, opened the window and, dropping her head onto the windowsill, rested quietly with her eyes closed" (218). She also places the typewriter so she can look over it through the window. And as she daydreams she imagines a male antagonist that she must defeat, a figure that supersedes the detective and mediates between him and Tony.

As usual in Jackson's fiction, writing is one of the primary activities of the characters. Natalie writes, both a "secret diary" that she nonetheless hopes to publish (37) and the "compositions . . . hidden in her desk" (29). In addition, the man who assaults her has heard that she is a writer.

Also, her writing facilitates her interpellation. Her identity is so bound up with writing that when Vicki and Anne enter her room (when Natalie is gone) to snoop and find out about her, they read her books. Moreover, her father the English professor publishes in the *Passionate Review* (Jackson's swipe at the cold war centrists at the *Partisan Review*) (135). And when she fantasizes that the campus is her estate, a new fantasy supplants the first one. The borders of the fictional estate (a reinscription of the imprint her father's neo-aristocratic holdovers have had on her) become the borders of a sheet of writing paper (over which she sees the window as a dream screen). Also, the title *Hangsaman* is from a playing card.

In addition, Vicki and Anne use writing to play pranks. For example, they write to a woman's date, pretending to be that woman, and cancel the date. When they send party invitations to the (all-male) faculty, they include orders for them not to bring their wives. Anne in turn seems to be a figure from a literal text reprinted in the social text: Natalie scornfully regards Anne as resembling something from *Little Women* (110).

Natalie, too, has an imagination mired not only in the oedipal social text but also in a masculine literal text. When she fantasizes that the detective interrogating her is her father, the detective's dialogue is the typical one from crime fiction. And not only does the murder occur in the study, but Natalie is also found sitting at the desk. The father whom the detective displaces is himself so textually constituted that he seems to be a living fiction.

The narrator's immersion in literature surfaces from the many allusions. When Natalie fantasizes that she and her family are unearthed a thousand years hence, she does so by reinscribing Hamlet's unearthing of Yorick: an archaeologist examines her skull. There are several allusions to writers of Jackson's region. Natalie's professor, Arthur Langdon, has the maiden name of Mark Twain's wife. (Twain and his wife are buried in her hometown of Elmira, just south of Rochester and Syracuse and just west of Bennington.) Jackson alludes to a writer to whom she is often compared, Nathaniel Hawthorne, by recalling Pearl's supernatural walking which, resisting gravity, borders on levitation. Tony walks in the forest "seeming not to put her feet down on the soundless moss" (272). The narrator alludes to other Gothic forbears, Edgar Allan Poe and Charlotte Perkins Gilman. In a scene lit by firelight, Poe describes the figure of the red death as *"untenanted"* (676). Gilman uses this same odd word to describe the house in "The Yellow Wallpaper" (39). Likewise, Jackson calls Natalie's absent space by the childhood home's fireplace "untenanted" (213). She also alludes to two of the primary writers who kept Gothic alive in her time. First she recalls William Faulkner's dichotomous Darl Bundren, who says that "our lives ravel out into the no-wind, no-sound" (191) by saying that Natalie wants to "sink away into that lovely nothing-space" (137).⁶ And in a pointed allusion to Blanche Du Bois, another victim associated with trees, Jackson has Natalie imagine that the detective tells her that she cannot "rely upon the generosity of strangers" (39).

Jackson also has two incidents resembling scenes from novels that her friends were writing at the time—novels that Jackson might have read while they were in progress. Ralph Ellison's modernized Gothic figure of the grotesque animated toy doll being sold on the street looks like Hangsaman himself: "Natalie stopped and stared at Tony's hanged man. It was a toy in the shop window, a tiny figure on a trapeze which turned and swung, around and around, endlessly and irritatingly" (248). And Jackson has Tony do something similar to what Holden Caulfield does when leaving school early in the morning. Holden wakes up the others by yelling *"Sleep tight ya morons!"* (52). To get the same effect, Tony slams the door: "Tony let the door slam behind them in a gesture calculated to awaken every sleeper within hearing" (233). Likewise, Holden's ostensible dislike for the movies appears with Natalie "resenting . . . the movie word 'frosh'" (73).

*Hangsaman* features Jackson's most ambitious syntax. Nowhere else does she use as much parallelism, balance, introjectories, and suspended predication. Nowhere else does she use as many cumulative sentences, piling on participials and appositives. In addition, her free indirect discourse distances the reader from both the third-person narrator and Natalie, and yet it immerses the reader in both. The effect is to make the narration even more undecidable; it makes the third-person report less reliable by making it seem more like it is coming from Natalie, and it makes Natalie's thoughts more reliable by making them sound more like they are coming from the third-person (most reading communities condition the reader to trust a third-person narrator).

As language, this novel is Jackson's most complex. But as psychology, her next novel, *The Bird's Nest*, is even more complex than *Hangsaman*.

## CHAPTER SEVEN

# The Bird's Nest

Published in 1954, Shirley Jackson's third novel continues its predecessor's focus on textuality and subject formation. The importance of class exhibited in the first novel will not return until her fourth. *The Bird's Nest* features Jackson's most ambitious use to date of the Gothic motif of the house to figure the self. Eight years before Ken Kesey's *One Flew Over the Cuckoo's Nest*, the bird's nest is a metaphor for insanity. But whereas Kesey uses the metaphor to refer to the house of many patients, Jackson uses it to refer to the patient as housing many personalities—the self as a heteroglossia of introjected Others. The protagonist, Elizabeth Richmond, is another one of Jackson's disunified subjects, but this time she contains four personalities (Elizabeth, Beth, Betsy, and Bess). And instead of one antagonist there are two. She conflicts with not only the father figure but also with the phallic mother figure. While Jackson does not develop the subject formation of these personalities in quite the linguistic depth shown with Natalie in *Hangsaman,* the novel as a whole is Jackson's most intertextual to date. In addition, the focalization here is more complex than in any other Jackson novel. The third-person narration not only switches between each of the protagonist's four various personalities as the point-of-view character, but also alternates with the first-person narration by the patient's therapist.

This therapist, Victor Wright, is a pompous, manipulative, pretentious know-it-all. As such, he reprises Arnold Waite from *Hangsaman* as a satiric parody of Stanley Edgar Hyman. However, Wright is not as grotesque as Waite is, and the parody of Hyman is subtler here.[1] Dr. Wright is a semiretired physician who has largely given up that profession to dabble in psychology and literature even though he is incompetent at both. He thinks his testimony is authoritative, as if he is the only witness. But his account is superseded by that of the third-person narrator, who often reports on the personalities when they are out of the doctor's sight, thereby putting him into the mix not as the authoritative voice but as one of five disturbed personalities. If Wright could read the third-person narration, he would feel neutralized. He is as unaware of many of the facts arising from the third-person testimony as each personality usually is of the other three. Although Wright, like Waite, is Jackson's creation, the third-person narrator is much closer to the voice of the implied author.

Wright's narration is suspect. It is not just that he fails to understand his patient, but also that he fails to understand himself—to understand that his hypocrisy often extends to dishonesty. In other words, he recuperates his own lies. For example he says, "I am an honest man" (35) but he contradicts himself when he says he was "afraid" of Betsy and then, two sentences later, says he "was not afraid of her" (155). Similarly, at first he does not like Elizabeth's Aunt Morgen. He describes her as not just "unattractive" (184) but a "fright" (143), even "a dragon" (83). For him, to be conversing with her in her home is to be "thoroughly wound about with spider webs" (187). But in the end, he is trying to get her to marry him so that (reminiscent of Hyman) he can spend her money. He even prides himself on how he uses his dishonesty (although he would not call it that) as a therapeutic technique. He says that his patient is so stupid that he needs to use only "perfunctory deviousness" (43). Right before he asks "Can we not talk together as friends, Betsy?" (75) he tells her, "If I find that you are of no use to me in my investigations, I will surely send you away and never let you come again" (74). Nonetheless, he states that he told Betsy (while she was hypnotized) that he is trustworthy: "'A doctor's first duty is to establish trust between himself and his patient,' I said . . . when she was . . . in my power" (47). With that last phrase, he unwittingly reveals himself as a parody of a Gothic mad scientist. He even tries to fool the reader with false modesty. He says, "Perhaps my literary style will leave something to be desired" but he is clearly impressed with his belletrism, which he takes for literary expertise (35).

He is oblivious to his inconsistencies. He makes Betsy keep her eyes closed, even when she is writing him notes, and then says without irony, "I could write a better hand with my eyes shut" (65). He remarks that Bess is foolish because she would do away with the other three personalities so that she can have all of the money: "She would willingly sacrifice three-quarters of her conscious life, if she might only be allowed to hold onto four-quarters of her money" (171). But Wright's solution is to repress all but the personality called "Beth" so that he can gain access to the fortune.

He surmises that the origin of her split into a multiple personality "must date from the most patent emotional shock in Miss R.'s life, the death of her mother" (69). He never realizes that the worst shock, which occurred earlier and began the splitting, was being sexually assaulted as a child. This trauma occurred at the hands of her mother's androgynously named boyfriend, Robin, who robbed her of far more than her virginity, thereby engendering this bird's nest of personalities. The most common cause of multiple personalities is childhood sexual abuse. Wright never realizes the etiology of his patient's condition because he is squeamish about Freudian reductionism: "I am not one of your psychoanalysts, but merely an honest general practitioner." He tries to erase the traces that would show him how this patient was inscribed: "Analytical nastiness has no place in the thoughts of a decent and modest girl like Miss R" (37). And finally, this would-be detective of the mind does not realize that, as his own discoveries will show, his client has committed matricide and her aunt is an accessory not only for that murder but also for Elizabeth's rape.

Dr. Wright classifies his profession as exclusively male. He links his practice with maleness when Morgen challenges him: "I had been insulted in my profession, my manhood" (200). When she directs the conversation, he feels "unmanned" (186). It is not only medicine but also writing that he defines as male: "a good writer is much the same as a good doctor; honest, decent, self-respecting men" (36). His confusion of himself as Wright the writer, as well as Wright the victorious righter of physical and mental wrongs through the rites of medicine, appears in his account of his patient's neurosis:

> I may liken this state and its cure to (if my reader will forgive such an ignoble comparison) a stoppage in a water main; Miss R. had somehow contrived to stop up the main sewer of her mind (gracious heaven, how I have caught myself in my own analogy!) with some incident or traumatic occurrence which was, to her mind, indigestible, and could not be assimilated or passed through the pipe. This stoppage had prevented all but the merest trickle of Miss R.'s actual personality from getting through, and given us the stagnant creature we had known. My problem was, specifically, to get back through the pipe to where the obstruction was, and clear it away. Although the figure of speech is highly distasteful to one as timid of tight places as myself, the only way in which I might accomplish this removal is by going myself (through hypnosis, you will perceive) down the pipe until, the stoppage found, I could attack it with every tool of common sense and clear-sighted recognition. There; I am thankful to be out of my metaphor at last, although I confess I think Thackeray might be proud of me for exploring it so persistently. . . . Let us assume, then, that the good Doctor

Wright is steeling himself to creep manfully down a sewer pipe (and I wonder mirthfully, whether by calling poor Miss R's mind a sewer I might not be approaching wickedly close to your psychoanalytic fellows, those plumbers to whom all minds are cesspools and all hearts black!). (47–48)

All of that from one who shrinks from "analytical nastiness" (163). Thus he is infelicitous both as a writer and as a therapist.

His incompetence as a psychologist is largely a result of his paternalism, which is at best condescending. He says of his patient, "I thought of myself, frequently, as fatherly, and often found myself addressing her as a fond parent speaks to a precious child" (51). But he is more often controlling and threatening. In his paternalism, he imagines that he is responsible for one personality's existence (as if she did not exist before him). He calls the personalities forth by first hypnotizing whichever personality is out and then commanding whomever he wants in his harem to come forth. He cajoles the personalities he does not like, Betsy and Bess, to keep their eyes closed—thereby keeping them in the dark. He prides himself on his control. He says of Elizabeth, "I could . . . subdue her into the trance state at will. . . . She could no longer revolt against my treatment" (58). This satiric parody of a doctor anticipates the comic doctors who figure in much of postmodern fiction.[2] He also recalls Jackson's actual doctors, who prescribed her pain pills, diet pills, antidepressants, and tranquilizers. (When she died, her daughter found her not breathing and called Dr. James Toolan, who was taking a nap; he told her to call an ambulance, and then he went back to sleep.) (Oppenheimer 269)

Wright speaks of himself as godlike. Regarding the appearance of the personalities, he compares himself to the Creator: "I had, with a magic touch, called them into active life" (69). Similarly, he says to Betsy, "It was I who brought you here in the first place" (74). When he is not God, he is God's agent: he describes his meeting with Elizabeth as "a cross-examination of which the Spanish Inquisitors might have been proud" (43–44). He uses a military and yet sexual metaphor to describe his treatment of his patient. He will "lead an unscrupulous flank attack upon her" (170). He threatens a personality he does not like with sadistic punishment: "If I had my way, Miss, you would be soundly whipped and taught to mind your manners" (157). The dark humor, of course, is that by whipping her he would be whipping all four. Furthermore, by stating that he can reunify the patient by leaving out a personality he does not like, he threatens one personality with what to her is death. He shouts at Bess, "Without my aid you will . . . cease to exist!" (201). For the good doctor, then, Wright makes might. And he ignores his own evil by projecting it onto his patient. Betsy, he says, was "a wicked and mischievous creature, bent on making trouble, and with what fearful designs in that black heart I could not begin to imagine" (76). In the end, he ostensibly cures his patient by keeping only the personality that is most tractable and compliant and passive and happy, and by effectively killing off the personalities that he does not like: Elizabeth, because she is a depressive, neurasthenic complainer; Bess, because she is concerned with preserving her inheritance, which the doctor tries to get; and Betsy, because she is the most pre-oedipal.

ᛟᛈᛟ

*The Bird's Nest* amplifies the Gothic metaphor of the building as the subject.[3] The building this time is a museum, which allegorizes the archaeology of the protagonist's selves. Although uncovering Jackson's allegorical treatment of the building makes the analogy seem obvious, the text hides her design and tool marks. As the building consists of four floors (a basement and three storeys), so the protagonist consists of four personalities. Analogous to the basement and foundation, Betsy is the pre-oedipal child of the Imaginary; analogous to the first floor as the first visible storey, Bess is the early adolescent whose first concern is the commodities fetish; on top of that, Beth is the late adolescent who has learned to negotiate the Symbolic by being a feminized "lady"; and as the last storey of the finished construction, Elizabeth is the young adult, the college graduate working in the pink-collar ghetto as a wage-slave secretary whose mind and body are cracking under the stress.

As the top floor begins to slant, so Elizabeth begins "to slip at about the same time" (5). As the museum's "foundations had begun to sag" (3) because it was constructed from weak materials, so Elizabeth's precarious four-part self cracks up because she was constructed out of several traumas. As the building gives way because of "the extraordinary weight some of the antiquities contained therein," so the weighty remnants of her past (as you will see, her mother's boyfriend has raped her and the mother has committed matricide) contribute to her fall (4). As the museum's artifacts are an arsenal from the Civil War, so Elizabeth was constructed from the civil war of the family, which began as a struggle not of brother against brother but of sister against sister. As the effort to rebuild the museum begins by sinking a vertical shaft from the top floor to the basement, so does Wright drill down through the layers of personalities. As "the wall had been taken away . . . directly to the left of her desk, and within reaching distance of her left elbow as she typed," so the wall of this character has such a big hole in it that it is in effect gone. As the new shaft suggests a deathblow (which will come to three of the personalities) because it leaves "the innermost skeleton of the building exposed," so Elizabeth feels "an almost irresistible temptation to hurl herself downward into the primeval sands upon which the museum presumably stood" (5). As the museum is administered by the paperwork on the top floor, so Elizabeth (the educated personality) is the secretary handling that paperwork. As the first and second floors contain the "unperishing remnants of the past" (4), so Elizabeth's repressed personalities reveal the family secrets. As "Elizabeth's office allowed of no concealment" of the entrance to the shaft while the entrances on the lower floors were hidden, so it is a hole in Elizabeth that leads down to the hidden holes. As the hole into the shaft on the second floor leads through a sarcophagus, so the mother's murder leads to the construction of Beth. As the hole into the shaft on the first floor is behind a door marked "Do not enter," so Bess is a young adolescent jealous of her turf and possessions—just the kind of character to have such a sign on her door, especially in Jackson's fiction (5). As it falls to the feminized "daughters of the town" (4) to raise the funds for rebuilding the museum, so Elizabeth's most feminized personality, Beth, will have to be the structure that holds the new Elizabeth together.

The plot is generally the reverse of the story. While the story of the construction of Elizabeth's personalities developed like one storey growing out of another—the basement first and the top floor last—the plot mostly reverses that development: Elizabeth appears first. At the beginning of the plot, she is twenty-three; at the end, twenty-four. According to the third-person narrator, Elizabeth's mother has died four years previously, which would be when Elizabeth was eighteen or nineteen. Elizabeth herself says the death occurred "over four years ago," which increases the chances that she was actually eighteen at her mother's death (69). Elizabeth is nondescript, a cipher, her identity stripped to that of a miserable bureaucrat whose initials suggest that she is a kind of emergency room: "The letters signed 'per er' and the endless listings of exhibits vouched for by E. Richmond were the outstanding traces of her presence" (6). It is this personality that first goes to Wright with complaints of headaches, backaches, nausea, and fatigue. Wright pities her, but he does not sympathize or much less empathize with her, never realizing that her work is insufferable. While his dislike of her is not as strong as his dislike of Bess and Betsy, he still prefers Beth.

Beth, the personality that developed just before Elizabeth did, is his favorite because she is the most "ladylike"—passive, compliant, and cooperative. He says that Beth, "although weak and almost helpless, was at least possessed of a kind of winsomeness, and engaging in her very helplessness" (153). She is as passive as Elizabeth, but does not complain. She often compliments Wright, but politely, without playing up to him. Like Elizabeth, she has no sense of humor or irony. What he does not like about her is that she is weak. He wants her to be strong so she can become the dominant personality and keep the others repressed. But that is a tall order when he also expects her to be passive. She says she was "inside" on the day her mother died, which implies Bess was "out" when the host body killed the mother (71).

Bess, the early adolescent with the commodities fetish, is motivated by greed. Starting with this novel and continuing through to Jackson's last, someone (in time-honored Gothic technique) kills someone else for the family fortune. Bess shakes her debilitated alcoholic mother to death (245). Morgen has told Bess that the reason why Bess's mother did not desert Bess for one of the mother's many boyfriends is that the mother had to stay with the daughter to keep access to the money the father entrusted to his daughter until she was to turn twenty-five. But because Bess says that Morgen's ostensible devotion to her is really a ruse so that Morgen can keep the money, the aunt may be guilty of what she accuses the mother of doing. Bess says, "Everyone thinks they can play tricks on me to get money" (173) and that Wright and Betsy "plot against" her to take the money (175). She is correct. But she is not believable as far as time and her age are concerned. She thinks she is nineteen (209) but also thinks it has been three weeks since her mother died (152) when it has really been about four or five years.

In some respects, Jackson's characterization of this multiple personality is psychological realism. An individual with a multiple personality can continue to live in the present even while out of touch with much of the present, with the result, as with Bess, of being obsessed by a trauma as if it just happened, and yet still being aware of other things that happened years later. Each personality of a multiple personality, then, is itself susceptible to the same kind of splitting. New personalities can appear when old ones splinter. Also, some of the personalities can know nothing, something, or everything about none, some, or all of the other personalities. In this case, Bess knows something of each of the others but they know little of her, which suggests that a woman defending her financial independence is repressed in the others; Elizabeth and Beth know something of each other, which suggests that Elizabeth is Beth broken down; and Betsy knows everyone, which suggests that she is the first personality, the pre-oedipal child. Betsy does not know when she was born (something an older personality would usually know). But she thinks she is about sixteen, which suggests that she quit growing a year or two after the development of Beth (who developed after Bess killed her mother). Bess replaced Betsy when the latter could not fully develop mentally after Robin, her mother's boyfriend, raped her. Wright asks her, "Why did Robin run away?" She answers, "Because I said I'd tell my mother what we did" (124). Typical of children who have suffered sexual abuse, her comment places the blame equally on her and Robin; she says the event was "what we did" rather than what Robin did to her. (Similarly, Natalie Waite in *Hangsaman* describes herself as blameworthy.) Elsewhere Betsy takes most of the blame. Hallucinating, she imagines that a man in a hotel is Robin, speaks to him as if the fault is mostly hers, and then defends against the fact that her mother was the enabler: "I won't let you, not ever any more, . . . and neither will my mother" (134). When she repeatedly touches on the topic of Robin with a waiter in the hotel, the waiter asks, "The one you had such trouble getting rid of?" Betsy's response to the waiter shows that her adaptation is to repress enough of the memory to minimize the shock, but to retain enough of the memory so that she will always know that Robin is dangerous: "Betsy nodded violently, swallowed, and said, 'But I don't have to remember that part, I decided on the bus. One bad thing about Robin ought to be enough, don't you think?'" (111).

In fact, just as one event with Robin can be a metonym for all sexual events with him, so he can serve as a metonym for all of the mother's boyfriends, and even for other men, some of whom might also have sexually assaulted Betsy. When she thinks that the man in the hotel is Robin, she cries out, "Not *this* one, not Robin again?" (134). She thereby implies that Robin is one of many; similarly, the question mark implies that she is asking the woman she addresses if Betsy has to submit to Robin, as if the woman is a displacement of an enabling mother who cooperated in the abuse of her child. Indeed, Betsy has gone to New York and to this hotel in search of the mother who abandoned her and whose death is unknown to Betsy (because she represses the memory). Betsy has told the woman, a hotel clerk, that Betsy's mother is in the rose room, so the clerk has taken her there. Apparently her mother spent a lot of time with different men, so hotel rooms therefore could have been a part of Betsy's childhood. The man's real name is Mr. Harris (recalling the recurrent demon lover who appears to Jackson's women as their savior prince but then turns into a monster). If Betsy has regressed to the point that the man looks like Robin, the woman would understandably look to her like her mother. Betsy flees the room and yet says to Mr. Harris, "Robin darling, call me Lisbeth" (the mother's nickname) (135).

Her fear evidently traces to an earlier attempt to solve the oedipal crisis by identifying with the mother as Robin's love object: "I want Robin to call me Lisbeth too. Because whatever he calls you he's got to call me." Her oedipal confusion of herself and her mother appears in such desperate musings as this one, which suggests that this personality contains an oedipal triangle of Robin, the mother, and Betsy: "If I had a husband then my mother could marry him and we could all hide together and be happy." Two sentences later, she confuses herself with her mother: "My mother's name is Elizabeth Richmond, Elizabeth Jones before I was married." In the sentence after that, she goes from identifying with her mother while addressing Robin, to identifying with her mother while the mother displaces Robin with Betsy as the love object: "Call me Lisbeth like you do my mother, because Betsy is my darling Robin" (107). Other times, Betsy just denies the whole complex. She tells a waiter, "My mother left me with Aunt Morgen, . . . but she didn't go with Robin" (111). Tamar Heller writes of traditional female Gothic,[4] "Feminist critics have read the female Gothic as a narrative about mothers and daughters, in which a daughter who has lost her mother either discovers that she is not dead or finds mother substitutes in her place" (2). Betsy's substitute is Robin.

Betsy is childish. For example, she likes to sing nursery rhymes, including one about a mockingbird, appropriately enough. Similarly, she recites a nursery rhyme that captures her status as one of the eggs trying to hatch: "Put her in a pumpkin shell, and there she kept her very well" (76). The egg metaphor of four birds and one nest is implicit in her reworking of an old nursery rhyme: "Elizabeth, Beth, Betsy, and Bess, they all went together to find a bird's nest."

Betsy likes to play childish tricks on people. She tells the hotel waiter, "I'm the gingerbread boy" (112), another indication of her loosely gendered oedipal state. Usually her playfulness is oppositional. She does not like Bess (who is unaware of Betsy's existence) so she puts ink on Bess's head. Bess thinks she has just inexplicably poured ink on herself. Betsy directs much of her disruptive play toward Wright. Because he at first will not let her come out unless she is hypnotized and keeps her eyes shut, she calls him "old eye-closer" (81). To cajole him into letting her open her eyes, she tries to charm him with a nursery rhyme: "Do you remember the man who was wondrous wise and jumped into a bramble bush and scratched out both his eyes . . . may I open my eyes now?" (ellipses in original 75). When the doctor tries to get Bess to help him repress Betsy, Betsy impersonates Bess and fools Wright into thinking that he is conspiring with Bess without Betsy knowing (85). Betsy knows that she must be repressed if her host is supposed to act like Beth. She tells Wright, "You have no place for me in your pretty little world" (73). When he tries to charm her, she resists: "Do you suppose that I could learn to love *you*, Doctor Wrong? When

you wish me evil?" (67). In a scene of wild inflation in which she fantasizes becoming as gigantic and threatening as adults seem to her, she
threatens to eat him and Elizabeth. (Natalie Waite has a similar fantasy
of inflation and incorporation.)

On the surface, the plot is resolved to please those who want a
happy ending; the good doctor puts this Humpty-Dumpty back
together again. The doctor believes he has restored this living museum
by tossing out the bad and realigning the good: "We are able, as few
others have ever been, . . . to select what is finest and most elevating
from our own experience and bestow" (268). Like a social Darwinist
sacrificing lesser sorts, he has no qualms about killing off three personalities: "Each life, I think," said the doctor, "asks the devouring of
other lives for its own continuance; the radical aspect of ritual sacrifice,
the performance of a group, its great step ahead, was in organization;
*sharing* the victim was so eminently practical" (273). He sounds like a
character from "The Lottery."

It is not only the doctor but also the aunt who engenders this new
American Eve. They rechristen her Morgen Victoria. That the aunt dominates is clear not just from her getting top billing. The aunt, sounding
like Geraldine Jackson, is only partly joking when she tells Wright, "You
can be her mommy, and I'll be her daddy" (268). But this new Eve,
ostensibly restored to prelapsarian innocence, remembers some of her
past and therefore something of her prior selves. Her confused memory
is still schizoid. She says she can remember but then thinks, "I am
through with remembering" (253). Her memory confuses past and present: "When she sat down in the doctor's office she wondered always if
she was sitting down this time or just remembering sitting down the last
time." She also confuses herself with the new parental dyad:

> She was clouded with memory, bemused with the need for discovering
> reason and coherence in a patternless time; she was lost in an endless
> reflecting world, where only Aunt Morgen and Doctor Wright followed
> her, as she pursued them. When she turned to Aunt Morgen, crying her
> name, Aunt Morgen might answer from fifteen years ago." (252)

So instead of chasing her mother and Robin, she chases Aunt Morgen
and Wright. Without any glimpse inside Morgen Victoria, the deep
structure of the plot resolution surreptitiously suggests that the resolution of the plot is false, that Wright's heroic rescue has failed and the
maiden is still controlled by Betsy. When Morgen Victoria gets her hair
cut, ridding herself of what grew out of her past, she is ostensibly sig-
naling her new identity. But her roots still grow from the same skull.
Wright only partly perceives that it is the masculine Betsy who is again

asserting herself. Complaining that Morgen Victoria got a haircut without his permission, he calls her "shorn and bold" (255). Moreover, she regains her masculine assertiveness. In addition to calling herself the gingerbread "man," she signals that she is resisting Aunt Morgen and Wright: "I've run away from a little old woman and a little old man" (262). At first she says the other personalities are "gone," but then corrects herself by saying she has "eaten them all." She pretends to be ironic and poking fun at Betsy when she goes back to calling him "Dr. Wrong," and he does not see that it is he, not Betsy, who is the butt of the joke—indeed that Betsy is the author of this irony (257).

Aunt Morgen exacerbates Morgen Victoria's regression because as the mother of Morgen Victoria, she reprises her role as Betsy's surrogate mother. First, the aunt fancied the man who would become Betsy's father, but then the aunt lost him to her sister. When he died he left his fortune not to his wife Lisbeth, who he knew would drink it up, but in a trust for the daughter to be administered by the aunt. Morgen provided most of the care when Betsy was a child. The mother, usually away on a drunk, provided only enough care to maintain access to the fortune. This aunt sees herself as her sister, as married to the father. Referring to herself, she says, "living on my income," but then catches herself: "Your mother's income, I should have said. Mine only . . . because I outlived her" (11–12). And finally she will marry the "father" of the new daughter, Morgen Victoria.

The mother lays the foundation for Betsy's gender confusion. From the child's perspective, the mother disappears as did the father. The mother names the daughter Elizabeth after herself. More importantly, the mother not only treated the daughter as if Betsy were the mother's love object, but also as if the daughter is a successful rival for Robin's affection. According to Betsy, the mother said, "Let's take your poor Robin along with us, Betsy, my girl. Because poor old Robin is lonesome and he is Elizabeth's darling" (98). Betsy's repetitive ruminations, in which she alternates between the positions of child, mother, and boyfriend/father, reveal her obsessiveness about her dissociations—the eternal return of her repressed:

> My name is Betsy Richmond, Elizabeth Jones before I was married. "Betsy is my darling," my mother used to say, and I used to say "Elizabeth is my darling," and I used to say, "Elizabeth likes Robin best."
> I don't even know where Robin is, anymore, she thought, and he wouldn't remember me any more than anyone else, even if he saw me Robin would think I was someone he didn't know at all, and if my mother knew about him he'd be sorry. My mother loves me best, anyway, Betsy told herself forlornly, my mother was only teasing about not

loving me best, my mother pulled my hair and laughed and said "Elizabeth loves Robin best," and my mother loves me better than anyone. My name is Betsy Richmond and my mother's name is Elizabeth Richmond and she calls me Betsy. Robin did everything bad. (96)

Betsy's ruminations also take her back to the scene of her competition against her mother for Robin's affection. At the beach, after a picnic of hard-boiled eggs and peanut butter sandwiches (eggs hardened and nuts softened) the mother tells Betsy to get lost. When Betsy returns too soon, possibly witnessing the primal scene, she hears Robin say, "Leave the damn kid with Morgen next time." As if fragments of herself are confused with other fragments, she talks about herself/her mother in the third person: "I love coffee, I love tea, I love Betsy and Betsy loves me" (99). She is in denial of her mother's death, and her unresolved oedipal situation leaves her obsessing about going back to New York and finding her mother there as if the mother is the "center of the maze" (103).

❦

The most important nonfictional work enabling this novel is the definitive work of the time on multiples, *The Dissociation of a Personality* by a doctor named Morton Prince. Jackson studied it assiduously before writing this novel, and Dr. Wright cites it as well (64). Prince's work, too, is the study of a young female with four personalities. The dominant personality in each is also bookish and becomes unfit for work due to headaches. And each patient is a somnambulist whose other personalities come out while the dominant personality believes she is asleep. Wright dwells on the oppositional personality (Betsy) as does Prince. Like Betsy, Prince's pre-oedipal trickster makes the other three personalities do what they want not to do, and not do want they want to do. Jackson makes this conflict more comic; when Betsy tries to throttle Bess, the body is actually strangling itself.

Not only does Jackson's patient resemble Prince's, but Jackson's doctor also resembles Prince. As with Wright after him, Prince emplots his narrative with himself as the heroic healer whose agon is the resisting irrational female. Also as with Wright, his voice is that of the detective, and his method is that of the verbose pedant, citing his notes as if they are evidence of the objective world rather than his construction of it. Both are so impressed with themselves that they are oblivious to their unwitting self-revelations. And Prince declares the normal as true, good, and beautiful. He says that his task is "to determine which personality was comportable with abnormality and which with normality, and so find the real self " (241). Both Wright and Prince overlook their coercive tactics. Like Wright, who will not let his hypnotized patient open her eyes, Prince does the same, even to the point of "often using physical force" (91). Prince flaunts his power even as he denies it. He tries to put the pieces back together by throwing away most of them.

Yet Prince appears to have helped Jackson understand her own life. She has Wright use Prince's term *aboulia,* which Prince defines as "an inhibition of will by which a person is unable to do what he actually wishes to do" (15). Deflating the myth of self-fashioning is one of Jackson's recurring motifs. An obsessive-compulsive, Jackson must have been struck by the fact that she was unable to refrain from certain destructive behaviors, primarily overeating, at the same time that she was unable to refrain from certain productive behaviors, primarily writing. No wonder she is unsurpassed at representing the sense of being controlled by demons that seem to originate outside of the body or outside of consciousness. Her diminished choice was both her blessing and her curse.

Thus as before, Jackson's characterizations almost constitute psychological realism, but not exactly, because her unsteady characters in general are like her protagonist here, who is simpler than Prince's patient (and simpler than Jackson herself). The fictional character is thus allegorical—neither a mimesis of a multiple nor a fully developed extended metaphor of one, but in between. The dominant, conscious personality is not the cause of events but the effect; the will lies less with the conscious than with the unconscious; and there is not a self but selves. This allegorical quality corroborates Howard Nemerov's statement that Jackson was a fabulist.

Several other enabling texts inform this heteroglossic novel, all of them canonical. Wright compares himself to Dr. Frankenstein: "I saw myself, if the analogy be not too extreme, much like a Frankenstein with all the materials for a monster ready at hand" (154). He says, "I had made a monster and turned it loose upon the world" (202). He thereby inflates himself because of his great deflation. (This kind of scientist/villain is familiar in such tales as Herman Melville's "The Bell-Tower" and Nathaniel Hawthorne's "The Birthmark" and "Rappaccini's Daughter.")

Alongside these canonical texts, Jackson incorporates fairy tales. When Wright puts Elizabeth under hypnosis, he says that "she is like a sleeping beauty" (55) and "like a princess in a fairy romance" (68). And he can implicitly recast himself from Frankenstein into a medieval hero: "Perhaps I saw myself—even I!—as setting free a captive princess" (59). More specifically, he recasts himself as a knight: "I found myself angry rather than frightened, much in the manner of a knight (rather elderly, surely, and tired after his long quest) who, in the course of bringing his true princess home, has no longer any fear, but only a great weariness, when confronted in sight of the castle towers by a fresh dragon to slay" (62).

In addition, Jackson includes a nursery rhyme, from which the novel gets its title:[5] "Elizabeth, Beth, Betsy, and Bess, they all went together to find a bird's nest." Betsy, the personality who resists Dr. Wright and Aunt Morgen, and who detects their monetary motive, exposes the nursery rhyme to show its economic base. She says, "all went together to find a nestegg" (173) and "In came the doctor, in came the nurse, in came the lady with the big fat purse" (239). Jackson further deflates the privileged, innocent status of nursery rhymes by suggesting their devolution into popular songs of mass culture. As she falls asleep, Elizabeth murmurs a mélange of nursery rhymes, popular songs, and other tunes: "Elizabeth sang, wordlessly and almost without sound, to herself. The tune she used was of nursery rhymes, of faded popular songs, of whispers and fragments of tune she had heard long ago, and, singing, she fell asleep" (15). The linking of song and poetry appears when the aunt's silly friend, Mrs. Arrow, sings Rudyard Kipling's "The Road to Mandalay."

This novel is, then, one of Jackson's most intertextual. In her notes to her editor, she describes this novel as a combination of several genres, as being a "thriller" interpolated into a mystery: "i always wanted to write a mystery story. now i've got a beauty." While still drafting the story, she was sure that the ending would be indeterminate: "the final elizabeth personality is a secret. this is going to be a mystery story" (SJP Box 20). For Jackson, some parts of a mystery should remain indeterminate. Neither Wright as detective nor the third-person narrator divulges exactly what Morgen Victoria's psychology is in the end.

But reviewers, approaching this novel as a commodity in 1954, often regarded this intertextual anticipation of postmodernism in old-fashioned terms. One reviewer said of this novel, "It suffers from being unable for too long to make up its mind whether to be a tragedy or a comedy, finally settling on the fatal mistake of treating schizophrenia lightly" (Terral). For that reviewer, comedy cannot be serious, the comic and the tragic cannot coexist, and humor cannot be dark. Another reviewer found it "esthetically confusing" (Scott 4). Some were evidently confused by a narration alternating between Dr. Wright's first-person narration and the third-person limited omniscient narration. For example, the reviewer for *Punch* said, "How much better if she had given us a straightforward story!" (Manning 271). Similarly, another reviewer called it "plotless" (Shelton). Another reviewer missed the layered ambiguity of the ending: "I am not wholly sold on the simplicity of its resolution" (Fuller 4). Apparently trying to appeal not only to shallow readers but also to shallow agents, editors, and publishers, Jackson placed a happy ending on the surface: as in *Hangsaman,* the protagonist seems to be reunified in the end. But it is implied that she really is not reunified, and it is indeterminate which traits of the old personalities dominate. At any rate, many reviewers missed the stylistic and thematic complexity of this venturesome novel. Few were as perspicacious as Kenneth Burke, who wrote to Jackson and Hyman that he appreciated its "purgation scene" and "ingenious novelistic DIALECTIC."

Burke understood that this novel's poetics were not just a mixing of literary genres but a mixing of literature and social formation. Betsy uses not only nursery rhymes to negotiate with Wright but other language to negotiate institutions. When Betsy flees to New York in search of her not just absent but dead mother, she boards the bus with a periodical because her reading of the scene at the bus station reveals people reading printed texts: "She did not care to read, generally, but she . . . had observed that nearly all the people standing in the station carried magazines or books." She also carries a basic text to help her in communicating: "She had a book in her suitcase, a large dictionary for use in case she needed help in talking or writing or spelling." Moreover the book is a commodity that can be exchanged for goods and services: "The book, which was large and solidly printed, might be a source of money sometime if she needed it" (88). It is not just the one-paged texts—her dollar bills—that she can use as money. When she arrives in New York, she thinks of the hotel (the name of which suggests the origins of writing and painting) as a text: "The Drewe Hotel was a sign on an awning, a gold script on caps and vest pockets and matchbook folders" (102). When she sees a rack of postcards, she resolves to send good-bye cards to the two personalities she hates, Elizabeth and Beth.

The novel is replete with these comic treatments of how the personalities are articulated through writing, not only with each other but also with others outside their body. Indeed, the protagonist takes the writing cure (rather as Jackson did as a madwoman in the attic in college). The first contact between the protagonist and Wright begins with an information card written by his receptionist containing his new patient's basic biographic data (37). When he lets her collect herself, he says that he "let Miss R. compose herself" (56). When he commands the necessarily incoherent Betsy of the prelinguistic Imaginary, he says, "My dear Betsy, . . . do compose yourself" (154). When he visits Aunt Morgen to talk to her about her niece's case, he brings his notebook (188). And he often tells the reader that he is consulting his notes as he writes.

But more importantly, the emergence of each personality, and later much of the communication between them, results from writing. Like another of capital's alienated laborers, Bartleby, Elizabeth is essentially a copyist, so alienated from herself by her labor as a functionary in the machine of tradition that she needs only "a clear written hand and a moderate speed at the typewriter" (7). When she starts receiving strange letters, she does not know that she has other personalities who are sending them. (Jackson used to find threatening notes she had written to herself but could not remember writing them.) Despite their hostility, like a lover caressing an anonymous love note, she savors the strange writing and saves it: "Sitting in the drugstore Elizabeth touched the badly written words with her finger and smiled; she had very definite plans for this letter: she meant to take it home and put it into a box on the top shelf of her closet with another letter" (8). And what kind of a box does she put it in? A "red cardboard valentine box that had held chocolates on her twelfth birthday." And what else does this oedipal character keep in the box? A letter from her mother. And who is the letter to? The boyfriend. And what does it say? It tells Robin not to send any more erotic intimations—it is a letter about letters, writing about writing: "Robin, don't write again, caught my Betsy at the letters yesterday, she's a devil and you know how smart!" (9). As Jackson did in her letters and rough drafts, Betsy refers to herself with a lowercase *i*. Betsy projects her sexual guilt onto Elizabeth by repeatedly calling her "dirty lizzie" (20–22). Soon the official letters she types at work have been finished in longhand with a handwriting she does not recognize. Later when Betsy thinks Elizabeth is threatening to come back, Betsy throws one of bookish Elizabeth's prized possessions, a dictionary, through a mirror, trying to get rid of the image of Elizabeth and to establish herself as the brat of the pack: "That'll show you I'm *still* worse than you are" (123).

Betsy plays tricks with writing. When a note to Wright arrives at his office, it is signed "Morgen," but actually Betsy has written it trying to prevent the meeting between the doctor and the aunt (171). It is Betsy who writes the most. Like a child just learning how, she scrawls slowly and puzzles over her own markings: "Betsy's writing seemed to have a kind of horrid fascination for her, the kind of delight so many of us experience when told of our babblings when asleep, or the half-wary excitement of having one's fortune told" (which is done by reading cards, palms, tea leaves, etc.) (174–75). Betsy makes herself known to Bess (who at first cannot believe Wright who insists that she houses another personality in her psyche) through writing. Wright directs Bess, who is left-handed, to try automatic writing (which is both a surrealist and psychoanalytic technique for accessing the unconscious). At first writing with her left hand, Bess is stunned to see her right hand (Betsy's hand) take away the pencil and begin addressing her in a childish hand and rhetoric (172). Thus for Bess, the return of the repressed comes through writing.

Sometimes more than two of the personalities will vie for dominance through writing. When compliant and feminized Beth writes Wright a note, Bess takes a page from Betsy's book and adds a postscript; but then Betsy writes a separate note contesting the first two (181–82). At the hotel in New York, Elizabeth writes a note containing Wright's name and address and telephone number because she knows that Betsy is taking the rest of the personalities with her and running away to New York, and hiding a note that someone besides Betsy might find is as assertive as Elizabeth can get in trying to foil this kidnapping. But Bess comes out, finds the note, and does not understand it (because she is the narrowest personality, detaching herself from most things other than money):

> It was on the desk, among the broken pens and spilled ink, that she discovered the highly important paper which she knew was to be hidden among her things and delivered to someone as yet unidentified. Although she did not understand how anything of vast importance could be written on such a tiny slip, she knew perfectly that it must not fall into Betsy's hands. . . . It resembled the hundreds of small papers, which come into people's hands every day, enclosed in packages of laundry, for instance, recommending dry-cleaning of curtains for the spring, or the labels which certify that Easter eggs are pure, or the slip of paper enclosed in the theater program pointing out that there was an inadvertent mistake on page twelve, where Miss Somebody's name had been mistakenly rendered as Miss Something Else; at any rate, she could not read it. (135–36)

Appropriately, Bess pins the note to money. And it is also appropriate when the protagonist winds up in the hospital and the nurse addresses her not as you but as "We": "We were a pretty smart girl to be carrying around that little paper" (138).

The intertextuality of Jackson's next novel, *The Sundial,* alludes to fewer canonical texts but more of the dominant culture's social text. Her most satiric work, *The Sundial* undermines the myths and ideology implicitly reinscribed by not only modernist myth critics but also the conservative wing of the consensus historians.[6] As is appropriate for a proto-postmodernist satire, it also foregoes *The Bird's Nest*'s complex characterization of Elizabeth and creates caricatures akin to Dr. Wright and Aunt Morgen. As such, *The Sundial* anticipates such absurdist satires of the 1960s as Joseph Heller's *Catch-22*, Ken Kesey's *One Flew Over the Cuckoo's Nest*, and Kurt Vonnegut's *Slaughterhouse Five*. But the object of *The Sundial*'s satire is even more comprehensive. For Jackson undermines nothing less than the master narrative of America's dominant culture.

CHAPTER EIGHT

# *The Sundial*

---

Appearing in 1958, *The Sundial* is an allegorical satire on the central myths of America's dominant culture: that America is God's favorite nation (a city upon a hill, a beacon to all humankind); that America is a new world, an exception to the limits God placed on other civilizations; and that America is where the mission of God's chosen people (the new Elect, the new saving remnant) is to take the virgin land (the new Eden, the new promised land) and create nature's nation (a new garden, a new frontier, a paradise). This novel shows that Shirley Jackson's knowledge of the dominant culture's hegemonic discourse was as deep as that of many scholars then publishing on that topic. She even outstripped Stanley Edgar Hyman in this regard. Indeed, Kenneth Burke had written to Hyman in 1953, "All the time you're digging in remote corners for info on the emergence of myth, there's little Shirley showing you how myths arise." In fact, this novel is her first after she completed her nonfiction book on the Salem witch trials, a book that should have put to rest any notion that she took witchcraft literally. Both the nonfiction work and *The Sundial* demonstrate that she took witchcraft as a still living part of the America's hegemonic codes. As an allegorical satire situated in history, this novel features less undecidability than do her other novels. The narration will be Jackson's least unreliable, although the bizarre events alone will be, uncannily, both estranging yet recognizable. And as further befits a comic satire, especially an absurdist one, these characters are flat and static. Absent are the prior explorations of the linguistic nature of subject formation.

The middle-aged phallic matriarch, Orianna Halloran, is a bit of an exception, although her growth is, as Jackson entered in her notes for this novel, a "disintegration into paranoia" (SJP Box 28). Jackson uses the concept of paranoia not in the sense that Orianna is fearful but in

137

the sense that she has delusions of persecution and, much more strongly, delusions of grandeur—although in Orianna's case it might be more accurate to say delusions of adequacy. Totally self-interested, she has married a rich man for his money and has now killed their only child, a son named Lionel, ostensibly believing that this crime is necessary for her to keep the estate. She is also given to denial. For example, her body language contradicts her oral language when she claims not to like the inscription on the sundial: "'I do not care for it,' Mrs. Halloran said, caressing the W in WORLD" (168).

Her husband, ironically named Richard, is one of Jackson's several feminized father figures. Like Uncle Julian in *We Have Always Lived in the Castle*, Richard is a sickly old man confined to a wheelchair and under a blanket—literally under wraps. He is so senile that he cannot remember whether or not his recently deceased son is dead. This invalid is the son of the House of Halloran's founding father, the man who built the family estate.

Richard is cuckolded by thirty-two-year-old Essex, whom Orianna has hired ostensibly to catalog the library. Essex is one of Jackson's feminized young males, much like Luke in *The Haunting of Hill House*. Passive-aggressive, he has no goals and depends on women.

Essex is pursued by forty-eight-year-old Aunt Fanny, Richard's younger sister; she has never married. She has visual and auditory hallucinations, which she and the others take to be valid apocalyptic prophecies. She rationalizes that she should believe her crazy visions on the grounds that she would be crazy if she did not: "Somehow it must be real because if it is not real it is in my own head" (31). She says, "I was taught bridge by a professional. My father believed that no expense should be spared on my education" (63). Among this ship of fools, she is the biggest fool of all.

Maryjane is the late Lionel's wife. When a visitor asks Orianna who Maryjane is, Orianna answers, "She's what my son Lionel married" (58). As crass and selfish as the rest, Maryjane claims that the reason why she wants her mother-in-law to die soon is so that the estate will pass to Fancy, Maryjane's daughter. But as with Orianna, Maryjane's ostensible reason for committing murder seems like a rationalization. In each case, the death will not bring the inheritance they claim to think it will. So either they are unconsciously rationalizing their hostility, or they are consciously lying.

Fancy, the wormy apple of her mother's evil eye, has not fallen far from the tree. In the end, she kills Orianna by the same method Orianna used to kill Maryjane's husband (who was Orianna's son): by pushing the victim down the main stairs. As Orianna's crown is taken from her dead body and placed on Fancy, the bratty ten-year-old heiress says, "*My* crown, now" (239).

Augusta Willow is an old friend of Orianna's from the days when they were gold diggers of easy virtue. She has come for the explicitly stated purpose of getting money. She tells Orianna to pay her; otherwise she will not leave. Augusta brings her two daughters. In their presence, she calls Julia the smart one and Arabella the attractive one. It might be more accurate to say that Julia, who is nearing thirty, is less stupid than the others. She is the only one who does not believe Aunt Fanny's ostensibly supernatural prophecies. Arabella is past twenty-five. Like her sister, she is concerned primarily with landing a husband.

Five minor characters round out this menagerie. Gloria is a seventeen-year-old visitor, a daughter of one of Orianna's old boyfriends. The others use her to supplement Aunt Fanny's visions by having Gloria look into a horizontal mirror covered with opaque oil, wherein she sees that the world will end in a few weeks. Miss Ogilvie is Fancy's governess. The captain is breeding stock the governess picks up in town to help Essex repopulate the earth. The two Inverness sisters own the village library.

Doubling emerges through several techniques, for example, through the use of similar names. The founding father's wife, who was the mother of Aunt Fanny and Richard, was named Anna. The current matriarch is her daughter-in-law, Orianna.[1] Also, Orianna and Maryjane are both called "Mrs. Halloran." In addition, Frances is the real name of both Aunt Fanny and Fancy. Characters are also paired by behavioral traits. For example, the ineffectual Essex recapitulates the ineffectual Richard. Likewise, Orianna and Augusta are loud and greedy. Augusta's two daughters are younger versions of the Inverness sisters. Essex and the captain are the unlikely studs. And Aunt Fanny and Gloria are the blind seers.

The house, too, is a character of sorts. The narrator says, "The character of the house is perhaps of interest." The house is like the estate in *The Road Through the Wall*: "It stood upon a small rise in ground, and all the land it surveyed belonged to the Halloran family" (10). The estate's debt to the exploitation of wage slaves appears when the house is often called "the big house" (145, 169, 175, 188). It takes its identity from the man who built it and whose name it bears. Of course he has a portrait of himself over the mantel in the drawing room. His design for the house and landscaping is an exercise in conspicuous consumption. His wealth is matched only by his ignorance and tastelessness. Only because an architect persuades him to does he put in a library, and only when he hears what a grotto is does he tell the architect to build one. Appropriately, Aunt Fanny has an apartment in an upstairs wing that contains the family's most important furniture and mementos. Her house/self consists of traces of her parents' house/self. Fancy even has a doll's house containing replicas of this built-in museum's artifacts. Most importantly, it is the voice of the father's ghost that tells Aunt Fanny that the earth will be destroyed but that all those who stay in the house will be saved. So the house as the originating Mr. Halloran has enduring influence. It is the locale where the characters display their interpellation.

Most of the behavior of these characters is bizarre yet referential. For example, when after the funeral Aunt Fanny says of Orianna, "I will join her in grief after dinner," she reveals herself as the hypocrite who feels no sorrow (5). The same character trait emerges in Orianna when she says after the funeral, "My schedule has already been much disturbed today" (10).

As a reminder that civility was not always a trait among the royalty who these neo-aristocrats imitate, their forced politeness often gives way to their selfishness. For example, when Augusta asks if Orianna likes Augusta's daughters, the reply is, "Not so far" (52). When Richard asks Orianna if she married him for his money, she responds, "Well, that, and the house" (14). Real people are rarely so arrogant, but real people are often so close to this extreme that these characters are referential while nonetheless proto-postmodern caricatures. Jackson thereby achieves the distance necessary for comic absurdism without losing the referentiality necessary for satire. As Nathaniel Hawthorne refers to reality by mingling the marvelous, Jackson refers to reality by mingling not only the marvelous but also the absurd.

The absurd characters accompany an absurd plot. She treats American culture not only with comic satire, but also with magical realism, which begins with a fantastic premise and then develops that premise realistically. The destabilizing event that launches the plot is Orianna's murder of her son. Although her ostensible motive is to inherit her dying husband's estate, there is no reason for her to kill her son to get the estate. The Gothic motif of an unclear title is updated to an absurd premise. There is no statement of who has willed what to whom, only that Fancy ultimately gets it, although there is no indication why she would get it before her parents die. In fact, when Fancy says she will inherit the estate upon her grandmother Orianna's death, she adds that she knows that Richard actually owns it: "When my grandmother dies, no one can stop the house and everything from being mine. . . . Of course I know that it really belongs to Grandfather" (21). So there is no reason established for Orianna's motive. If the originating patriarch willed half to Richard and half to Aunt Fanny, killing Lionel would not give Orianna control of the estate. And if Richard inherited the whole estate, his wife would get it before his son would, unless he has willed otherwise, and there is no evidence that he has. If Richard has no will, Orianna would inherit the estate even if Lionel were alive.

Nonetheless, this destabilizing event of Orianna killing her son is what gives rise to Aunt Fanny's visions. As long as Fanny holds the key to salvation through her apocalyptic visions, Orianna hesitates to carry out her plan to lock Aunt Fanny in the tower. Further absurd plot developments surface. At the beginning, there apparently has been no police investigation of Lionel's murder. At the end, these characters believe they are god's saving remnant, yet they wait like Samuel Beckett's Lucky and Pozo or Saul Bellow's dangling man, Joseph. Aunt Fanny says, "We have *never* had anything to *do,* you know, but now we are waiting besides, and it is almost unbearable" (66). These heirs to the Puritan tradition are nonetheless a long way from the Puritan doctrine of preparation, according to which there was much work to be done. As Essex puts it, "We are . . . gathered here waiting, and yet we have no way to prepare" (65). Except for some last-minute purchases of meager provisions like instant foods (which allow for minimal preparation), they do not ready themselves for the new kingdom.

In addition, signs appear that the characters take as evidence that the earth really is approaching conflagration. First there are odd portents. After Aunt Fanny's initial vision, they regard a snake in the house and a crack in the front window as signs that the father's jeremiad was valid. Then in time-honored fashion, the signs come from nature in the form of foreboding, stormy weather. When some readers are still reading this absurdism literally, Jackson sabotages these foreshadowings by presenting a preposterous event that these characters take as a sign of impending social breakdown. Someone walks into a department store with a polar bear—groomed like a poodle—on a leash. Yet even Burke wanted Jackson to treat the ending more literally. In a letter to Jackson and Hyman, Burke said his wife had "also read the book, avec jouissance" but that he wanted Jackson to sustain the ending "note of ominous waiting" rather than "patter" at the end. What Burke did not realize is that because there is no end, Jackson satirizes even that note. The plot stops during the scheduled eve of destruction. If the plot continued, these characters would find that their spin on the American apocalypse (which, pace Lauren Berlant, can now be called a "national fantasy") was not validated.

One reason why readers willingly suspend disbelief of this unbelievable absurdism is that the narrator is rather reliable, especially for Jackson. The reports are pointed. For example, the narrator says outright that Fancy is a liar. Also, the narrator describes Augusta as "a large and overwhelmingly vocal woman, with a great bosom and an indefinable air of having lost some vital possession down the front of it" (51). She settles slowly into a chair, "listening for cracks in the wood" (57). On the other hand, the dialogue is decentered, sounding almost as much English as American, but it is just odd enough to underscore the satire's referentiality, yet not enough to undermine it. Only twice does the narrator focus so completely through a confused point-of-view character that the reader is also confused. Just before Aunt Fanny has her first vision, she is disoriented in the garden. Rather than clarify where Aunt Fanny is and what is really happening, the narrator immerses the reader in Aunt Fanny's consciousness (such as it is). Similarly, when Julia gets lost in a fog and stumbles through the countryside not knowing where she is, the reader cannot tell where Julia is either.

Thus only a few techniques of the fantastic appear. Yet what is peculiar for the reader is normative for the characters. Even Aunt Fanny's reports of the father's voice seem to them not supernatural but real. Yet they regard some possible events as supernatural. For example, Orianna tells Aunt Fanny, "You may very well have seen your father; I would not dream of disputing a private apparition. But you could not have seen a gardener trimming a hedge" (34).

This novel is not only Jackson's most comic, but also one of her most intertextual. Her allusions range from the canonical to the absurd, with the canonical always perverted by the leading characters. Of course one of the central enabling texts of the American culture's master narrative is the Bible. Jackson's satire concentrates on the belief in a chosen people in a promised land. In addition, Elizabethan allusions abound. In propaganda, poetry, pageants, and so forth, Queen Elizabeth was frequently referred to as "Oriana" and "Gloriana." (Spenser uses that name—as well as many other pseudonyms—to refer to her throughout *The Faerie Queene*.) Similarly, the "captain" suggests Francis Drake. Where the captain seems to be a gigolo in waiting, Drake was reputedly one of Elizabeth's lovers. And the Sir Francis Drake Hotel is an architectural landmark in San Francisco (the city where Jackson was born). But most importantly, he defeated the Spanish Armada, which enabled British colonization in America. The "captain" also suggests John Smith, whose promotion of America as a land of plenty resonates with the Hallorans' belief that nature will supply all that they want. And there are such names as Stuart and Essex. In addition to the Elizabethan allusions, one of the architects is constantly "maligning Horry Walpole" but nonetheless designs a home that reinscribes the Gothic grotesque (188).[2] And the Inverness sisters, exponents of prim propriety, "read a chapter from Henry James aloud every evening" (87) evidently never learning anything except how to decorate. In addition, the sundial bears an inscription from Chaucer. Mr. Halloran has very little idea what it means; it prophesies the alienation arising from avarice, and he and his heirs exemplify the prophecy. Orianna, who begins by coveting the estate but ends by trying to inherit the world, unwittingly sullies Virginia Woolf. When Orianna dreams that she is the old witch in Hansel and Gretel, she says to herself wistfully, "a place all my own" (113). And Essex often quotes from canonical British literature, for example, "Had we but world enough" (162). Believing that such belletrism elevates him, he does not realize that his desires are for world dominion and for time to revel in it. Jack London, a San Francisco Bay area native like Jackson, has his naturalist vision reduced to social Darwinism when Aunt Fanny tells the Inverness sisters that she wants a book that would tell how "to build a fire" (which is the title of one of London's stories) (89). Jackson also alludes to children's literature. For example, Orianna says that the only thing her party lacks "is the head of the Cheshire Cat looking down on us from the sky" (207). And Mr. Halloran's decor includes a framed copy of Rudyard Kipling's "If" (188). These allusions register both postmodernism's diminution of literature as well as modernism's reverence for it.

This novel's intertextuality even includes mass culture mendacity. For example, the House of Halloran competes against another apocalyptic group, "The True Believers," which is the title of a then-popular commonsense philosophy book by Eric Hoffer, a San Francisco longshoreman. In addition, Aunt Fanny says of hearing her dead father's admonitions, "Father knows best" (the title of a shallow television series that celebrated domesticity) (111). Jackson also alludes to one of the most noted television commercials of the day, in which a crown miraculously appears on the head of anyone eating Imperial margarine. Gloria tells Orianna, "You're a crazy old lady who sits at her dinner table with a crown on her head" (201) (and in the end Fancy puts it on and says "*My* crown, now") (239). Jackson also alludes to ostensibly nonfictional representations, exposing them to show their fictional components. For example, she incorporates the case of Lizzie Borden (whom she calls "Harriet Stuart"). She sets *The Sundial* outside Fall River, Massachusetts, where the Borden murders really occurred. This novel's villagers propagate oral and written stories about the case in an effort to capitalize on it by attracting tourists.

Jackson registers the state of writing with the fate of one of the estate's architects. This young man had a master's degree in literature from Columbia and wanted to write plays in blank verse. He read half of one scene to the founding Halloran in hopes of networking with Mr. Halloran's associates and acquiring patronage. But instead the aspiring writer got a job as a file clerk. Similarly, the current Hallorans burn almost all of the books on this roomy estate to make room for supplies such as toilet paper. Orianna claims that the books are not valuable because there are no first editions. The books that they keep are an embarrassment, and writing new texts—falling into history—is forbidden:

> The only books to be included were Aunt Fanny's *Boy Scout Handbook,* the encyclopedia, Fancy's French grammar—so that Miss Ogilvie could keep Fancy from forgetting the little she had gained—and a World Almanac. No writing materials of any kind were included, and gradually these books came to be called "unburnables" in order to differentiate them from the rest of the books in the library. (157)

Whereas their Puritan forebears saw signs in nature, these new redeemers read signs in representations, namely, print, television, movies, and music. They believe that bizarre Others (as if Others could be as bizarre as they) are a sign of the apocalypse. For example,

> A man in Texas won a divorce from his wife because she tore out the last chapter of every mystery story he borrowed from the library. A television set in Florida refused to let itself be turned off; until its owners took an axe to it, it continued, on or off, presenting inferior music and stale movies and endless, maddening advertising, and even under the axe, with its last sigh, it died with the praises of a hair tonic on its lips. (199–200)

These characters reinscribe characters from other representations. When the captain tries to leave the estate and Orianna protests that she is not trying to stop him, she asks, "Am I an ogre? Is this castle of mine guarded? Patrolled by dragons or leopards? Do we live under a spell, as in the city of Brass, or an evil enchantment?" (135–36). She is so literal minded that she cannot see that metaphorically the answer to all of those questions is yes. And when several of the characters make conversation by imagining themselves having fun, they cast themselves in a fairy tale. Gloria says,

> "We will find an ash grove for our shrine."
> "Are there reeds in the stream?" the captain asked. "We will make young Fancy here a flute, and she can pipe for us."
> Fancy giggled. "You will all have to follow me and dance," and Maryjane added shyly, "We can put flowers in our hair, those red ones, and dance under the trees." (198)

Similarly, Essex casts himself as the lead in an adventure story: "I am to be the huntsman" (130). He also likes to put on the locals by making up scandalous stories about others. For example, he tells Miss Inverness that Aunt Fanny "had been captured by pirates off the Mediterranean coast," implying that they raped her (214). He uses a Western version of the New England captivity narrative to suggest that the governess, too, was raped: "Miss Ogilvie as a child was violated by a band of Comanche Indians in a lonely farmhouse on Little Wicked Bend River" (207). He also uses the stock sensationalist plot from tabloids by claiming that the captain is a serial killer (215). In addition, Orianna says that on the day of reckoning the locals will be "wholly revised" (170).

These characters live in plots and settings from genre fiction. For example, Maryjane says that meeting her husband was "just like a movie" (217). Similarly, Arabella is excited about a movie she saw that employed a stock plot device: "They found the buried treasure right on that spot." She speaks in clichés, such as, "Isn't it *divine?*" (68).

In fact, these characters do live according to textual injunctions. Old man Halloran's decor includes several inscriptions that exhort the flock with platitudes. One inscription is "Hated by fools, and fools to hate, Be that my motto and my fate." They dined under a sign saying "Let none save good companions grace this festive board." Some of the signs contradict others. For example, they sleep despite a reminder of the work ethic, "Get up, get up for shame, the blooming morn Upon her wings presents the god unshorn," yet climb the stairs reading, "When shall we live if not now?" Some of these sayings are little more than white noise. For example, the "grotto-motto" is "Fear no more the heat of the sun" (188).

As every new dispensation requires codification, Orianna draws up a list of rules for the new world. Like Woodrow Wilson's messianic Thirteen Points, Orianna's list also contains thirteen points. Although hers are more clearly base and self-interested than his (one of her injunctions is that no one but her may wear a crown), one can say about hers the same that was said about Wilson's: God gave us ten commandments, and Wilson gave us thirteen.

Most importantly, Jackson also alludes to America's master narratives. As an allegorical satire on American myths, *The Sundial* occupies a space between the satiric novel of manners and political satire. Jackson satirizes the ideology that underlies both manners and politics. Her absurdist characterizations feature automatons unable to do anything but reinscribe hegemonic codes. Such characterizations are consistent with allegory. As Angus Fletcher points out, allegorical characters are obsessive and act as if they have no choice (120, 305). In addition, to treat myth consciously—as fabulators such as Jackson do—is to write in the comic and allegorical modes. Robert Scholes states, "The really perceptive writer is not merely conscious that he is using mythic materials: He is conscious . . . that he is allegorizing. . . . Thus his use of myth will inevitably partake of the comic" (171). Jackson's novel is a satiric Marxist palimpsest written on the pages of the capitalist social text to which it refers.

The first tenet that this novel allegorizes is the belief in a "new world" (136–37).[3] Despite being chosen as the only survivors, they nonetheless believe that they have an enormous burden. Orianna says, "I will only point out once more that I have undertaken a tremendous responsibility in arranging to lead you all into this new world" (194). She describes the new social order as a "utopian community" (137). Nonetheless, they will take with them the riches of the corrupt world. Before the corrupt world is cleaned up, the chosen few will clean it out. In their commodities fetish, the new elect is like its founder. The founding patriarch "could think of nothing better to do with his money than set up his own world," which he does by building his little empire with imports of the fallen world's material culture and the beliefs implicit in them (11).

As in the dominant culture at large, the Halloran clan believes that the new world will be like a garden.[4] Orianna says, "Never before have I had any open, clear-cut invitation to the Garden of Eden; Aunt Fanny has shown me a gate" (47). Aunt Fanny's revelations occur in the garden. Or more precisely, they occur in ambiguous areas on the margin of the garden, as befits a satire on an industrial society ostensibly affirming pastoralism. The first occurs when she is lost in the garden and thinks she may have strayed into the family graveyard. The second occurs when she is lost in the maze (which consists of high hedges). The declension of the garden myth is implicit when Aunt Fanny complains, "I wish . . . that my father could see what has been done to the gardens" (24). The decline of the garden narrative is explicit in the final garden party. At a time when America promoted home bomb shelters, which would seal out one's neighbors, the Hallorans throw a party for those who will be annihilated because they will be locked out of the estate. Fanny wants to show the locals that the Hallorans "do not break faith with them, even now" (84). This parody of Thanksgiving belies the condescending contempt toward Others felt by both the early and the present chosen people. For all of her Victorian prudery, Miss Inverness is correct when she refers to Orianna's "baubles of rank and pride of place" (206).

Nevertheless, the Hallorans reinscribe the narrative of America as nature's nation. Aunt Fanny says that future generations will find "all their wants supplied from nature" (122). Orianna is literal minded about providence. When she sees Aunt Fanny stocking up on canned peaches, Orianna says, "Surely we are entering a land of milk and honey? Must we take our own lunch?" (118). Essex envisions the new world in the same terms that F. Scott Fitzgerald has the Dutch sailors envision it. Whereas the sailors see it as "the fresh green breast of the new world" (182), Essex depicts the new world as "fresh, untouched, green, lovely" (161).

A contemporary turn on the myth of a new world is that it might take place in the new frontier: outer space. In the science fiction version of the new world garden, transcendence occurs in the heavens. The other doomsdayers, The True Believers, contend that they will be transported into literal skies. Recycling clichés from 1950s outer space movies, their leader says, "We go to Saturn where we get translated into a higher state of being" (102). Orianna rejects the competing prophecy: "Those people are perfectly capable of sending their saucers just anywhere, with no respect for private property" (104). The hysterical optimism and denial of death implicit in the escape to outer space emerges in the captain's question, "How can the *world* end? There's no *sense* to it" (138). The real question is, How can it not end? As with Kurt Vonnegut's Billy Pilgrim, the captain's childish answer is that, saved by the new magic and witchcraft of technology, we will take the world with us on spaceships— new Arbellas. One of the young sisters meant to repopulate the world is named Arabella, which suggests *Arbella,* the ship on which John Winthrop began the metaphor of "the citty upon a hill." And her question, "Isn't it divine?" reveals the secularization of the originating vision.

Like the many saving remnants before them, they regard themselves as a chosen people.[5] Aunt Fanny says, "Those who survive this catastrophe . . . will be free of pain and hurt. They will be . . . a kind of chosen people" (second ellipses in original). Both Aunt Fanny the percipient and Orianna the recipient believe that they have not chosen their mission but that it has chosen them. Aunt Fanny says, "It's not as though *I* had any choice in all this, I *only* say what I'm told" (43). The narrator says that Aunt Fanny "was completely subject to some greater power, . . . her own will somewhere buried in that which controlled her" (41). Likewise, Orianna says, "I have no choice" (47). As the new elect, they have a mission to redeem the earth.[6] The narrator says, "They were charged with the future of humanity" (40). Aunt Fanny says they will "breed a new race of mankind" (41).

As separatists, they believe that they are exceptions to the corruption of others. Interpellated fully into the value of greed, but interpellated less into the original doctrines that rationalize greed, Fancy realizes that her elders' attempts at saving the world are attempts at saving themselves:

"What makes anyone think you're going to be more happy or peaceful just because you're the only ones left? . . . You all want the whole world to be changed so *you* will be different. But I don't suppose people get changed any by just a new world" (165). Even if there could be a new world, it could not remain new once people come because they bring their old selves and history into it. Indeed, the idea of a new world is an idea that comes from the old world.

Another chapter in America's master narrative is that the new world will bring regenerative purification. Aunt Fanny says, "Evil, and jealousy, and fear, are all going to be removed from us" (42). In their minds, "When they came forth from the house it would be into a world clean and silent" (40–41). Similarly, Maryjane thinks the apocalypse, since it will remove disease, will cure her of her asthma. Jackson further satirizes this notion of purity by having the prophet of perfection, Aunt Fanny, speak imperfectly: "Harmony is to be restored, inperfections erased" (45). Their desire for purification is a projection. After Aunt Fanny hears her father's voice, the clan relies on Gloria's projections. To see into the future and divine the date of the conflagration, she looks at a mirror that is lying flat with olive oil on it. What one sees in a mirror, of course, originates in oneself.

Their vision of purification exemplifies what Richard Slotkin calls "regeneration through violence." This clan believes that purity can be reached only after all but they are killed off. Aunt Fanny announces that "the beings who created" the earth will "burn it" (43). (The adults pass this vision onto Fancy, who kills Orianna.) The emphasis on the cataclysmal aspect of the new world appears in the frequent allusions to *Robinson Crusoe*. As soon as he hears of Aunt Fanny's vision, Richard wants it read to him. *Robinson Crusoe* figures modernity's eschatology of alienated bourgeois individualism. Aunt Fanny reinscribes this enabling text by storing "a keg of nails, since the bag of nails which Robinson Crusoe brought from the ship had proved so comforting; mindful of Robinson Crusoe, Aunt Fanny had added a grindstone, and, with some embarrassment, several shotguns and an assortment of hunting knives" (156).

Yet they are in denial about the real destructive horror of the apocalypse.[7] Reinscribing exceptionalism, Orianna says that the conflagration will not hurt them: "The peril is for others: we are safe" (231). Nonetheless, she wants no one to witness it: "We don't want to see any of it, and we don't want to hear about it, either" (233). So she decrees that no one is to listen to the radio during the conflagration and that they must keep the windows covered. And she cannot be thinking what the world will look like on the morning after the conflagration. She tells the others, "Dress yourselves . . . with an eye to our appearance tomorrow and the good impression we must create" (236).

The declension from purifying revelation into hypocrisy appears in the characters' willing suspension of disbelief. At first, they do not accept Aunt Fanny's vision as the gospel. The narrator says, "Not one of the people around Aunt Fanny believed her father's warning" (39). But they will live as if they do believe it. For example, Essex says it is "claptrap" (47) but he cannot face the fact that he is pursuing a fiction: "That world *must* exist. . . . It *must*; we cannot be promised such a thing, like children, and see it withdrawn" (161). They do not believe Aunt Fanny until they see the promise for self-aggrandizement.

The declension from revelation into hypocrisy also appears in their willing suspension of belief. They accept this reinscription of the original social text just as the characters in "The Lottery" accept theirs. The narrator notes, "Not one of the people in Mrs. Halloran's house could have answered honestly and without embarrassment the question: 'In what is it that you believe?'" (38). Until the crisis invoked by Aunt Fanny's vision, Orianna has literally forgotten about the Bible: "Mrs. Halloran sat long alone, her open hand resting on the pages of a Bible she had not opened, or even remembered, for many years" (41). The motif of a chosen few on a mission for the new promised land is further implicit in the last supper at the Halloran estate, which includes twelve people—Richard, Orianna, Aunt Fanny, Maryjane, Fancy, Essex, the Captain, Miss Ogilvie, Augusta, Arabella, Gloria, and Julia. Significantly, the lord (Lionel) is dead. And it was the thoroughly secular Madonna who killed him. The declension is so great, the affirmation of the horological so extensive, that Christianity has become witchcraft. For example, Maryjane and Fancy engage in this conversation:

> "Fancy, dear, would you like to see Granny drop dead on the doorstep?"
> "Yes, mother. . . ."
> "I am going to pray for it as long as I live," said young Mrs. Halloran, folding her hands devoutly. (3)

The decline from transcendental purpose to a displacement of the sacred with the profane is enjoined by their founder's motto: "*WHEN SHALL WE LIVE IF NOT NOW?* was painted in black gothic letters touched with gold over the arched window at the landing on the great stairway" (4). The originating Halloran did not like that motto, preferring the more frank version, "You can't take it with you" (188). So despite the other injunctions to rectitude, it comes as no surprise that the new world garden will be a libertarian one. Aunt Fanny says that unlike the first Eden, theirs will be without prohibitions (122). There will be no prohibition against greed—no warning about the difficulty of getting a rich man (or woman) into heaven. One reason why Orianna eventually accepts the vision is that she believes it will allow her to keep her wealth: "I would not be so willing to believe in Aunt Fanny if her messages dictated that I give away all of my earthly possessions." Or, putting it more simply, she says, "I cannot afford to ignore her" (47).

To preserve privilege, one of the first features of the old world to be maintained in the new is class exploitation. The chosen few turn out to be not the whole saving remnant, but only the privileged. Aunt Fanny says, "Miss Ogilvie, in this finer world of ours you do not suppose that we, you and I, will work with our hands? Surely you appreciate the need for a . . . what shall I call it? . . . a servant class? (ellipses in original 133) (Matters of class in *The Sundial* are more explicit than in the two preceding novels, *Hangsaman* and *The Bird's Nest*.)

In their commodities fetish, they continue the tradition of conspicuous consumption. The original "Mr. Halloran had directed that the carvings on the roof be flowers and horns of plenty" (12). The original Mrs. Halloran's dying words were, "Take care of my things" (175). Thus their new world would look a lot like the old one, in which Augusta shows up and says, "There must be someone you can help us get a dime out of" (58). Along with the commodities fetish goes the power fetish. Another reason why Orianna believes is that she will retain power: "Authority is of some importance to me. I will not be left behind when creatures like Aunt Fanny and her brother are introduced into a new world" (47).

As in the society that they think they are leaving, the new saving remnant believes that they will achieve timelessness, that they will step out of time and be immune to the foul contagions of the Other.[8] Ironically, they would step out of time by bringing the best of the past with them, by preserving the sacred (which they unwittingly define as secular). Their continuation of their founder's vision exemplifies Sacvan Bercovitch's arguments that succeeding generations in America regard themselves as links in a chain that reaches back through key events in American and world history all the way to creation, and forward to future generations *(Jeremiad)*. This saving remnant still thinks in biblical terms. For example, Orianna says of the vision of the future, "Our ark has landed" (127). Similarly, Gloria says that they "look at cave paintings or catacombs or ancient palaces" the way future generations will look back at them. Likewise, Aunt Fanny believes that future generations will regard Halloran House as a "shrine of their gods." Tourists visiting the scene will be engaged in a holy ritual:

"They will come on a kind of pilgrimage." In turn, the future generations will insert this saving remnant into new narratives: "They will
tell stories about . . . us" (123). Essex envisions the return to paradise
as "the kind of life and world people have been dreaming about ever
since they first began fouling this one" (161).[9] Jackson uses the family
to figure this confusion of timeless continuation with timeful change.
"'The essence of life,' said Mrs. Halloran gently, 'is change, you will
all, being intelligent people, agree. Our one recent change . . . the
departure of Lionel . . . has been both refreshing and agreeable'" (17).
In addition, Aunt Fanny has kept all of the furniture and knickknacks
from the founder's original apartment as a museum to remind her of
right conduct. Fanny is in thrall to the social text. For example, when
she reads *Alice in Wonderland,* she hears her mother's voice reading it
to her. When she is using her mother's name to run the maze, she gets
trapped: "This is my own maze, she told herself, this is the maze I grew
up in; I could not be a prisoner *here*; I know the way so perfectly, and
she turned and was further lost" (108–9). The key to negotiating this
maze is that it is based on the palindrome structure of the first Mrs.
Halloran's name: "Like all mazes, it went to a pattern, and the pattern
had been, romantically, built around the name of Aunt Fanny's
mother, Anna. One turned right, left, left, right, and then left, right,
right, left, and so on, alternating, until the center of the maze was
attained" (106). Pursuing the quest in the name of the mother leads
her back to her childhood. When the father speaks, she listens "with a
child's care" (40).

Thus the search in accordance with the mother also leads to the
father. It is in the maze that she hears his voice for the second time. He
enforces the cult of domesticity. He says, "The father will guard the children" but only if they stay in his house (32). Her other auditory hallu-
cination occurs at the sundial, the decentered centerpiece of the founding Hallorans' estate. Her prophecy expresses her political unconscious:
"It is as though something I had known all my life, and believed without ever really knowing what it was—some lovely, precious secret—had
suddenly come into the open. When my father spoke to me he only
reminded me of what I had always known, and forgotten" (43).

Disseminating the Halloran representations, Aunt Fanny uses this
museum for Fancy's interpellation. She takes Fancy there as "a way of
establishing one strong direct line from the first Mrs. Halloran to
Fancy." Aunt Fanny sits in her mother's chair and has Fancy sit in Aunt
Fanny's chair. Then Aunt Fanny tells her, "You must be me, little
Frances" (182). (They are doubles, as you have seen, both named
Frances and each despicably shallow and self-centered.) However, Fancy

declares that her lineage is not through Aunt Fanny, but rather through
Fancy's mother: "I am my mother" (183). Of course, the lineage does
not matter.

The sundial figures the inevitable imperfection of the timeful world.
Amid the house and grounds, which are as obsessively symmetrical as
any construction of the enlightenment (whose aesthetics are unbalanced
about balance), only the sundial is an exception. It is set off-center. The
titular figure of this novel, then, is decentered time. At first, the founding Halloran did not like the aphorism on the sundial:

> He had half hoped that the inscription on the sundial—left to the dis-
> cretion of the people in Philadelphia who knew so much about that
> kind of thing—would be "It is later than you think," or perhaps even
> "The moving finger writes, and having writ," but through the fancy of
> someone in Philadelphia—and no one ever knew who—the sundial
> arrived inscribed WHAT IS THIS WORLD? (12)

Those key words come from Chaucer:

> What is this world?
> What asketh man to have?
> Now with his love,
> Now in his colde grave,
> All alone, withouten any companye!
>
> ("Knight's" lines 2777–79)

Because the moral of this epigram—which bespeaks medieval centered-
ness—is inconsistent with Orianna's worldliness, she also dislikes it.
Nevertheless, Orianna's eye is drawn to the sundial: "If the sundial were
taken away I, too, would have to avert my eyes until I saw imperfection"
(14–15). She does not realize that her attraction to imperfection would
mark her life even in the new world. In fact, she inadvertently awaits the
new world by lying next to the sundial. After Fancy kicks her down the
stairs, Essex and the captain dump Orianna's body next to the sundial
in the hope that the conflagration will dispose of the body so that they
will not have the unpleasant task of having to bury her on the first
morning of the new world.

Jackson's reviewers, as well as later scholars, fail to understand this
novel. Several reviewers deflect Jackson's attack away from America's
dominant culture and toward all people. For example, one complains
about the novel's "contempt for the human race" (Swados 20). Likewise, another says that her target is "mankind" (Peden 18). Yet another
says, "If this is indeed Miss Jackson's concept of humanity, . . . then *The*

*Sun Dial* (sic) can be interpreted only as a complete and unswerving statement of misanthropy" (Grebstein 37). As mystifiers often do, they replace the target of history with the target of nature. Another mystifying operation, one habitually performed on Jackson even by her admirers, is to deflect her fiction out of the material world and into the epiphenomenal. For example, one reviewer (who also mistakes these characters as representative of the damned human race) claims that this novel is a fantasy because it departs from mainstream realism, as if those two modes are the only options and are in opposition (Girvin 5). Similarly, William Peden describes the founding Halloran's messages as coming "from the spirit world" (18) without attending to the myths of the spirit world. The messages are coming through what we mystify as a spirit world. The messages, then, are coming from history. Like Jackson's biographer, Peden treats demons as if they originate in the private sphere of the self-fashioning individual. Ironically, another way to obscure Jackson's referentiality is to police her novel with the order of realism. For example, Lenemaja Friedman complains about the "many symbols" and "artificial manipulations" (120). She also complains about "the difficulty of sympathizing with the protagonist, Mrs. Halloran" and the fact that "there is no person with whom the reader can identify; for the characters . . . are not nice people" (121). Even if Friedman realized that it is a proto-postmodernist allegorical fable, she would presumably reject this novel on generic grounds, thereby masking (like the reviewers) her anxiety over having the dominant culture exposed. Not until John G. Parks's article in 1978 did this novel receive any perceptive analysis, and there has been none since.

For its cultural work, this novel is Jackson's greatest achievement. By comparison, "The Lottery" only adumbrates this novel's exposure of American assumptions. In addition, for its intertextual, comic, and parodic absurdism, this novel anticipates the beginning of postmodernism's outpouring of satiric absurdist fiction.

## CHAPTER NINE

# The Haunting of Hill House

Published in 1959, just one year after *The Sundial, The Haunting of Hill House* relinquishes the dark humor and cultural satire of its predecessor. Instead of continuing the dialogue with myth and myth criticism, it resumes the dialogue with Gothic. For *The Haunting of Hill House* is Shirley Jackson's most Gothic novel. It features her fullest development of the house as a metaphor for the disunified subject. To that end, it returns to the theme of language as the means of subject formation. It returns to the psychological fabulation of *Hangsaman* and *The Bird's Nest*, maintaining their theme of interpellation through the family.[1] It also resumes a radically unreliable narrative point of view by focalizing through a delusional character. And it leaves some plot developments undecidable.

John Montague, an anthropology professor investigating an allegedly haunted house, is another satiric parody of Stanley Edgar Hyman. "Round" and "bearded," Montague is "a little man both knowledgeable and stubborn" (60). Full of himself, John Montague talks down to people as if he is lecturing. In Jackson's notes, he is the "voice of knowledge scholarship learning."[2] Yet in other ways, Montague is Hyman's mirror opposite. Jackson tweaks Hyman by having her narrator and characters almost always call Montague "Doctor," rubbing in the fact that Hyman had no doctorate. Similarly, she gives his parodic twin the last name of the anthropologist Ashley Montague, who was known as one of Bennington's most effete faculty members.

John Montague's patina of empiricism and objectivity deflect any penetrating view of his underlying commitment not to investigate reports of ghosts but to endorse them. He not only believes in poltergeists, but also ascribes motive and agency to them. He says, "Poltergeists like to turn people out of bed violently" (141). Another of Jackson's comic proponents of the supernatural, he reveals that he believes that Hill House is literally haunted. He says, "The evil is the house itself" (82) and "We have only one defense, and that is running away. At least it can't *follow* us, can it?" (124). This belief in ghosts is a trace of his youth: "He had been looking for an honestly haunted house all his life." As such, it was not anthropology that led him to this belief. Rather, it was this belief that led him to anthropology: "In this field he might come closest to his true vocation, the analysis of true manifestations" (4).

His obsessive celebration of the rituals of rationality and empiricism is a reaction formation. He has an irrational fear of irrationality and fear. Appropriately, he stays in the yellow room. He says, "Fear . . . is the relinquishment of logic, the *willing* relinquishing of reasonable patterns" (159). Besides endorsing the belief in the self-creating subject, this statement exemplifies the relinquishment of logic. As Jackson's oeuvre maintains, evil exists, and those who deny it relinquish logic, mystifying the logic of absurdity. For Montague, to uphold reasonable patterns is to keep doing the same thing even when logic dictates otherwise. He is possibly justified in sending the protagonist, Eleanor Vance, away when she grows increasingly incoherent, but he does so with such a punishing alacrity and dutiful insensitivity that it belies his hysteria. Like Hyman, in trying to contain the irrational, he becomes the container. And just as he is oblivious to his hypocrisy, he is oblivious to his treachery. To relieve his insomnia, he reads *Pamela,* which features a protagonist like Eleanor who is victimized by a cad like Montague. If he would handle her anxiety with less of his own, she would not kill herself in the end. But he has to rid Hill House of this foul contagion of irrationality, no matter how irrationally he does it. In making the supernatural and ghosts the specialty of such an academic, Jackson continues to push the margins of ritual, myth, and symbol into the text.

Montague's wife is his helpmeet in researching the spirit world. She makes no pretense of academic rationality. As Jackson's mother introduced her daughter to planchette, so Montague's wife introduces it in this novel. A device for contacting ghosts, it records the writing made when two people push around a small contraption that holds a pencil. When his wife arrives spouting nonsense about the spirit world, her ignorance and irrationality defeat his erudition at every turn. She is even more self-important and cocksure than Montague, with even less reason to be so. Like Aunt Morgen in *The Bird's Nest,* she is "dragon rampant" (236). Arriving a couple of weeks after the others, she displays her apparent cuckolding of Montague by bringing along Arthur, who obsessively displays his masculinity. For example, he patrols the house at night with a revolver. Mrs. Montague is another of Jackson's phallic mothers, though the most comic one.

Luke is the nephew of Hill House's owner. The narrator says, "Luke Sanderson was a liar. He was also a thief. . . . His dishonesty was largely confined to taking petty cash from his aunt's pocketbook and cheating at cards" (9–10). Apparently a gigolo, he also sells the watches and cigarette cases given him by his aunt's friends. In Jackson's notes, she describes Luke as "the voice of cynicism." Retrieving Eleanor, who has run uncontrollably up a rickety spiral staircase, he threatens to shove her back down. When she thanks him for saving her, he tells her he would not do it again.

Eleanor is a socially maladroit loner. At thirty-two, an appropriate age for one on the verge of martyrdom, she has spent the last eleven years caring for her invalid mother, who finally died three months before the start of the plot, after which Eleanor has slept on a cot at her sister's apartment, undoubtedly unwelcome. Inheriting only a pittance, Eleanor has lost her early adulthood and the chance at a career and permanent home while her older sister escaped caring for the mother and started her own family. Small wonder Eleanor cannot "remember ever being truly happy in her adult life" (6). In a restaurant, she sees a child who will not drink her milk because it is not served in her usual cup, which has stars on the bottom so that she can see them as she finishes drinking. Eleanor identifies with the child and silently urges her to resist. Thus Eleanor lives in her childhood world of fairy tales, imagining enchanted gardens as she drives through the country. She also lives in adolescent romances, imagining handsome males rescuing her from homelessness. Eleanor, then, is a *puer aeternus*. But more importantly, she recuperates the victimized heroines of eighteenth-century sentimental novels. Jackson says in her notes, Eleanor is the "voice of honor." As Elizabeth MacAndrew and David H. Richter argue, the sentimental heroine is not the simplistic stereotype that scholars such as Leslie Fiedler make her out to be, and she is central to the development of Gothic fiction.[3]

But Eleanor is not pure innocence. She hated her mother and hates her sister. She is morbidly self-conscious, deploring her clothes, wrinkles, dishpan hands, awkwardness, and penury. Her incipient paranoia emerges from her grandiose assumption that romance is waiting for her behind every tree, and from her assumption that others persecute her. Each assumption is a reaction formation to the fact that others barely notice her. In recounting the places she drove through to get to Hill House, she reconstructs the journey so that she is the instrument of great agencies. She thinks, reminiscent of the Hallorans in *The Sundial*, "I am the one chosen" (147). She projects her hostility onto the waitress and onto the customer in Hillsdale, and onto the caretakers at Hill House, as if all of the quirks of these simple folk are emblems of their hostility toward her. She stops romanticizing Luke as soon as he whines that he never had a mother.

Much of Eleanor's depressive paranoia is bound up with her guilt. She blames herself for her mother's death. She says her mother died because she slept through the mother's knocking on the wall for help. But if Eleanor knew that her mother was knocking and if Eleanor did not help, Eleanor could not have been asleep. On the other hand, if Eleanor slept through her mother's death, how would Eleanor know that her mother had been knocking? Her account of the mother's death may be a fantasy of blameworthiness—of the kind that several of Jackson's characters exhibit. Fantasies of blameworthiness in her other characters often accompany compensatory fantasies of empowerment, which deny weakness. Eleanor could be a survivor of child abuse. She has a dream that suggests a trace of resentment over being the victimized child by featuring herself as the rescuer of the victimized child. In the dream, she believes she hears a child crying and that she will intervene: "I will not go along with the hurting of a child, no, I will not; I will by God get my mouth to open right now and I will yell I will I will yell 'STOP IT'" (163).

There are some moments when she believes her behavior to be a willed choice, for example, when she and Theodora, her double, are fleeing the forest: "She felt every slow step as a willed act, a precise mad insistence upon the putting of one foot down after the other as the only sane choice" (175). Other times she feels that her body will not obey her mind, for example, when she is tempted to investigate the horrifying noise outside her bedroom: "Eleanor knew that, even if her feet would take her as far as the door, her hand would not lift to the doorknob" (130). Sometimes she will repress content and blame it not on her mind but on the content, for example, when she cannot remember the rest of the words that come after "Present mirth hath present laughter": "She was sure that the rest of the words must be most unsuitable, to hide so stubbornly from her memory, and probably wholly disreputable to be caught singing on her arrival at Hill House" (32). More typically she wonders why she said something but she does not blame some Other: "'I'm thirty-four years old,' Eleanor said, and wondered what obscure defiance made her add two years" (137). (She denies her anxiety about approaching the age of Christ's martyrdom.) Similar fractures occur: "'I am learning the pathways of the heart,' Eleanor thought quite seriously, and then wondered what she could have meant by thinking any such thing" (164). Her usual sense of agency is that it is Other and hostile. She says of the house, "It wanted to consume us, take us into itself, make us a part of the house, maybe—oh, dear. I thought I knew what I was saying, but I'm doing it very badly" (139). At moments like that, she distances one part of herself from another part of herself.

For Eleanor is another of Jackson's disintegrating protagonists. Losing control, she tells herself that she is presiding over her own dissolution: "I will relinquish my possession of this self of mine, abdicate, give over willingly what I never wanted at all; whatever it wants of me it can have" (204). Soon she is hearing voices that no one else hears, and she believes they are real. She says of the "chairs and tables and windows," "When I am afraid I no longer exist in any relation to these things" (159). As her condition worsens, she says, "I *hate* seeing myself dissolve and slip and separate so that I'm living in one half, my mind, and I see the other half of me helpless and frantic and driven and I can't stop it" (160). As she kills herself in the end, she applauds herself for doing so but then immediately wonders why she is doing it: "I am really doing it, I am doing this all by myself, now, at last; this is me, I am really doing it by myself. . . . *Why* am I doing this? Why am I doing this? Why don't they stop me?" (245–46).

Cruelly, Eleanor's final dissociation arises from the others' frustration of her desire to associate with them. She is heartened by the sense of belonging that she feels at first: "Eleanor thought, I am the fourth person in this room; I am one of them; I belong" (60). In a placid moment, she thinks, "You are happy, Eleanor . . ." (137). After Luke spurns her, she tries to get close to Theodora,

> each of them moving delicately along the outskirts of an open question, and, once spoken, such a question—as "Do you love me?"—could never be answered or forgotten. . . . They could only wait passively for resolution. Each knew, almost within a breath, what the other was thinking and wanting to say; each of them almost wept for the other. (174–75)

Eleanor says she wants to go home with Theodora, but Theodora also spurns her.

Although the house estranges her, it gives Eleanor an uncanny shock of recognition because it is a figuration of her.[4] Jackson wrote in her notes, as if she discovered this point while rereading her drafts, "Eleanor *IS* house." Likewise, Jackson wrote in her notes that Eleanor is "ALL DISTORTED *LIKE HOUSE.*" By the end of the novel, the identification of Eleanor and the house are clear. It turns out that the house's foundation and construction allegorize Eleanor's psychological foundation.

The development of that motif is gradual. When Eleanor first enters the house, she sees her reflection, although not in a mirror. Instead, she sees the reflection of her hand as it appears to sink below the floor into the foundation and basement. Entering, she is "watching the wavering reflection of her hand going down and down into the deep shadows of the polished floor" (37). The house, then, is both a mirror reflecting Eleanor and a window in which she sees herself in the depths of the house. That vertical image doubles a horizontal image of the self in the recesses of the house. Some rooms contain other rooms. More importantly, the first-floor rooms comprise a series of concentric circles; the inner rooms have no windows. As a result, she cannot see the inner self from the outside; she must go there. And getting there is problematic because the passageways do not go to places where they appear to be going. That is because, as Montague says, "Angles which you assume are the right angles you are accustomed to, and have every right to expect are true, are actually a fraction of a degree off in one direction or another" (105). The result is that walking through a series of rooms leads to an unexpected place. Also, the doors and windows are off-center, so that they can open or close on their own.

On the other hand, while the foundation is fixed, the top is structured haphazardly, in effect, unfinished just as Eleanor's induction into the Symbolic is unfinished. Eleanor perceives the house's tenuous construction: "She had a quick impression of the builders finishing off the second and third stories of the house with a kind of indecent haste, eager to finish off their work without embellishment and get out of there, following the simplest pattern for the rooms." What started as Victorian rococo ended in a heteroglossia of architectural voices, the "clashing disharmony that marked Hill House throughout" (38). Appropriately, the unbalanced Eleanor occupies an unbalanced room: "It had an unbelievably faulty design which left it chillingly wrong in all its dimensions, so that the walls seemed always in one direction a fraction longer than the eye could endure, and in another direction a fraction less than the barest possible tolerable length." Of course the color of her room is blue. In addition to blue wallpaper with blue flowers, there are "blue dimity curtains, . . . and a blue figured rug on the floor, and a blue spread on the bed and a blue quilt at the foot" (40).

Eventually Eleanor begins to splinter. For example, at the end the house dances, and the formerly repressed Eleanor follows suit: "Hill House went dancing" (205); Eleanor goes "dancing in the hall" (229). But in redesigning Eleanor, the house robs her of her self as she is constituted at the start of the plot: "When she tried to speak, her voice was drowned in the dim stillness" (37). Ultimately the house draws her out of herself in a way she does not need. She desublimates but returns to the place of domestic interpellation. Domestic ideology makes her believe she is free when in fact she is trapped: "I have broken the spell of Hill House and somehow come inside. I am home, she thought, and stopped in wonder at the thought. I am home, I am home, she thought; now to climb." She climbs the tower where an earlier resident hanged herself. She erases the past while keeping it in the present, and she keeps the past in the present by forgetting the present: "Time is ended now, she thought, all *that* is gone and left behind" (232).

The house also figures Eleanor's mother. Jackson wrote in her notes, "leaving house = betrayal of mother." Hugh Crain built the house for his wife, who died early, just like Eleanor's mother. When Eleanor cannot bring herself to go into the library, she is repelled. She is repulsed by the "cold air of mold and earth which rushed at her." Faced with these aggressive signifiers of death, Eleanor cannot speak—or even think— about her association with the mother: "'My mother'—she said, not knowing what she wanted to tell them" (103). As Judie Newman argues, Eleanor associates the library (because her mother forced her to read to her) and the nursery—the two rooms most significant to Eleanor—with her unmothering mother and herself as an unmothered child.

The mother is one of Jackson's obsessive themes. In *The Road Through the Wall*, Harriet Merriam's mother is phallic. In *Hangsaman*, the mother is feminized. In *The Bird's Nest*, Elizabeth Richmond's multiple personality derives from maternal doubles, her feminized mother and phallic aunt, both of whom are too present in some ways and too absent in others. In *The Sundial*, the phallic mother is a murderess who kills her own son. And in *We Have Always Lived in the Castle*, Merricat has killed her mother (and father and aunt) just to be closer to her sister. Newman recognizes the problematics of mothering in *The Haunting of Hill House*:

> The source of both the pleasures and the terrors of the text springs from the dynamics of the mother-daughter relation with its attendant motifs of psychic annihilation, reabsorption by the mother, vexed individuation, dissolution of individual ego boundaries, terror of separation and the attempted reproduction of the symbiotic bond through close female friendship. (123)

For Newman, the inchoate postmodernism of this novel lies in its "anticipation of revisionist psychoanalytics" (133).

Newman's analysis is also relevant to Jackson's relationship with her phallic mother. Jackson's mother was the father she never had. Moreover, her father was the mother she never had. As Newman states, the too-absent or feminine father plus the too-present or masculine mother problematizes the daughter's subject formation:

Daughterly individuation may be inhibited by paternal absence and by overcloseness to mothers, who tend to view their daughters as extensions of themselves.

Conversely, coldness on the mother's part may prevent the loosening of the emotional bond because of the unappeased nature of the child's love. (122)

In Jackson's notes she said of Eleanor, "betray mother by being born." (Jackson's mother told her that Jackson was a failed abortion.) On Eleanor's journey in which she can only go home again, she imagines homes in which a maternal figure cares for her.

Theodora is her double. As Jackson wrote in her notes, "theo *is* eleanor." When they are about to share not only a room but also clothes, Theodora says, "'We're going to be practically twins'" (158). She wears Eleanor's clothes. When Mrs. Montague arrives, she thinks Theodora is Eleanor.

More importantly, Theo knows what Eleanor is thinking, as if Theo is inside Eleanor's mind, which, allegorically, she is—like Tony in *Hangsaman*. For example, Theo tells her, "You're afraid everyone's going to laugh at your clothes" (46). Similarly, when Mrs. Montague arrives and Eleanor thinks to herself, "I wonder how long she is going to stay," Theodora whispers to Eleanor, "I wonder how long she is going to stay?" (184). Theo also apparently divines that Eleanor had an uncle like Jackson's Uncle Clifford: "Did you used to have a comic uncle?" (53). Theo is the first to posit that it is Eleanor who has written the mysterious messages on the wall. She is also the only one with whom Eleanor apparently shares a supernatural experience. In a deserted forest at night, they stumble across children at a sunlit picnic: "The path led them to its destined end and died beneath their feet. Eleanor and Theodora looked into a garden, their eyes blinded by the light of sun and rich color; incredibly, there was a picnic party on the grass in the garden. They could hear the laughter of the children" (176).

The house allegorizes Theodora as Eleanor's double. In a letter to Hyman and Jackson, Burke wrote, "the behavior of your House scenically parallels the relationships btw. Theodora and Eleanor (as though it were expressing what in them is left somewhat latent)." Theodora's room connects with Eleanor's through their bathroom. They are at their closest figuratively when they are at their closest literally, sleeping in the same room in adjoining beds. When Eleanor dreams she is holding Theodora's hand but then awakes alone and too far from Theo to have been holding Theo's hand, Eleanor asks, "Whose hand was I holding?" (163).[5] The answer is that if she was actually holding someone's hand, it had to be her own. It is impossible that she could have been holding anyone else's. In her notes, Jackson deemed this line the most important one in the novel. And it is, for it allows us to follow the connection of her right hand (traditionally the side associated with rationality, consciousness, and light) across to the left hand of darkness.

As Eleanor's double, Theodora is also Eleanor's mirror opposite. Theodora expresses Eleanor's repressed feelings. Jackson's notes say that Theodora is the "voice of emotion." Theo says people fear knowing what they "really want" (160). Theodora knows what Theodora desires and pursues it. She is also sensuous. She likes colorful clothing and flamboyant grooming. She says she wants "to look as bright as possible" (47). She shows Eleanor how to paint her toenails bright red. She strokes Eleanor's cheek and presses her own cheek against her hand.[6] However, in her sensuousness she is self-centered. In Jackson's notes, her last name is Vane. Eleanor is correct when she recognizes Theodora's "iron selfishness" (147). As the narrator puts it, "Duty and conscience were, for Theodora, attributes which belonged properly to the Girl Scouts" (8).

In her selfishness, she can be cruel. When Eleanor tells her desperately that she wants to go home with her, Theodora asks, "Do you *always* go where you're not wanted?" (209). Even before that, as Eleanor disintegrates and is absorbed into the house, Theodora relishes the thought of Eleanor's destruction. Theodora says that her role in Hill House is destructiveness. The house, she says, is "a little hideaway where I can be alone with my thoughts. Particularly if my thoughts happened to be about murder or suicide or—'" (43).

Thus Theodora is the projection of Eleanor's denied self. As Eleanor's alter ego, she embodies Eleanor's repressed eroticism and assertiveness. Eleanor is very uncomfortable with Theo's bright clothing. She recoils when Theodora tries to paint her toenails. And she apparently smears menstrual blood on Theodora's clothing and then blocks out any memory of doing so. Theodora is also a projection of Eleanor's denied assertiveness. Knowing Eleanor's disempowering unconsciousness of Eleanor's agency, Theo says, "We never know where our courage is coming from" (50). Like many of Jackson's decentered subjects, she experiences motivation as arising from without. What little courage Eleanor has comes from Theodora. But Theodora also figures Eleanor's self-destructiveness. This demon turns against her as surely as the demon lover turns against Jackson's other protagonists, and as surely as Tony turns against the similarly suicidal Natalie in *Hangsaman*. Small wonder, then, that Eleanor thinks of Theo as "someone whose anger would be frightening" (49).

Theodora and Eleanor as a pair are doubles of two other pair of sisters, Eleanor and her older sister, and the Crain sisters. In her notes,

Jackson wrote "THEO = SISTER." Just as the Crain sisters disagree over who owns the house, so Eleanor and her sister disagree over dividing their mother's estate. Eleanor's sister, who is older, corresponds to the older Crain sister.

When everyone else rejects her, Eleanor finally gives in to the seduction by this novel's oldest character: Hill House. At first she resists the siren call of the house, which appears written on the walls, first in chalk, later in what is apparently menstrual blood: "HELP ELEANOR COME HOME ELEANOR" (155). But the more dislocated she becomes, the more she wants to stay there. (Jackson wrote in her notes that Eleanor is "ALL DISTORTED *LIKE HOUSE.*") The house, then, is another of Eleanor's dark doubles, another siren ostensibly promising assistance but actually calling her to destruction.[7]

As she often does, Jackson uses the Gothic convention of giving the house human attributes. First, it looks like a human. It has a "face," a cornice like an "eyebrow" (34), and a "dormer like a dimple." Second, it has physical power. For example, the narrator states that this house "seemed somehow to have formed itself" (35) and that the tower is "held . . . tightly in the embrace of the house, in the straining grip of the house" (231). The house also has the power to grip Eleanor. By using metaphors ambiguously, Jackson suggests that the power is literal: "Hill House came around her in a rush; she was enshadowed" (36), and "the house had caught her" (35).

The house also has attitudes. Montague says the house has a cold spot at its "heart" (119). When Eleanor feels the cold spot in the hall, she says, "It doesn't seem like an *impartial* cold. . . . I felt it as *deliberate*" (120). The house also has suspicious intent. For example, Dr. Montague says it "watches every move you make" (85). Montague thinks the house wants to isolate Eleanor: "Doesn't it begin to seem that the intention is, somehow, to separate us?" (135). As a result of such perceptions, Eleanor quickly evaluates the house as diseased and "vile" (33). The third-person narrator, taking on Eleanor's bias, reports that the house is "evil" (an anagram of "vile") (34) and "arrogant and hating" (35).[8]

Jackson (apparently unconsciously) inscribes herself into the house. Her several sketches of the two-storey house exhibit traces of her body (SJP Box 22).[9] The front view of the house exaggerates the round front porch so as to make it look like teeth (several years earlier, she had all of her upper teeth pulled). In addition, the roof looks like the rounded top of a skull with a hair on top—the same single strand of hair she used in many drawings of herself. This single strand of hair reappears in some of her sketches of the top view of the second storey. If the viewer turns up the right side of such sketches and looks at the sketch with the right side as the top, the *W* for west looks like the single strand of hair atop her head.

But more important, the top views register further traces of anxiety about her orality—her dental problems, overeating, obesity, and colitis. With the top views turned right end up, the general outline of the house resembles a blockishly stout person with the tower now looking like a round head. Furthermore, the top view of the floor plan shows a hallway that suggests her esophagus and digestive tract; this hallway even makes a right turn (like the large intestine coming out of the stomach) and goes past the "nursery" (the womb) and exits the building through a bottom-rear outlet she labeled *back stairs*. Jackson felt a personal connection between this house and herself. After deciding to use a magazine picture of an old California house as her model for Hill House, she asked her mother to get information about it and found out that her grandfather, an architect, had designed the house. Like Eleanor, Jackson was erasing yet also reinscribing representations left by her patriarchs.

Like her other novels, *The Haunting of Hill House* features writing about writing. But the setting of this one is more suffused with precise genres (e.g., fairy tales and didactic primers) and specific texts. The result is not just more allusions, for Jackson's allusiveness is not an end in itself but rather a means for leading to larger discursive practices. Where in *The Sundial* the allusions connect with America's master narratives, here they connect with subject formation, as they did in *Hangsaman* and *The Bird's Nest*. The difference between the allusions in those two novels and in *The Haunting of Hill House* is that here subject formation issues from not just the prison house of language in general but from specific texts in particular. This strategy suggests that Jackson came to regard the role of discourse in subject formation and interpellation as not just a general process but rather a very precise one, in which not merely language in general but genres and even just a few specific texts directly determine much of the subject.

The destabilizing event that begins the plot is Dr. Montague's use of writing to assemble a team of fellow investigators. In search of volunteers, he combs "the records of the psychic societies" and "the back files of sensational newspapers" (5). Eliminating from his list the names of people who are dead, he contacts the rest by letter. After assembling a team of four, Montague learns by telegram that one is backing out. Montague tells the remaining members that the burden of their activity will be not so much on detecting alleged haunted activity, but on comparing events in the house to stories about the house: "The purpose of their stay, the letters stated clearly, was to observe and explore the various unsavory stories which had been circulated about the house" (5). And although Montague says "a deranged house is a pretty conceit" (70–71), and that as for secret chambers, "no such romantic devices exist here" (66), he believes what he calls "stories" (69).

The story that Montague wants to explore is the traditional ghost story. What he knows of the house's alleged haunting he gets from an old newspaper account, which certainly amounts to a paucity of documentation, thereby making his story more of a legend. Two sisters named Crain inherited a family estate and, in a Gothic convention, disagreed over who owned the "title" to it. After the younger sister got old, she was displaced by the older sister's friend, who had designs on the title.

Montague finds Eleanor through a newspaper story that claims that her childhood home was peppered for three days by an inexplicable shower of stones (7). When Eleanor tells her sister that she wants to go to Hill House, the sister reads Montague as a villainous mad scientist, installing him in a mad-scientist narrative: "Perhaps Dr. Montague—if that really *was* his name, after all—perhaps this Dr. Montague *used* these women for some—well—*experiments. You* know—*experiments,* the way they do" (8).

Once Eleanor begins her journey, writing continues to be a central part of the plot. A road sign foreshadows what will be her fatal attempt to compensate for her marginality; it is a billboard advertising "daredevil" car races, but the second *d* is missing (19). Eleanor will dare evil and the vile devil, and she will see through the veil, but she will not live to tell about it. Another foreshadowing occurs when Mrs. Montague says that spirits often appear around books: "Books are frequently very good carriers, you know. Materializations are often best produced in rooms where there are books" (186). When Eleanor finally succumbs to the house's seduction, it is in the library. Indeed, when Eleanor is caught frantically roaming the house at night, she uses the library as a pretext, a cover story: "I came down to the library to get a book" (237).

Allusions are also frequent. For example, Theodora wonders if Dracula lives here (48). Theodora's mate has ripped up a volume of Alfred de Musset, which had been a birthday gift from Theodora (9). Dr. Montague has brought *Pamela* and *Sir Charles Grandison.* After some reflection, he proffers the obvious: "A Fielding novel . . . would never do for very young children. I even have doubts about Sterne—" (90). Dudley looks to Eleanor like a "sneering Cheshire cat" (32). Oscar Wilde's "Canterville Ghost" is a favorite of Montague's, and the doctor's Shakespearean name suggests fatal family repressiveness. Also, Eleanor's thoughts, returning obsessively to Shakespeare's ballad "O Mistress Mine," dwell on the line "Present mirth hath present laughter," which seems to be another of Jackson's allusions to architecture in New England writers, in this case Edith Wharton's *House of Mirth* (*Twelfth* 2.3.42). Probably the most tongue-in-cheek allusion is to Theodore Dreiser: Eleanor's sister's name is Carrie.

It is not just for Montague that Eleanor lives in a text. On her journey to Hill House, she daydreams several narratives about herself. For example, when she sees a "tiny cottage buried in a garden" (22) she inserts herself into the setting for this scenario: "People will come to me to have their fortunes told, and I will brew love potions for sad maidens; I will have a robin . . ." (ellipses in original 23). She rehearses the classic tale—a staple in her dominant culture—that she is a lonely wanderer, a pilgrim reborn by escaping: "I am a new person, very far from home" (27). She knows herself well when she says, "What I want in all this world is peace, a quiet spot to lie and think, a quiet spot up among the flowers where I can dream and tell myself sweet stories" (194–95). The story she rehearses, then, has a burial plot.

The textual form that dominates her ruminations is the fairy tale. On her way to Hill House, Eleanor stops and walks into oleander groves and imagines castles, magic spells, stone lions, jewels, kings, and princesses, all of which constitute her "soft green picture from a fairy tale" (20). Romantic love is one of the fairy tales she imagines. For example, she pictures herself wandering in the woods. She imagines that she will wander, "chasing butterflies or following a stream, and then come at nightfall to the hut of some poor woodcutter who would offer her shelter" (17). Eleanor's fairy tale of desire reinscribes Hill House "into a fairyland." She wonders,

> Once I have stepped between the magic gateposts, will I find myself through the protective barrier, the spell broken? I will go into a sweet garden . . . and find one path . . . and it will lead me directly to the palace which lies under a spell. I will walk up low stone steps past stone lions guarding and into a courtyard where a fountain plays and the queen waits, weeping, for the princess to return. . . . The enchantment is ended and . . . we shall live happily ever after.
>
> No . . . once the palace becomes visible and the spell is broken, the *whole* spell will be broken and all this countryside . . . will return to . . . a soft green picture from a fairy tale. Then, coming down from the hills there will be a prince riding, bright in green and silver with a hundred bowmen riding behind him, pennants stirring, horses tossing, jewels flashing. (20)

But the true nature of her journey—that the lovers meeting are women who will meet in death—is foreshadowed in her imaginary fairy tale in the house she is driving past: "A little dainty old lady took care of me. . . . I dined upon a bird, and radishes from the garden, and homemade plum jam. . . . When I died . . ." (ellipses in original 18). She doesn't finish this fairy tale. But she does continue to respond to actuality from her position within fairy tales. For example, "This is where the princess comes to meet the magic golden fish who is really a prince in disguise" (52).

The fairy tale is closely associated, of course, with the dream text; both are narratives of wish fulfillment. Sometimes the narrator describes Eleanor's fairy tale reveries as if they are dreams. It is in the sense of dream as the encoding of desire and the Imaginary that Jackson not only opens the novel but also closes it. She uses the opposition of reality and dream in the first sentence: "No live organism can continue to exist sanely under conditions of absolute reality; even larks and katydids are supposed, by some, to dream. Hill House, not sane, stood by itself against its hills, holding darkness within" (3). The use of "sane" in the second sentence seems inconsistent with its use in the first. But the apparent contradiction is only that. The first sentence is consistent with the dominant culture's romantic dream that one needs to dream for sanity (dream deprivation was a hot topic in the 1950s). But what Jackson adds is that just because dreams are necessary for sanity does not mean that they are sufficient. It is not just Gatsby's dream that is puerile but his whole life. Moreover, if dreams are necessary, then sanity requires estrangement (although again it is not sufficient).

Eleanor's inscription into the social text issues from the book of instruction that Hugh Crain assembled as a collage, "MEMORIES, *for* SOPHIA ANNE LESTER CRAIN; *A Legacy for Her Education and Enlightenment During Her Lifetime From Her Affectionate and Devoted Father,* HUGH DESMOND LESTER CRAIN; *Twenty-first June, 1881*" (167–68). The recursiveness interpellating Eleanor surfaces from the year of publication; a palindrome, 1881 goes back to its origin. The construction of this book is literally intertextual; it is a collage made from other representations. The father has assembled prior texts in the form of prints and plates of paintings, etchings, and illustrations, plus original drawings perhaps his own. Under them are carefully hand-printed maxims that are possibly plagiarized, but even if they are his original words they are not his original ideas. He and his wife have let the Symbolic speak for them. One aphorism figures his daughter as a text that her parents have written: "Honor they father and thy mother, Daughter, authors of thy being, . . . that they lead their child in inno-cence and righteousness." To that romantic innocence, he adds Calvin-ist natural depravity. Under a color plate of a snake pit this adage appears: "Eternal damnation is the lot of mankind; neither tears, not reparation, can undo Man's heritage of sin." He enjoins her to remain a virgin. Under a Goya etching he writes, "Reflect, Daughter, upon the joy in Heaven as the souls of these tiny creatures wing upward, released before they have learned aught of sin or faithlessness, and make it thine unceasing duty to remain as pure as these" (168). Elsewhere he writes, "Daughter, hold apart from this world, that its lusts and ingratitudes corrupt thee not; Daughter, preserve thyself" (168–69). Part of a page is burned away with the following explanation: "Daughter, could you but hear for a moment the agony, the screaming, the dreadful crying out and repentance, of those poor souls condemned to everlasting flame! Could thine eyes be seared, but for an instant, with the red glare of wasteland burning always!" (169). This primer goes on with illustrations and quotations regarding the seven deadly sins. Hugh Crain has written the last page in blood. After all of this fear and guilt, he admonishes her: "Fear and guilt are sisters" (172).

Eleanor's introjection into the house as text surfaces in writing. When some unknown agent writes the message "HELP ELEANOR COME HOME ELEANOR" on a wall twice (155), Eleanor's identification with a prior resident of the house (probably the sister cheated out of the estate) surfaces as she goes downstairs to get a book. As with many of Jackson's characters, her unconscious surfaces in association with sleeping and continues with rationalizations by the conscious mind that obscure the fact that the unconscious is directing the behavior:

> She had awakened with the thought of going down to the library, and her mind had supplied her with a reason: I cannot sleep, she explained to herself, and so I am going downstairs to get a book. If anyone asks me where I am going, it is down to the library to get a book because I cannot sleep. . . . She went barefoot and in silence down the great staircase and to the library door before she thought, But I can't go in there; I'm not allowed in there—and recoiled in the doorway before the odor of decay, which nauseated her.
>
> "Mother," she said aloud, and stepped quickly back. "Come along," a voice answered distinctly upstairs, and Eleanor turned, eager, and hurried to the staircase. "Mother?" she said softly, and then again, "Mother?" (228)

She then starts her frantic scramble about the house and grounds.

The writing about writing makes this a heteroglossic novel. The reader reports regarding an early draft of the novel show how little the editors of the time understood the intertextuality. One wrote, "I can't figure out what she wants to do with the story. Mystery? Spoof? Psychomystery? Gothic horror?" The answer, of course, is all of these, plus fantasy, fable, dream, myth, and fairy tale. It is also, as Tricia Lootens points out, a ghost story, but it is also a parody of the ghost story (for reasons that you will see later). At this point it is enough to note that just as Jackson wrote about witchcraft without taking it literally, she wrote about ghosts without taking them literally. In her letter to her editors, she says that she is writing against "the truly incredible notion that there are ghosts." When the book appeared, Maxwell Geismar's review objected that it did not conform to any preceding genre: "The author is not altogether fair with us. After the crime tales of a William Roughed, or the mystery tales of Henry James himself, we are bound to expect a 'rationale' of even the supernatural." Geismar, unprepared for nascent postmodernism, sees form as timeless, ahistorical; if he had been a contemporary of James he would have said that his work did not conform to precedent. For Geismar, the rulebook is constant, and we are "bound" by it. He also provides a taxonomy of genres that places what he calls "supernatural" as a "restricted and peculiar medium" (31).

In addition to engendering anxieties about genre, Jackson also alienated some by destabilizing dominant modes. Another reader report objected to indeterminacy: "Beware of suggesting symbolism. . . . Great danger this will baffle people, as her last book did, by not making clear what to look for." One example of indeterminacy that troubled the publisher's editorial readers was the "symbolism" of giving two females androgynous names. In the early drafts of this novel, the protagonist and her double were named Theodora and Erica, but Jackson changed the name "Erica" to "Eleanor." She also dropped Theodora's last name of Vane, possibly because someone did not appreciate how it doubled Eleanor's last name of Vance.

Those enforcing hegemonic codes of realism as an apology for the dominant culture also miss the satiric parody of the realistic novel of manners. In his review of this novel, Geismar misreads Jackson's use of Gothic to defamiliarize. Privileging realism, Geismar concedes that she is sometimes capable of approaching it: "The opening sections seem almost . . . familiar. . . ." Geismar complains that Jackson is usually outside of the familiar: "If Miss Jackson is proficient in describing the alarums and excursions of human pathology, she is correspondingly weak on the 'normal' world of human relationships, or even of ordinary social gossip" (19). Of course, Jackson does not subscribe to the opposition of the normal and the pathological. As Joanna Russ notes, Jackson transcended realism "because conventional forms simply will not express the kind of experience she knows exists" (xiii).

In addition, by complaining about the "excessive glibness of the principals," the publisher's reader misses the satiric parody of the dialogue of romantic love. Jackson's dialogue is stilted because these characters are pretentious. They inflate their diction. And this stilted quality comes from interpellation in modes other than realism and in genres other than the novel of manners. The characters sense that they are characters constituted by prior texts. For example, Theodora tries to appear witty by saying that there is a "witch in the tower, and a dragon in the drawing room" (142). And Luke bows "as befitted one off to slay a giant" (144). In a conversation between the four principal characters, they all try to be witty and charming and ironic by posing as stock fictional characters. Eleanor tells Luke, "I live a mad, abandoned life, draped in a shawl and going from garret to garret." He responds by asking, "Are you one of the fragile creatures who will fall in love with a lord's son and pine away?" Montague's contribution to this attempt at wit is that he is a "pilgrim" and "wanderer," and Luke's is that he (conditioned by the Ernest Hemingway mystique) is a bullfighter (62).

After rehearsing roles from melodrama and romance, they shift their lame repartee to another genre. Theodora says, "What a good time for a ghost story" (69). In this comic parody of the unfunny, Jackson must present enough of the quotidian to interest readers conditioned by realism, and yet establish a subtext of these characters as twits—all without undermining reader interest. Audiences are now used to such galleries of absurd antiheroes, but as Geismar and the editors exemplify, satiric parodies of the absurd in an intertextual relationship with the novel of manners were too dialogic for many in the 1950s.

Undecidability of narration helps achieve undecidability of genre and mode. One reason for the third-person narrator's unreliability is, of course, that the point-of-view character is fragmented. Her basic perceptions are wrong. By sometimes reporting from outside of the viewpoint character, the narrator is clear that Eleanor is misperceiving. For example, she is not really holding Theodora's hand but "*perceiving* that she was lying sideways on the bed in the black darkness, holding with both hands to Theodora's hand" (163). Other times the narrator reports not that something happened but that Eleanor sees or feels it. When she moves toward a stationary object, the narrator reports the action as if the object is moving toward Eleanor, for example, as she drives along: "Hillsdale was upon her before she knew it" (23). Similarly, as she makes her entrance at Hill House, she thinks, "Hill House likes to make an entrance" (27). Reports sometimes reflect her confusion of inner and outer: "It was warm, drowsily, luxuriously warm" (228). Part of that dissociativeness is that she confuses herself with the house. For example, she projects much that the narrator reports. When she notes, "They made houses so oddly back when Hill House was built" she is also remarking on herself (32). Another reason is that the narrator's omniscience is so limited that it cannot know some things. For example, the narrator does not know what has become of several people: "To his dozen letters, Dr. Montague had four replies, the other eight or so candidates having presumably moved and left no forwarding address, or possibly having lost interest in the supernormal, or even, perhaps, never having existed at all" (5).

Yet at other times, the omniscience is so unlimited that the narrator reports on things far away. For example, within two paragraphs the narrator reports on what the doctor is doing in his room, then what Luke is doing in his room, then what Mrs. Dudley (the servant) is doing six miles away, then what the owner is doing three hundred miles away, and finally what Theodora's friend, the doctor's wife, and Eleanor's sister are doing in different cities. Another reason is that the narrator can, like a narrator in classic fantastic, believe in the marvelous. As a result of this guileful narration, it is undecidable whether a haunting actually exists—whether, for example, Eleanor frightens the other characters with her pounding and giggling, or whether there is a ghost who haunts Hill House—because the narrator cannot or will not say.

But of course the undecidability about the marvelous cannot hold. In the modern fantastic, the referent is not a ghost but the unconscious. The mode, then, is allegorical. There is no haunted house; Eleanor haunts herself, or rather the traces of history make one part of herself haunt the Other part—the conscious being Other to the real home of the subject: the unconscious.

Like the unreliability of the narration, the indeterminacy of the plot further contributes to the multivocality of genre and mode. Jackson said in her report to the publisher, "I absolutely refuse to include any rational explanation, like an escaped lunatic, or a gang of international jewel thieves." This novel finally emerges as a parody of ghost stories when the wise helper turns out to be Montague's literal-minded wife. It is impossible to take the supernatural seriously when this *alazon* is the guide to the spirit world.

Similarly, the plot parodies the archetypal hero journey. At first, the plot adheres to the archetypal events analyzed in Joseph Campbell's *The Hero with a Thousand Faces* (which Viking once promoted along with *The Lottery* in a display advertisement in the *New York Times Book Review*) but slowly undermines them (SJP Box 22). When Eleanor first hears the call to adventure, she has to overcome her sister to make the journey. Then a seemingly crazy warning figure appears, a crone on the street who says she will pray for Eleanor. But she is a parody of a witch. She calls Eleanor "dearie" (14). An old woman on the streets of an

American city would not call someone "dearie" no matter how many times she had seen *The Wizard of Oz*. True to the archetype, Eleanor gets past the guardian of the gate, the figure who tries to prevent the questing hero from entering the kingdom or arena of trial. But the guardian of the gate here is comic and literal. It is the bumbling Dudley, a parodic name for a melodramatic villain.

So in this novel, Jackson has two stories going at once: the manifest text (a parody of the Gothic ghost story) referring to the latent text (a parody of that manifest text that replaces it with a Gothic allegory of the uncanny).[10] When the narrator says that Hill House is "hiding its mad face in the growing darkness" (56), Eleanor is also hiding her mad face (as well as her mad interior). When Eleanor says, "I am disappearing inch by inch into this house, I am going apart a little bit at a time" it is into her Imaginary that she sinks. The bicameral nature of the story is implicit when Eleanor says of the threatening nocturnal sounds, "How can these others hear the noise when it is coming from inside my head?" (201).[11] On the manifest level, the others cannot hear what is in her head. This whole text comes from her head. As for the psychological referent of her allegory, Jackson wrote to her editor, "The ghost promotes a connsumation (sic) deeply desired by the percipient." And as for the nonrealist form of this novel, she added, the "ghost is a statement and a resolution of a problem that cannot be faced or solved realistically." As such, she reveals her true ideas about the supernatural. In addition, she once again anticipates not only Roth's and Barth's claims that realism cannot represent reality, but also Oates' claim that Gothic can.

So *The Haunting of Hill House* focuses on intertextuality, in particular the conventions of Gothic and the role of language in subject formation. As a psychological fable of interpellation through the family, it explores gender more than class. Indeed, this novel has attracted more feminist criticism than any of her other works. And the next novel, *We Have Always Lived in the Castle*, finishes a strong second. The increased focus on gender in these two novels accompanies a decreased focus on class. For although *We Have Always Lived in the Castle* problematizes class more than *The Haunting of Hill House* does, these two novels simply do not sustain the theme of class established in *The Sundial*. Indeed in the final analysis, *We Have Always Lived in the Castle* reveals the cracks in Jackson's Marxist foundation, which was not solid in the first place.

CHAPTER TEN

# We Have Always Lived in the Castle

Published in 1962, three years before her death, *We Have Always Lived in the Castle* is Shirley Jackson's last completed novel. At 214 small pages of large print, it is also her shortest. (Each of her novels is shorter than its predecessor.) It resumes *The Sundial*'s satire on myth and ideology, although not as explicitly. It continues the Gothicism and architectural allegory of *The Haunting of Hill House,* although not as extensively. And it shows the protagonist's mind as linguistically constituted, although not as specifically. But unlike them, it features one of Jackson's few first-person narrators (outside of her domestic narratives) and one of her few young female protagonists who are less victims than victimizers.

Uncle Julian is the most darkly comic character in Jackson's oeuvre. When he was in his middle fifties, six years before the start of the plot, his niece Merricat, who is the protagonist, poisoned him with arsenic (along with her father, mother, brother, and Julian's wife). Only Uncle Julian survived, but with brain damage. So the darkly humorous comic butt of the novel is an addled invalid. He is so confused that he thinks the niece who poisoned him is dead even though she lives in the same house with him. Prematurely senile, he is given to excessive sleeping, unintended lapses from politeness, nonsensical statements, and comments that are irrelevant to the conversation at hand. He cannot even feed himself. In the context of the possibility that Jackson had been molested by her uncle, it is significant that Jackson's most feminized male is an uncle.

Charles Blackwood is the cousin of Merricat Blackwood and her sister, Constance. Charles is the Gothic intruder, the would-be usurper of the sisters' inherited estate, the male seducer looking for sex from Constance and money from them both. He assumes the patriarchal position by moving in to the room of the sisters' dead father and wearing his watch and chain. Merricat perceptively suspects that he will try to cast Constance as the dead father's wife by putting her in the dead mother's jewelry. Like Luke Sanderson in *The Haunting of Hill House,* he is a wastrel who capitalizes on his family. He is interested in the family heirlooms not as mementos but as commodities. When Merricat damages the watch, he complains, "We could have sold it" (112). When he sees a Dresden figurine, he asks if it is valuable. He also wants to wear the fine clothes left by the sisters' father. Merricat is right when she tells him he should not try to take the property of others. He assumes that he can get at the money through an incestuous marriage to Constance. In addition, he wants to send Merricat away. He taunts her by asking, "What would poor cousin Mary do if Constance and Charles didn't love her?" (113) and wondering out loud who will be there in a month, him or Merricat. Similarly, he has no sympathy for Uncle Julian. When he first arrives, he is incredulous that anyone would have this disgusting inconvenience nearby. He asks pointedly, "Does he always eat with you?" (102). After being apprised of Julian's infirmities, Charles says, "He just likes to be waited on," which of course is true not of Julian but of Charles (117).

Constance Blackwood, twenty-eight, is agoraphobic (as was Jackson at the time she wrote this novel). But strictly speaking, Constance does not have pure agoraphobia because her fear of the town is not wholly unreasonable (and neither was Jackson's). Merricat Blackwood says, "Constance never went past her own garden" (2). Charles is right when he says she "works like a slave" (117). She stays home and does all of the cooking, cleaning, and gardening, as well as lovingly caring for Julian and Merricat, welcoming all sorts of impositions with unconditional love. After the townsfolk have destroyed almost all of the sisters' property in the end and they are living in rags in the burned-out shell of their former home, there are only two tea cups left with handles, and Constance is in "terror" lest one of them break and she be forced to use damaged tea service (212). According to Claire Kahane, "The heroine's exploration of her entrapment in a Gothic house . . . can be read as an exploration of her relation to the maternal body" ("Maternal" 243). Constance's relation to her dead mother is to displace her by obsessively repeating her mother's domestic drudgery in all ways except marriage.[1] This blond domestic angel plays her mother's harp in front of the dearly departed's portrait. What Kate Ferguson Ellis says of sentimental heroines applies to this satiric parody of one: "By acting like Pamela, they can purify the fallen aristocratic castle and make it into a home worthy of the name. This is the premise that the Gothic novel takes up" (8).

Despite her amiability, she is a passive-aggressive enabler who unconsciously uses her cloying sweetness to get the dark Merricat to do her dirty work. She is the one who taught Merricat about poisons. And Merricat administered it by slipping it into the sugar that Constance put on the table.[2] In addition, no one disputes Mrs. Wright when she says that Constance "told the police those people deserved to die" (53). Covering for Merricat, Constance took the fall but was acquitted. Nonetheless, the villagers believe Constance did it. The sisters suppress the fact that Merricat is the culprit, not mentioning it until the end, and agreeing never to talk about it again. When Uncle Julian dies in the end, Constance shows no remorse, only a predilection for conforming to the manners expected of a deceased's survivors.

While Constance is the long-suffering, dutiful housewife, Merricat Blackwood has only a few female identifications. Although she is childlike and sometimes even maternal, and although she despises every male except her cat and often flees to her vaginal hideout, a riverside cavern that is covered with bushes,[3] Merricat is generally more male-identified. She plays the husband's role by taking her sister as her partner. Appropriately, she likes the way a serpentine chain wraps around her arm: "I liked the watch chain, which twisted and wound around my hand when I picked it up" (111). And she performs the manly duties of carpentry, trading downtown, and killing people. On the first page, she announces her predilection for the deadly mushroom *Amanita phalloides* (a man-eater phallic). Later she uses this knowledge to threaten Charles: "The *Amanita phalloides*, I said to him, holds three different poisons. There is amanitin, which works slowly and is most potent. There is phalloidin, which acts at once, and there is phallin, which dissolves red corpuscles, although it is the least potent" (104). She thereby leaves no doubt about the impressiveness of her mushroom. She also imagines poisoning people in the village: "I always thought about rot when I came toward the row of stores; I thought about burning black painful rot that ate away from inside, hurting dreadfully. I wished it on the village" (9). She imagines the market strewn with dead villagers, even children: "I wanted them doubled up and crying on the ground in front of me" (22). Her fantasies take on biblical proportions: "Their throats will burn when the words come out, and in their bellies they will feel a torment hotter than a thousand fires" (24).

Merricat is home to a menagerie of neuroses, beginning with obsessiveness. Although her most common musings are the hostile fantasies, she repeats other thoughts. For example, she tells herself several times to be "kinder to Uncle Julian" (116), but she never is, and in fact she causes his death in the end. Also, she mentions the garden many times. And she repeatedly listens to her cat, thinking it talks to her. She is also compulsive. She fears that putting on a ring would trap her: "I would not touch the ring; the thought of a ring around my finger always made me feel tied tight, because rings had no openings to get out of " (111). In addition, she dislikes bathing. Her fear of dirt masks her commitment to it. Rather than clean the house, she prefers to "neaten" it (60, 149, 182).[4] Her resultant filthiness she projects on others. She regards the Harlers and other locals as dirty, and she speaks of firefighters as "dragging their hoses, bringing filth" (149). Her complaint about the dirty village's appearance is that it is grey, "put together out of old grey wood" (15). Similarly, she disdains the village women for their "grey evil weariness" (4). She is evidently unaware of the fact that grey results from a combination of black and white, as in black wood and sugar. She is likewise oblivious to the implication when she says that Charles "blackened" the world (137) and that the house after the fire consists of "black and twisted wood" (167).

Occasionally, Merricat Blackwood is delusional. She believes that her left eye works better by day and sees gold, yellow, and orange, while the right eye works better by night and sees blue, green, and grey. She takes her vision literally. For example, she thinks Charles is getting bigger when he is simply getting closer: "He stood up; he was taller now that he was inside, bigger and bigger as he came closer to me" (82). Her paranoid ideation overrides her perception. Because she believes him to be a demonic ghost, she thinks she is watching a shapeshifter. In addition, she gets her Sunday sermon from her cat: "On Sunday morning I lay there with Jonas, listening to his stories. All cat stories start with the statement: 'My mother, who was the first cat, told me this,' and I lay with my head close to Jonas and listened" (76). She believes that the river might not be there if she does not see it—that it depends on her ideation for its existence. Looking back on the night she killed her parents, brother, and aunt, she imagines not that they resist her but that they obey her. Her mother says to her husband, "Mary Katherine should have anything she wants, my dear. Our most loved daughter must have anything she likes." The father responds, "Lucy, you are to see to it that our most loved daughter Mary Katherine is never punished." The wife answers, "Mary Katherine would never allow herself to do anything wrong; there is never any need to punish her" (139). Thus Merricat rehearses her delusions of grandeur—her right to kill and yet to glory in her high moral stature— by reinscribing the murder scene from six years ago. Similarly, she recalls the previous night's death of Julian from a fire that she caused: "I sat by the creek, wishing that I had been kinder to Uncle Julian.

Uncle Julian had believed that I was dead, and now he was dead himself; bow your heads to our beloved Mary Katherine, I thought, or you will be dead" (164).

Despite her delusions, Merricat's narration is less unreliable than that of many of Jackson's narrators, whether first-person or third. One interesting problem bearing on the narrator's stance is her situation and audience. Where and to whom would she be addressing herself? Is it the general audience that Ralph Ellison used in *Invisible Man*? Or is Merricat, like Holden Caulfield, addressing someone in an institution? Given what might befall a character in this situation, she is probably addressing some official, such as a lawyer or psychotherapist. Indeed, it seems that her auditor must already know important facts that the reader does not know. Most importantly, the reader does not know until page 43 that the sisters' parents, brother, and aunt died of arsenic poisoning and that Constance was acquitted. (Similarly, that the murderer was Merricat does not emerge clearly until page 161.) As a result, the plot structure includes several darkly comic incidents in the first 42 pages that the reader cannot understand on the first reading. The result is that the reader is the butt of dramatic irony. For example, when Merricat says that the people in the store recoil when she buys lamb and sugar, the reader does not yet know that lamb was the last supper for the Blackwoods, and sugar the medium for the poison. Later, the reader catches on when the two busybodies come for tea:

> "Sugar?" I asked her; I couldn't help it, and besides, it was polite.
> "Oh, no," she said. "No, thank you. No sugar." (40)

Moreover, Jackson shows her readers that they can be sympathetic to a young woman who appears to be a victim ("No one would ever offer to help me") but who is actually a mass murderer—the ultimate antihero (13). For indeed, as Lynette Carpenter shows, Merricat has admirable traits. Foremost among these is that she resists Charles. She is also willing to resist all of the other males. And she is devoted to her sister. The reader remains so sympathetic to Merricat that not only the perversity of her psyche but also the absurdity of her situation disappears. Whereas *The Sundial* proceeds from an absurd premise, this one ends with an absurd conclusion. Merricat would have the reader believe that she and Constance lived happily ever after in a house that has had its roof and second storey burned away. She says nothing about rain and snow, nor does she say what they did for heat and light. At the same time, however, the reader does not ask about such things, and should not ask, because this novel is a fabulation.

This novel continues Jackson's writing about writing. Textuality suffuses the setting. As with Jackson's home, the Blackwood home is replete with books. The father's books alone cover two walls. Similarly, his daughters make regular use of the village library. In addition, Uncle Julian believes he is writing a book about the murder, and he is pleased to see Merricat with a book; he does not realize that it is a cookbook. Merricat associates books with her delusions of grandeur. When recalling the family she decimated, she imagines her father telling his wife to get Merricat a new book.

Textuality also marks the village. In fact, textuality leads the reader on a trail to the village. As Merricat walks to town, she imagines she is making moves on a game board. Also, the sisters receive hostile letters from the townies. And visitors write their names on the Blackwood home and fences. For example, the Mueller boy's initials are on the library porch. In addition, the town newspaper was full of stories about the murder and trial, so now the sisters never read the paper. Even the origins of writing appear. A boy has left his handprint in the sidewalk. Even the family name, Blackwood, suggests the source of paper. In fact, Merricat defensively mentions that another family owns the paper mill. When the locals destroy the Blackwood home, they ruin almost everything except the library books.

Reviewers and critics have recognized this novel's similarity to those of other writers. Guy Davenport and Arthur Hammond compare it to the work of William Faulkner and Edgar Allen Poe. They might have added that Jackson alludes to Poe with the sisters' family name, which is the namesake of one of Poe's organs of publication, *Blackwood* Magazine.[5] They might also have added Nathaniel Hawthorne and the many producers of Gothic before him, for here Jackson again uses the family estate with a disputed title. Set in a contested old manse, this novel is in dialogue with the Gothic tradition, but Jackson also continues her dialogue with updated Gothic absurdism[6] by implying that it is not just the Blackwoods who have lived in the castle since their Adamic arrival in it with no apparent forebears. Rather, Jackson implies that the dominant culture, too, has habitually lived in Franz Kafka's *Castle*. In David W. Noble's terms, the American Adam believes that he is an exception to history rather than an extension of it (*Eternal* and *Death*). And as ever, one subgenre Jackson uses is the eighteenth-century novel. Davenport states, "Jackson is interested in driving to some. . . . Crusoe island" (517). Jackson alludes to Crusoe directly when the sisters discuss what to wear after their apocalyptic conflagration. Merricat tells Constance, "Robinson Crusoe dressed in the skins of animals" (200). In an interview, Jackson stated that Crusoe was an important part of the novel's theme. She described her novel as "a kind of Robinson Crusoe setting of a private little world," but quickly added, "I am not coming out in favor of that" (M. M.). Also as before, she reaches for the noncanonical end of the spectrum. Merricat regrets that she was not born a werewolf. A newspaper reviewer in Jackson's hometown of Bennington failed to appreciate the intertextual nature of this novel. She complained that it "falls somewhere between a novel and a horror story that does not allow full satisfaction in either genre" (Tate 12).

It is just this juxtaposition of modes and genres that perceptive readers lauded, particularly this novel's dialogue between tragedy and comedy. For example, one reviewer described it as "A Sunny, Cheery Horror" (Safford W-18). The dark humor is in dialogue with the other fictions of 1960's fabulation. Of course, the characterization of Julian is among the most mordant of the era. In addition, after the house is burned down and the sisters have little left except the basement, kitchen, and living room, Merricat reflects on things the kitchen needs: "It would be nice to have a fireplace in here, I thought; we could sit beside a fire, and then I thought no, we have already had a fire" (185). Even Jim Donell, the crass fire chief, gets off a couple of good lines. When taunting Merricat by saying that she and Constance should leave town, he says facetiously, "It's too bad when the old families go," and then adds, "although you could rightly say a good number of the Blackwoods are gone already" (19). It is the bitterly dark comedy of two neurotic women and their daft uncle struggling to reinscribe domestic bliss at the setting of the gentry's collapse that moved Dorothy Parker to write, "This novel brings back all of my faith in terror and death" (44).

With proto-postmodern irony, this novel not only privileges writing but also satirizes it, especially nonfiction. (Several of Jackson's parodic patriarchs are scholars like her husband.) In an interview to publicize this novel, Jackson laughed at her husband for taking thirteen years to write his latest book (M. M.). Similarly, Julian has been trying to write a book about the murders ever since they happened six years previously. He complains that a writer's work is never done. He has saved news clippings about the murder and trial, and he has also made notes about both. Now he is trying to arrange them into the draft of a book. Julian calls it "one of the few genuine mysteries," and to him it is indeed a mystery, one to which he has no clue (43). Jackson undermines the alleged nonfictional aspect of scholarship by having Julian say, "I shall be forced to invent, to fictionalize, to imagine" (95). And as Stanley Edgar Hyman fictionalized Jackson by promoting her as a witch, Julian now announces that he will fictionalize his wife by saying she was beautiful. Similarly, when the data fail him totally, he moves from fictionalizing to falsehood: "I shall commence, I think, with a slight exaggeration and go on from there into an outright lie" (90). And Jackson even inscribes herself in Julian's work. He repeatedly announces that he is writing chapter 44 (87, 90). When Jackson was writing this novel, she was 44.

As before, an important form in Jackson's intertextuality is the fairy tale. When Merricat comes out of hiding to see that the conflagration has resulted in the destruction of her estate, she experiences the shock of recognition as if it is an unsatisfactory fairy tale: "I thought that we had somehow not found our way back correctly through the night, that we had somehow lost ourselves and come back through . . . the wrong fairy tale" (67–68). Merricat's penchant for fairy tales leads her to try to remake reality by representing it as a fairy tale: "When I was small I thought Constance was a fairy princess. I used to try to draw her picture, with long golden hair and eyes as blue as the crayon could make them" (28). By translating writing on paper on the one hand to drawing on paper on the other hand, she uses the intermediary of the crayon, which is halfway between pencil and paintbrush; she restores ideograph to pictograph.

In the end, the sisters become part of the social text of the madwomen in the attic (although in this case they are so mad that they have burned up the second floor and the attic and now live on the ground floor and in the basement—in Jackson's recurrent architectural metaphor, their higher consciousness is destroyed). The locals read them as legends, and even tourists know the story. In time, the legends grow. One woman says, "The local people tell some tall tales" (206). Another says, "They hate little boys *and* little girls. The difference is, they eat the little girls" (207). Visitors treat the ruin like a museum or battle site. One says, "I've heard that it was quite a local landmark at one time" (206). Another says that the staircase was made of carved Italian marble. Visitors bring their picnics to the lawn. They come to have their pictures taken here as if it is a shrine. In addition, guilty pilgrims bring offerings of food and clothing, leaving them by the door where the sisters will fetch them under cover of darkness—they only come out at night. And like many sacred sites, this one is desecrated. Visitors write their names on the house. Moreover, people let their dogs run free in the garden. They even take mementos.

As ever in Jackson, writing is associated with the attempt to lift sensational events up to legendary status. Nursery rhymes facilitate this elevation of the sisters into secular sainthood. From Merricat's entry into the village at the beginning (with all but an *A* on her breast), through the fiery stoning of the house at the climax, to the development of legend at the end, the children (including boys with the recurrent name of Harris) chant such ditties as this one:

Merricat, said Connie, would you like a cup of tea?
Oh, no, said Merricat, you'll poison me.
Merricat, said Connie, would you like to go to sleep?
Down in the boneyard ten feet deep!

(22–23)

Merricat's witchcraft rituals often involve textuality. She believes that to say something three times is to make it real. She has three magic words, which she believes protect her from change. Her obsessions about these words are contradictory—she must always remember them but never forget them: "I would not forget my magic words, . . . but I refused to let them into my mind" (73). In a witchcraft ritual for preserving the purity of the estate from outside interference, she nails her father's account book to a tree. To purify her father's room of Charles's influence, she first removes all of her father's books. And to further defeat change, she erases Julian's death by putting his pen into the river: "I went down to the creek and buried Uncle Julian's initialed gold pencil by the water, so the creek would always speak his name" (201).

Merricat feels haunted by Charles, who is both a disruptive agent of change and an embodiment of the past. She calls him a "ghost" (88). She fears him as a patriarchal figure who will take her back into the past that she escaped when she killed her parents and brother and aunt. To stay in never-never land and not finish the oedipal project, Merricat needs Constance, and Charles threatens to come between them. So she performs her rituals to get rid of him and to prevent that change. For example, she breaks her father's watch.

One of Merricat's defenses for maintaining her obsession with time is to deny it. She notes those things that will always last. She says that their library books will "stand forever" (2). She also says that they "closed the drawing-room door behind [them] and never opened it afterwards" (176). To keep time at bay, they agree never to mention the murder again. In addition, she thinks she has made Julian immortal. But to keep things forever is to keep the past in the present. Even the name "Julian" is associated with time (and text) in the form of the Julian calendar. She has no answer when Constance asks, "How are we going to know what time it is?" (182). Moreover, the sisters have given up observing birthdays. Even the story she tells largely ignores the period in time that is most important, the slaying and trial. Merricat tells us about the aftermath, the denouement. She also projects time onto the Other. For example, she is disgusted that the village's grayness is unchangeable. She mystifies and naturalizes time by saying that the sisters have "always" lived in the castle and that the locals have "always" hated them (6).

Although she would prevent the intrusion of the past by preventing the intrusion of the future, she depicts the present as a repository of former times. For example, she says that their silverware has "been in the house for generations of Blackwood wives" (168). And they will subsist largely on the "preserves" their foremothers have left in the basement (168–69). These sisters, then, will be eating history even as they try to eliminate it. At the same time that they are living after the end of history, they are living at the beginning of it; they are simultaneously postlapsarian and prelapsarian—like the Hallorans in *The Sundial*. As Nick Carraway says, they are born back ceaselessly into the past, not knowing that the past is ahead of them.

To deny time even as she represents it, Merricat twice uses a spatial metaphor that obscures the confusion of the postlapsarian and prelapsarian. Moreover she uses this same time-denying metaphor to account for the change wrought by the fire. Of the fire's alteration of their previous life, she says, "Although I did not perceive it then, time and the orderly pattern of our old days had ended" (171). Of their new life after the fire, she says, "Slowly the pattern of our days grew, and shaped itself into a happy life" (193). Their domestic sphere is the heart of innocence, the place where the purity not just of the virgin land but of these two virgins preserves moral superiority. Merricat sees the house as an arena for the struggle between good and evil, and she says that she would aid her sister in that struggle: "It was as though she had been expecting all her life that Cousin Charles would come, as though she had planned exactly what to do and say, almost as though in the house of her life there had always been a room kept for Cousin Charles" (92). She tries to expel him with rituals of exorcism.[7] Likewise, when his pipe leaves an infernal hole in a chair, she hopes that the damage will help her get rid of him: "I hoped that the house, injured, would reject him" (114). Ellis writes,

> The foregrounding of women as subjects through which the experience of salvation is conveyed raises contradictions about the enclosed space she "rules." A space where "terror, doubt, and division" cannot enter is a place where innocence cannot be undermined by the "rough world" outside it. But walls that cannot be penetrated become a prison. A castle turned into a prison and reconverted into a home (or destroyed so that its prisoners can establish a home elsewhere) is the underlying structure of the feminine Gothic. But not all enclosed spaces can become homes. Walls can confine and conceal as well as protect, and evil can flourish in a climate of privacy no less easily than good. Where the home is destroyed utterly and the destroyer continues to wander upon the face of the Earth, we have the Lewisite or masculine Gothic. (44–45)

Jackson puts the feminine and masculine Gothic in dialogue by having the home destroyed partially and having one of those responsible, Merricat, roam the ruin while the locals wander the larger arena.

The figuration of the domestic sphere as the place of purification begins with Merricat's anthropomorphizing of the house. She says their house has a "stern, unwelcoming face" (28). Also, she refers to "the heart" (79) and "bones" of her house (151). In addition, she says that after the fire, "the house seemed to shiver" (167). Merricat projects herself onto the house. When she and her sister are anxious about being exposed to the firefighters, Merricat says, "The front of the house was white and pale and uncomfortable at being so clearly visible; it had never been lighted before" (149). After the fire, she unconsciously associates the ruin with the Blackwoods twisted up from the rot she has put in them: "Today the house ended above the kitchen doorway in a nightmare of black and twisted wood" (167). The burning away of part of the house and their refuge in what is left suggests the mutilated psyche of each. Likewise, the burning away of the top storey of their house figures the loss of their rational minds; and their descent into the lower regions of the house suggest that they live only in rationalizations of base motives. As Chris Baldick notes, the Gothic figures "old buildings as sites of human decay. The Gothic castle or house is not just an old and sinister building; it is a house of degeneration, even of decomposition, its living-space darkening and contracting into the dying-space of the mortuary and the tomb" (xx).

As with the Hallorans, Merricat's vision of the purified future is another spin on the quest for Eden. In a review entitled "In a Garden of Eden," Paul Carroll notes, "Mary Katherine loves her Eden, where all is ritual, food, incest, and peace" (16–B).[8] And as you have seen, Guy Davenport notes that the sisters are restored to the Edenic innocence of "a Crusoe island." Consistent with the Crusoe version of Eden, Merricat fashions a toga made of a tablecloth. And Constance says, "I will wear leaves" (199). After fleeing to Merricat's hollow after the fire and sleeping there all night with her, Constance looks like a primitive Eve: "There were leaves in her hair and dirt on her face" (165). In this retrograde setting where foliage overtakes the house, they look like American Eves restored to a primitive Eden: "No one ever saw our eyes looking out through the vines" (213). But Eden is disrupted by evil in the form of the working-class villagers in general and Charles in particular. His presence in the garden warps the apple trees: "Even the garden had become a strange landscape with Charles' figure in it; I could see him standing under the apple trees and the trees were crooked and shortened beside him" (115). Richard Slotkin shows that evil in the

American Eden necessitates regeneration through violence. With her fire, Merricat destroys Eden to save it. Like members of the culture of which she thinks she is innocent, she is attracted to apocalyptic scenes. As Davenport notes, one of Jackson's themes is "some last stand" ("Dust" 516). As such, the sisters constitute a satiric parody of one of the hallmarks of America's social text, what Malcolm Bradbury calls "a new world fable of prelapsarian man beginning again, the new Adam in the new Eden" (vi).

Recalling *The Sundial*'s True Believers, Merricat conceives of her heaven on earth as if it is the moon. In a letter to Jackson and Hyman, Burke applauded the "idyllic" end in "womb-heaven." Early on, Merricat tries to convince herself that her fantasy is real: "I am living on the moon, I told myself, I have a little house all by myself on the moon" (20). The two most important features in her vision are the fireplace and the garden: "I liked my house on the moon, and I put a fireplace in it and a garden outside . . . and I was going to have lunch outside in my garden on the moon" (21). In the end, she believes she really is on the moon. She tells Constance, "We are on the moon at last" (165). But Merricat is disappointed: "I am thinking that we are on the moon, but it is not quite as I supposed it would be" (195). Consistent with the myth of the new Eden as paradise regained, she sometimes represents the moon as paradise lost: "On the moon we wore feathers in our hair, and rubies on our hands. On the moon we had gold spoons" (87). But to have rubies on their hands, they would have to wear rings. Merricat thus inadvertently expresses the desire for entrapment that she disclaims, a desire that she finally fulfills by burning down the house and thereby leaving her sister and herself bound even more tightly together in even more restricting circumstances.

Again Jackson subverts myth by rooting it not just in personal fantasy—private demons—but in traces of the public. Indeed, Merricat announces right away that her favorite genres are not just fairy tales but also history. Lauren Berlant says of Nathaniel Hawthorne that his production is marked by not just individual vagaries but by traces of a mythology we can now call a "national fantasy." Similarly, Sacvan Bercovitch has detailed how the dominant culture encourages identification of the private with the public through rituals of consensus *(Rites)*. The place that Merricat wants to go is consistent with the dominant culture's social text not only of conflagration but also of a New Frontier witnessing a man on the moon. Merricat's fantasy anticipates that of Kurt Vonnegut's Billy Pilgrim, who also imagines his separate peace as taking place in outer space.

As part of Jackson's nascent postmodern subversion of myth criticism, she places myths and rituals alongside fairy tales, legends, and nursery rhymes. What is even more important, she devalorizes myth criticism by breaking the opposition of myth and ritual on the one hand, and magic and witchcraft on the other. Jackson, the wife of a scholar who studied folklore and ballads and collected folk music and blues, thereby demystifies the myth critics' tendency to obscure ideology under valorized canonical myths and to separate those privileged myths from other beliefs and practices they called "folklore."

Similarly, she also linked myth and ritual to ideology, for this novel is a case study in the neo-aristocratic haute bourgeois exploitation of the petit bourgeois and the lower class. The Blackwoods own a huge tract of land, with their own river running through it. Their father displays his conspicuous consumption by getting the first piano in the village. Merricat is so rich that she can destroy wealth, such as silver dollars and jewelry, in her witchcraft rituals. In addition, she looks down on the nouveau riche: "The Clarke's house is newer but no finer than the Blackwood house." Likewise, she looks down on the petit bourgeois and "their dirty little houses" (5). She covets even their meager holdings. Of the rundown Rochester House she says, "I wondered sometimes if the Harler people knew that they lived in a house which should have belonged to Constance" (7). The only reason she gives for her assertion that her sister should own what is left of the Rochester House is that their "mother had been born there" (4). Apparently Merricat wants to have it just so no one else will.

Merricat's parents raised her to believe herself superior. After the Blackwoods fenced people out of the Blackwood land and thereby make them walk next to the dangerous main road, Merricat's mother used to say, "The highway's built for common people" (26). Merricat says of the villagers, "Our father said they were trash" (15). As a result, she divides the world into the "rich" people like herself versus everyone else:

> When I was small I used to lie in my bedroom at the back of the house and imagine the driveway and the path as a crossroad meeting before our front door, and up and down the driveway went the good people, the clean and rich ones dressed in satin and lace, who came rightfully to visit, and back and forth along the path, sneaking and weaving and sidestepping servilely, went the people from the village. (26)

Her property assists her as a bulwark against evil: "We had always a solid foundation of stable possessions. . . . As soon as a new Blackwood wife moved in, a place was found for her belongings, and so our house was built up with layers of Blackwood property . . . keeping it steady against the world" (2). For Merricat, a woman's home is her castle.

Her interpellation prevents her from perceiving her class privilege. In fact, she sees herself as disadvantaged: "I have had to be content with what I had" (1). She denies that the shabbiness of the village might have anything to do with the fact that she inherited the wealth it would take to make the village attractive. "The blight on the village never came from the Blackwoods" (9). She is oblivious to the fact that she has never had to work, that she lives on wealth that her forefathers extracted from the locals. So she sees no hypocrisy in telling Charles, "Next time don't go around taking other people's things" (130). She is as hypocritical as Julian when he says, believing Charles is Julian's brother, "You are a very selfish man, John, perhaps even a scoundrel, and overly fond of the world's goods; I sometimes wonder, John, if you are every bit the gentle-man" (134). She is oblivious to the fact that the Blackwood sisters are the deadwood sisters. By saying that they "have always lived in the castle," "always had plenty of money" (9), and "the people of the village always hated" them, she erases the story of how this class arrangement origi-nated (6). She also obscures the fact that the hatred must have intensified when Constance beat the murder charge. Merricat says nothing of what the villagers must have regarded as another unearned privilege of the rich paid for by the commoners. Moreover, she overlooks the fact that the object of the proletarians' wrath is not the sisters but their property. The villagers do not harm the sisters; what they destroy is the sisters' store of commodities. For all of the anxiety and fear that Jackson felt as a result of her dealings with small-minded people in Bennington, her final repre-sentation of small towners is more sympathetic than not, at least implic-itly. (An important qualifier is that the townsfolk accept Charles the usurping patriarch.) Despite momentary lapses in her life when her emo-tions quite understandably got the best of her temporarily, her considered opinion as it emerges in the deliberative act of writing expresses not her childhood as a privileged bourgeois but her adulthood as one aware not only of gender and psychology but also class.

However, Jackson's class-consciousness is not unlimited and uncon-flicted. Like anyone else, of course, she does not totally escape the ide-ology that interpellated her. Probably more than any of her other texts, this one most belies the erosion of her Marxism. For despite the legion of Merricat's faults, she remains (as you saw) rather sympathetic and even somewhat heroic. Therein lies part of the haunting quality of the book, for the reader keeps rooting for Merricat. Perhaps part of the rea-son is that Merricat's motive for murder does not emerge clearly, which is in keeping with the illegibility of evil and subject formation in Jack-son's fiction. And Merricat's identification with the Blackwood property makes the attack on it seem almost as disturbing as the stoning in "The

Lottery." An even more important reason for Merricat's qualified admirableness is that Jackson has put a lot of herself into Merricat. Both are borderline multiple personalities. Also, Merricat expresses tendencies that Jackson represses. And Merricat, like Jackson, is an effective rhetorician. For in spite of all the evidence against herself that Merricat divulges, she evinces the proto-postmodern antihero's ability to seem to rise above the ostensibly respectable characters in the story. So this novel is probably where a thoroughgoing deconstruction of Jackson would be most telling. For Jackson's respect for Merricat may conceal a respect for some of Merricat's questionable values.

Nonetheless, her last completed novel is one of her most class conscious, even though Jackson's own disunified subjectivity may be more visible here.[9] For if, as Mary Poovey claims, Radcliffean Gothic undermines capitalist ideology, so too does Jackson's. But the Gothic intertextuality of some of her fiction enables some critics to misread her as the poet of privacy. Such critics believe the fiction Hyman and Jackson created about her. They read Shirley Jackson's fiction through the fiction about Shirley Jackson.

Jackson was right when she wrote in her diary, "Insecure, uncontrolled, I wrote of neuroses and fear and I think all my books laid end to end would be one long documentation of anxiety." But Jackson did not select her own society and then close the door. Society selected her as its object, and her production is the record of its contradictions. Then criticism selected her as its object—a simple and apolitical sensationalist entertainer who also wrote nifty domestic narratives (never mind that she despised them)—and then closed the door on some of her most complex and penetrating novels: *Hangsaman, The Bird's Nest,* and above all *The Sundial.*

# AFTERWORD

Until just after her death, Jackson received commentary from such luminaries of the time as John W. Aldridge, Cleanth Brooks, Guy Davenport, August Derleth, Chester E. Eisenger, Leslie Fiedler, Maxwell Geismar, Ihab Hassan, Granville Hicks, Gilbert Highet, Alfred Kazin, William Kennedy, Stanley J. Kunitz, John O. Lyons, Dorothy Parker, Louis Untermeyer, and Robert Penn Warren. But soon after she died, she was contained, domesticated, and marginalized even by those who would celebrate her. (If, as David W. Noble says, we have historians against history, we also have literary critics against literature) *(Historians.)* Critics began to take seriously her least serious work, the domestic narratives. Jackson was not hurt by critics who lacked high regard for her cash crop but rather by critics who did. Meanwhile, the regard for her serious fiction fell as her critics masked her techniques and themes by focusing on her sensational aspects, and celebrated her for being popular. For example, Lenemaja Friedman, who wrote the first book on Jackson, applauded her as being an "entertainer" (Preface).

The first error of Jackson criticism is the same as that applied to other proto-postmodernists such as Kurt Vonnegut and John Barth: the notion that they write private, apolitical fiction.[1] But the opposition of self and public breaks down. Even the unconscious, of course, is political. The site of contending subject positions known as Shirley Jackson did not result in the production of what her biographer calls "private demons." Likewise, Friedman is wrong in finding that Jackson "creates microcosms, private worlds set apart from the larger universe of crowds and cities, pushing-and-shoving functional people; away from the problems of ecology and population growth and urban housing renewal" (44). Writing about "The Lottery" at the end of the Vietnam War, which was waged largely by men who objected to it but went anyway, Friedman claims, "If anything is illogical about the total ritual, it may be the stoicism of the participants and their complete willingness to sacrifice themselves or members of their families" (67). Such misreadings are a long falling off from Kenneth Burke's comment about Jackson's first novel, that central to it is "the way she gets at the mystery of social class."

Likewise, students of Jackson long overlooked her themes of gender. Michael L. Nardacci states, "one gets the feeling that the subject of Women's Liberation would have meant nothing to her" (15). Similarly, Friedman states that "Miss Jackson avoids sex altogether" (158). On Jackson's writing about "lesbians," Judy Oppenheimer claims, "it is highly unlikely that . . . she even knew precisely what the word meant" (40). But in her diary Jackson writes about her friend at Rochester, Jeanne Marie Bedel, a French student regarded by the locals as a Communist: "my friend was so strange that everyone, even the man i loved, thought we were lesbians and they used to talk about us, and i was afraid of them and I hated them, then i wanted to write stories about lesbians and how people misunderstood them. and finally this man sent me away because i was a lesbian."

Some scholars missed not only the message but also the code. Friedman is incapable of seeing Jackson in the context of the transition from modernism to postmodernism. She dismisses Jackson's dialogic anti-realism as "artificial manipulations" (126). Similarly, Michael L. Nardacci misses the dialogic style of *The Haunting of Hill House* by complaining that the "satiric passages seem to grate on the rest of the work" (26).

There are similar misreadings of Jackson's life. Thousands of college students are introduced to Jackson by headings like this: "Shirley Jackson lived a quiet life" (Clayton 642). Oppenheimer elides the worst to be found in the Stanley Edgar Hyman and Jackson archives, and then whitewashes the rest of the evidence. She passes over Jackson's diary entries about suicide: "The suicide attempt she mentions was not a serious one; her parents possibly never even knew about it" (40). Similarly, Oppenheimer dismisses any possible significance of the attempted suicide by Jackson's daughter, who was found full of Jackson's pills and with one of Jackson's books across her chest. This suicide attempt occurred just two weeks before Jackson died at forty-eight of a heart attack. Friedman romanticizes Jackson's death by claiming something that no one knows: "Miss Jackson had died peacefully in her sleep" (40). Likewise, students of Jackson idealize her conflicts. Despite Jackson's frequent theme of domestic servitude, Friedman concludes that Jackson's own housewifery did not restrict her writing.

With the earliest Jackson studies leading readers away from her most significant work, it is no wonder that the first four novels have been largely ignored. Often readers give up on Jackson before getting to them because the domestic essays and Gothic novels are promoted as her best. Fortunately, some recent scholarship has been a marked improvement.[2] For example, the studies by Dale Frederick Bailey, Marta Caminero-Santangelo, Lynnette Carpenter, Joan Wylie Hall, Tricia Lootens, Judie Newman, Roberta Rubenstein, and Andrew J. Schopp are marked advances. And Jackson is the subject of a recent essay by Jonathan Lethem, winner of a National Book Critics Circle Award. By providing a new overview of Jackson's fiction, this study hopes to reorient Jackson criticism and encourage the attention that she deserves.

# NOTES

INTRODUCTION.
SHIRLEY JACKSON AND PROTO-POSTMODERNISM

1. A copy of the syllabus that includes Jackson is in the Shirley Jackson Papers, Box 31, Library of Congress, Washington, D.C., hereafter cited as SJP. The SJP contains a box of diaries, two boxes of Jackson's family correspondence, nine boxes of professional correspondence, two boxes of poems and articles, five boxes of short stories, and on average about a box of manuscripts and clippings for each volume she published—a total of forty-one boxes.

2. A copy of "Reading Recommended by the Book Committee" is in SJP Box 31. The month and day are missing.

3. "Come Dance with Me in Ireland" was reprinted in *Best American Short Stories, 1944*. The *New York Times Book Review* named *The Lottery* to its list of "Best Fiction of 1949"; "The Lottery" was reprinted in *Prize Stories of 1949: The O. Henry Awards*. "The Summer People" was included in *Best American Short Stories, 1951*. *Time* and the *Yale Review* both listed *Hangsaman* as one of the best books of 1951. "One Ordinary Day, with Peanuts" was included in *Best American Short Stories, 1956*. The *New York Times Book Review* put *The Haunting of Hill House* on its list of the "Best Fiction of 1959." In 1960 it was nominated for a National Book Award. In 1961 "Louisa, Please Come Home" won the Edgar Allan Poe Award. *We Have Always Lived in the Castle* was named by *Time* as one of the "Ten Best Novels" of 1962, included on the *New York Times Book Review*'s list of "Best Fiction of 1962," and nominated the next year for a National Book Award. "Birthday Party" appeared in *Best American Short Stories, 1964*. In 1965 "The Possibility of Evil" won the Edgar Allan Poe Award. In 1966 *The Magic of Shirley Jackson* was named to the *New York Times Book Review*'s "Best Fiction of 1966." The *New York Times Book Review* listed *Come Along with Me* in "The Best Fiction of 1968."

4. Noted scholars of the time who wrote criticism on Jackson include John W. Aldridge, Cleanth Brooks, Chester E. Eisenger, Leslie Fiedler, Gilbert Highet, Alfred Kazin, John O. Lyons, and Robert Penn Warren. Eminent scholars who reviewed her books include Guy Davenport, Maxwell Geismar, Ihab Hassan, Granville Hicks, and Louis Untermeyer. Prominent creative writers discussing her work include August Derleth, William Kennedy, Stanley J. Kunitz, and Dorothy Parker. Some of the venues that reviewed her books are *Commonweal, Nation, National Observer, New Leader, New Republic, New York Times Book Review, New Yorker, Punch, Saturday Review, Spectator, Time, Times Literary Supplement, Virginia Quarterly,* and *Yale Review.*

5. For the historical context of the transition from modernism to post-modernism, see Boyer; Limon; Olster; Schaub; Stevick; Waugh; Wilde. For studies of the forms and themes of postmodernism, see Kuehl; Maltby; McHale; Nash; Saltzman; Scholes; Slethaug; Stonehill.

6. According to William Patrick Day, "The other in the Gothic is always the self as well" (18–23). Similarly, Rosemary Jackson contends that "fantasies structured around dualism . . . reveal the *internal* origin of the other" (55).

7. Jacques Lacan posits that the mind or self, which he calls "subjectivity," consists of the Imaginary, the Symbolic, and the Real. We enter the Imaginary between the ages of six and eighteen months, during what Lacan calls "the mirror stage," when the child identifies with the image of itself as a whole entity separate from the mother. The Imaginary leads the ego to mistake the self as coherent and self-creating. In the mirror stage, the child recognizes differences between itself and others such as the mother and father, aggressively desires other people and other things, yet fears the aggressive desires of others. When the child outgrows the Imaginary (or rather adds to it) by entering the Symbolic, the child gains linguistic competence and functions in a world of signifiers.

For Lacan, boys have an easier transition into the Symbolic because they have had to submit to what he calls "the law of the father" that the boy not possess the mother, who used to be coterminous with the self. He agrees with Nancy Chodorow, who believes that girls do not separate as easily from the mother because society encourages girls to identify with their mothers, and that therefore girls do not enter the Symbolic as easily as boys do.

8. Some scholars hold that individuals do not choose to be what they are, have little free will, are not unique, and are effects more than causes. Many of these scholars prefer the term *subject* because it calls attention to the fact that language makes people (and literary characters) what they are—people are in subjection due to linguistic constructs. Some of these scholars oppose the common definition of the subject as "self-determining" by questioning what they call "self-fashioning." See Greenblatt.

9. John Barth says, "Reality is more preposterous than realism—wilder and less plausible" (Murphy 37). And according to Philip Roth,

The American writer in the middle of the 20th century has his hands full in trying to understand, and then describe, and then make *credible* much of the American reality. It stupefies, it sickens, it infuriates, and finally it is even a kind of embarrassment to one's own meager imagination. The actuality is constantly outdoing our talents, and the culture tosses up figures almost daily that are the envy of any novelist.

Such attitudes inform the postmodernism's rationale for using the nonrealist forms of fable, allegory, Gothic, and the fantastic to feature disunified characters, discontinuous plots, absurd settings, and unreliable narration.

10. Gaston Bachelard says, "The house image would appear to have become the topography of our intimate being" (xxxvi). Similarly, Sandra M. Gilbert and Susan Gubar state that "houses, nests, shells, and wardrobes are in us as much as we are in them" (7). Day says of *The Mysteries of Udolpho,* "The castle functions as the externalization of Emily's own imagination, the Other, as physical environment, made into a double" (22). And Richard Wilbur points out that "the House of Usher *is,* in allegorical fact, the physical body of Roderick Usher, and its dim interior *is,* in fact, Roderick Usher's visionary mind" (107).

11. Louis Althusser uses the term *interpellation* (to be moved into) to describe the process by which ideology uses language to impose identity on a subject: interpellation moves the subject into discourse. Through interpellation, ideology in effect says, "When I want your opinion, I'll give it to you." Usually, the subject's seemingly chosen beliefs are largely the ones to which ideology has subjected her. Interpellation calls attention to the competition of discourses and the decentering of the subject—the displacing and deprivileging of the subject— by seeing people less as creators of meaning and more as created by meaning. See Althusser, 160–65.

12. By contrast, Rosemary Jackson agrees with Tzvetan Todorov that the fantastic disables allegory: "As Todorov points out, the fantastic cannot be placed alongside allegory or poetry, for it resists both the conceptualizations of the first and the metaphorical structures of the second" (41). But Shirley Jackson writes not pure allegory but rather the allegorical. On the other hand, Rosemary Jackson's contention that the fantastic resists metaphor does seem applicable to Shirley Jackson, who uses metonymy more than metaphor.

Rosemary Jackson also contends that "the basic trope of fantasy is the *oxymoron.*" Such an argument also fits Shirley Jackson, for her fiction exhibits the conflicts enabled by oxymoron, which Rosemary Jackson defines as "a figure of speech which holds together contradictions and sustains them in an impossible unity, without progressing towards synthesis" (21).

For the most detailed analysis of the fantastic's importance in Shirley Jackson, see Reinsch, 6–9, 20–21.

13. A phallic mother subscribes to the dominant phallocentric ideology (which privileges beliefs and values associated with males, principally the belief

in a unified, independent, self-determining subject. For a discussion of the phallic mother in *Wuthering Heights*, see Kavanagh. See also Michie.

14. Sigmund Freud worked archaeologically, uncovering the patient's unconscious by starting with the most recent contents and working down to their foundation in childhood. Appropriately called "depth psychology," the Freudian model of the unconscious was vertical, with consciousness as the top storey growing out of many hidden storeys below. These hidden storeys consisted of innumerable stacks of untold condensations and displacements. Freud likened condensation to metaphor (whereby the unconscious hides one thing by merging it with another thing) and displacement to metonymy (whereby the unconscious hides the similarity of two things by separating them). Influenced by structuralism, poststructuralism, and linguistics, Lacan argued that the unconscious is structured like a language. Applying Jacques Derrida's argument that language is an undecidable chain of signifiers, Lacan argued that the unconscious is an undecidable chain of metaphor and metonymy. In Jackson's case, her fiction in general and her characters in particular feature metonymy more than metaphor. That is, she emphasizes discontinuity. Metonymic plots, narrators, settings, and characters are fractured; their connections are more tenuous and undecidable. If, as in Aristotle's definition, metaphor is a yoking of opposites that reveals their similarity, then metonymy is an unyoking of similarities that conceals their similarity.

15. For readings that applaud the domestic narratives, see Joshi, "Domestic"; LeCroy; Reinsch, 3; Walker.

16. For other statements against the notion that Jackson believed in witches and the supernatural, see Nichols, 8; Reinsch, 1, 8, 9, 11–12, 33, 36; Sullivan, 121.

17. On the other hand, Judy Oppenheimer claims that three of Jackson's children believe she was psychic. But Oppenheimer's discussion is so ambiguous that it might not accurately reflect the views of Jackson's children. More specifically, it could be that they regard their mother as not literally psychic but virtually so by dint of her extraordinary mind. At any rate, the views of her children recalling the perceptions of childhood seem less reliable than the views of Jackson's adult contemporaries.

## CHAPTER ONE.
### SOME CONDITIONS OF PRODUCTION

1. All references to Shirley Jackson's letters to her parents are to SJP Box 3.

2. Stanley Edgar Hyman Papers, Box 4, Library of Congress, Washington, D.C.; hereafter cited as SEHP. All references to Stanley Edgar Hyman's diary are to SEHP Box 3.

3. All references to Jackson's diaries are to SJP Box 1.

4. In a letter to Hyman dated April 12, 1964. All references to letters from Kenneth Burke are to SEHP Box 4.

5. In fairness to Jackson and her doctors, they were not atypical of their time. Doctors did not know at first about the dangers of these drugs. So Jackson and Hyman did not know how damaging and addicting these drugs were. Nor did many others who used them, such as John Barth and John Kennedy.

6. All references to her mother's letters are to SJP Box 2.

7. Her slight English accent is evident in *Shirley Jackson Reads "The Lottery."*

8. So as not to appear older than Hyman, Jackson gave the year of her birth as 1919. Actually she was born in 1916.

9. Joan Didion and David Wyatt analyze pre-World War II California as paradisal, especially for those who grew up there and then had to live someplace else.

10. The social text is culture considered as discourse. That is, all social forms signify (not just literal texts and speech but also everything meaningful— from sports to advertisements to architecture). Interpellated into the social text, people are ruled not just by government, business, and nature, but also by regimes of discourse, largely because the values and beliefs of the social text are taken not as constructed but as given, unproblematic, and natural.

## CHAPTER TWO.
### THE LOTTERY OR, THE ADVENTURES OF JAMES HARRIS

1. For a discussion of the postmodern use of the double, see King; Slethaug. For further discussion of the double in Jackson's short stories, see Joan Wylie Hall.

2. For the purposes of this study, other prominent proto-postmodernist anthologies include Eudora Welty's *A Curtain of Green* (1941), Jane Bowles's *Two Serious Ladies* (1943), Truman Capote's *A Tree of Night and Other Stories* (1949), Paul Bowles' *The Delicate Prey and Other Stories* (1950), Flannery O'Connor's *A Good Man Is Hard to Find* (1955), James Purdy's *The Color of Darkness* (1957), and Howard Nemerov's *A Commodity of Dreams and Other Stories* (1959). Significantly, most of the production of these authors after 1960 did not become postmodern and usually became less proto-postmodern.

3. Cannon Schmitt points out that critics "have sometimes neglected both the figurative nature of the feminine and the presence of feminized and suffering male characters" (11).

4. As Rosemary Jackson puts it, "The uncertain vision of the protagonist of the fantastic is spread to the reader through a conflation of narrator and hero" (30). In stories like this one, Jackson uses such narration without using other characteristics of the fantastic.

5. Cynthia Griffin Wolff writes, "A woman pictures herself as trapped between the demands of two sorts of men—a 'chaste' lover and a 'demon' lover—each of whom is really a reflection of one portion of her own longing" (213).

6. According to Rosemary Jackson, fantastic literature has become a fabulation of the uncanny (24). See also Alexander.

7. In *The House of the Seven Gables,* Nathaniel Hawthorne writes that the mirror "is always a kind of window or doorway into the spiritual world" (412). According to Eugenia C. DeLamotte, "Even in Hawthorne's darkest Gothic, the mirror world of the self-reflecting ego is, like all mirrors, a door into the spiritual world. . . . The self-reflecting world of the guilty ego is a prison, but like so many Romantic prisons, it somehow gives access—even special access—to what is beyond it" (116).

8. Among the authors showing that the stoning victim is more likely female are Kosenko; Oehlschlaeger; Whittier.

9. Joan Wylie Hall points out that absurdism marks several of the stories in this volume (14).

CHAPTER THREE.
COME ALONG WITH ME:
PART OF A NOVEL, SIXTEEN STORIES, AND THREE LECTURES

1. As such, this psychological fable constitutes what Robert Scholes calls one of the dominant forms of recent fabulation, the "allegorization . . . of the invisible world" (102).

2. In an essay not published until 1993, Shirley Jackson celebrated the lost Richardsonian Eden of "peace," "principle," and "kindness" ("Notes" 109–11).

3. According to William Patrick Day, Gothic inverts the romantic quest:

In the Gothic . . . there is no ascent from the underworld, nor is a new Eden established there. The hero never recovers his true identity. Once in the demonic underworld he becomes subject to endless transformation and metamorphosis, his identity permanently and completely fragmented in a world of cruelty and terror. . . . The Gothic does not simply create ambiguous or ironic romance, but subverts the mythology of the whole genre." (7)

Gothic, then, offers many techniques for postmodernism's pessimism about the subject's ability to learn or succeed. On terror and horror's view of the subject, see Grixti; Halberstam; Terry Heller; Kristeva.

4. Similarly, Juliann E. Fleenor writes, "The conflict at the heart of the Female Gothic . . . [is] the conflict with the all-powerful, devouring mother. This maternal figure is also a double, a twin perhaps, to the woman herself. For the mother represents what the woman will become" (16).

5. For Scholes, recent fables remain didactic: "Fables traditionally have lent themselves to preaching, either as exempla in medieval sermons or directly through moral tags appended to the tales themselves—or both. This didactic quality seems to me also characteristic of modern fabulation" (10–11).

6. Elizabeth Fox-Genovese writes,

> Class oppression . . . deprive[s] many women of the "protection" under which many middle-class women have chafed. Forced by economic necessity to work outside the home, frequently deserted or abused by husbands or other male kin, poor women have never been restricted to a domestic haven. . . . Indeed, women who belong to socially oppressed groups might understandably see privileged women as their oppressors or at least as beneficiaries of their oppression. (19)

Such statements reflect recent feminism's sensitivity to class.

7. Rosemary Jackson says, "The fantastic problematizes vision (is it possible to trust the seeing eye?) and language (is it possible to trust the recording, speaking 'I'?" (30).

8. Bierce lived in the San Francisco area until three years before Jackson's birth. S. T. Joshi deems Jackson "the twentieth-century Ambrose Bierce" ("Domestic" 27; see also "Bierce" and *Weird*).

CHAPTER FOUR.
*JUST AN ORDINARY DAY*

1. This protagonist exemplifies what Tony Tanner says of the heroes in Ralph Ellison, James Purdy, William Burroughs, and Joseph Heller, that they "share one dread—of being 'taken over' by some external force, of being assimilated to an alien pattern not of their choosing" (109). In this case, Shirley Jackson's protagonist is so overwhelmed that she responds to her persecutor by telling herself that she wants to give in to him. Like the characters in "The Lottery," she not only acquiesces in her own exploitation but is also unaware of her exploitation. See also Meyers; Koenen.

2. Similarly, George E. Haggerty says of Henry James's "Sir Edmund Orme," "What we perceive in this tale is how appropriate hauntedness can be

as a means of talking about characters' relations to the past and explaining their actions in the present" (150).

3. What Tamar Heller says of Wilkie Collins is true of Jackson. Each was "in both a masculine and feminine position" (9).

4. Elizabeth Fox-Genovese explains that "as a metaphor, sisterhood has evoked the purportedly noncompetitive, noncontractual bonds of familial affection and devotion" (20–21).

CHAPTER FIVE.
*THE ROAD THROUGH THE WALL*

1. In "Why Can't They Tell You Why?" Purdy creates a similar scene. A mother forces her son to throw into the furnace the only pictures—the only representations of any kind—of the dead father he must somehow grow up to emulate.

2. Pat Macpherson shows that Esther Greenwood in *The Bell Jar* (Sylvia Plath wanted to be the next Shirley Jackson) was matrophobic. Whereas Greenwood hates and fears her mother for being feminized, Jackson hated and feared hers for being phallic. Strictly speaking, matrophobia is not necessarily misogynist, since it is not femaleness that is the immediate object of the hatred. On the other hand, of course, "female" as a signified can metonymically displace both "feminized" and "phallic."

3. As Claire Kahane puts it, "While boys can use their maleness to differentiate themselves from an engulfing maternal-female presence, girls are locked into a mother-daughter confusion of identity by virtue of their gender, encouraged in that confusion by the tendency of mothers to see daughters as duplicates of themselves and to reflect that vision ("Maternal" 243).

4. Manfred Putz describes the origin and result of this process:

> Being given over, in whatever modified form, to the world, to society, to an antagonistic "other" that demands servitude and restrains freedom, the self remains in the circumference of alienated existence. Accepting this state and agreeing to a part reconciliation with the very powers that threaten to dominate it, the self agrees to even more than the abolition of its autonomy. It makes alienation the ultimate condition of its existence. (39)

This definition of alienation by absorption into the Other is essentially Lacanian.

5. Tod's alienation, originating in pre-oedipal object relations, proceeds by means of contiguous, metonymic associations. Patricia Waugh describes this phenomenon as follows:

"The infant becomes human through *absence* and the creation of *desire* rather than presence and the discovery of satisfaction. Desire cannot be satisfied." (55)

Compare with Putz in note 4.

6. William Patrick Day explains how the encounter with the Other desublimates the repressed, giving rise to scapegoating as a way of self-recrimination through projection: "The figure of the double transforms the self-Other relationship into a self-self relationship. . . . The other resolves itself into a version of the self, a fragmentation and externalization of identity that destroys the self as fully and as surely as the overt attacks of its nemesis (20)." Jackson's characters, then, resemble Flannery O'Connor's: both authors use doubles obsessively (as will Plath in *The Bell Jar*, whose protagonist is even writing a paper on doubles).

7. A legitimate anxiety figured in this text is the fear of households limited to the nuclear family. And small ones at that: these families average fewer than two children. As such, in these confining households, although they are neither architecturally Gothic nor holding people under a descending pendulum, most of these children are confined in various ways, especially psychologically. On the other hand, Jackson in her own life exemplifies the anxiety of having one's parents too near.

CHAPTER SIX.
*HANGSAMAN*

1.Kelly Hurley claims that the "sense of metaphysical estrangement instantiated by the fantastic enables one to distinguish it from such genres as the fairy tale and the allegory, in which supernatural or magical events are accepted by character and reader alike with a certain nonchalance" (15). Hurley is right about texts that adhere to one of those genres, but here Shirley Jackson uses techniques of the fantastic to construct a text that is largely a psychological allegory. For other important studies of the fantastic, see Atteberry; Rabkin; Siebers.

2. For a study of college women in fiction, see Marchalonis.

3. That line appears in Sylvia Plath's *The Bell Jar*. Esther Greenwood's prospective father-in-law completely misreads her. Thinking she wants to marry his son when she actually does not, he says, "I think we understand each other" (52). Plath's novel is also about a budding writer with a name suggesting callowness. And like Natalie, Esther is surrounded by doubles and is writing a paper on doubles. Plath had modeled herself after Jackson and had hoped to meet her when, like Greenwood, she was chosen for an internship at *Mademoiselle*.

4. Patricia Waugh writes, "We search not for the lost object but for its substitute by displacement. . . . This is what Lacan means when he argues that the

subject is determined by the chain of signifiers, and this signifying chain is itself the structure of the unconscious" (55).

5. The derivations of the term *inappropriate* and its cognates reveal that term's origins in the defense of property holders. *Inappropriate* pertains to those things that should not be appropriated, and points to the basis of our sense of what is proper—propriety.

6. In the 1940s, Jackson wrote a parody of Faulkner's prose ("Go").

## CHAPTER SEVEN.
### THE BIRD'S NEST

1. For a study of the grotesque as satire, see Clark.

2. For examples of postmodern versions of the mad doctor, see Dr. Marvin Rose in John Barth's *The Floating Opera* (1956), Doc Daneeka in Joseph Heller's *Catch-22* (1961), the psychiatrists and Big Nurse in Ken Kesey's *One Flew Over the Cuckoo's Nest* (1962), Dr. Bigelow-Martin in James Purdy's *Cabot Wright Begins* (1964), and Dr. Hilarius in Thomas Pynchon's *The Crying of Lot 49* (1966).

3. For three book-length single-author studies that focus exclusively on Gothic, see Fedorko; Wardrop; Weston.

4. For more on the female Gothic, see Wolstenholme.

5. Eight years later, Ken Kesey took the image of the cuckoo's nest from a nursery rhyme.

6. Bernard Sternsher makes an important distinction between consensus historians of the right (such as Daniel Boorstin) and the left (such as David W. Noble).

## CHAPTER EIGHT.
### THE SUNDIAL

1. "Ori" means "of" or "connected with." It is cognate with the suffix "ory."

2. For the American grotesque in the transition from modernism to postmodernism, see Meindl.

3. For analyses of the myth of the new world that appear before *The Sundial,* see Lewis; Miller; Smith. For myth and symbol studies published soon after *The Sundial,* see Baritz; Noble, *Historians;* Sanford. For recent studies of the decline of America's dominant narratives, see Douglas; Hume.

4. Myth and symbol studies of America as a garden that were published before *The Sundial* include Lewis; Miller; Smith; Sanford. For such studies published after *The Sundial*, see Fryer; Kolodny; Marx; Noble, *Eternal* and *End*. For a recent study of gender and the American landscape, see Westling.

5. For analyses of the chosen people published before *The Sundial*, see Tuveson, *Millennium*; Miller. For studies of the chosen people that were published after *The Sundial*, see Baritz; Bercovitch, *Puritan* and *Jeremiad*. For a recent example of the New Americanist approach to the identification of self with nation, see Pease.

6. For studies of America's redemptive mission published before *The Sundial*, see Goldman; Miller. For studies appearing after, see Bellah; Tuveson, *Redeemer*.

7. For studies of the apocalypse in American culture in general, see Boyer; Rabkin, Greenberg and Olander; Wojcik. For studies of the apocalypse in American literature in particular, see Dewey; Robinson. For studies of America's apocalyptic paranoia, see Melley; O'Donnell.

8. For studies of the dominant culture's pursuit of timelessness, see Noble, *End*, *Eternal*, and *Historians*.

9. Ernest Hemingway wrote, "Our people went to America because that was the place to go then. It had been a good country and we had made a bloody mess of it and I would go, now, somewhere else as we had always had the right to go somewhere else and as we had always gone" (285).

## CHAPTER NINE.
### THE HAUNTING OF HILL HOUSE

1. What Michelle A. Masse says of nineteenth-century Gothic obtains here: the terror is not delusional but referential, growing out of "the prohibition of female autonomy in . . . families" (12).

2. Except for the letters from Kenneth Burke (which are in SEHP Box 4) all references to Shirley Jackson's notes and letters regarding *The Haunting of Hill House* are to SJP Box 22.

3. David H. Richter's important and convincing argument is that Gothic reinscribes *Pamela* by separating hero and villain.

4. Allan Gardner Lloyd-Smith writes that because Gothic minimizes mediation between the reader and the uncanny, Gothic might be "more simply and deeply related to the affect of the reading experience than the apparently innocent mimeticism of realism" (13). By reading the house, Eleanor can read herself—or at least come as close to reading herself as she can get. Eve Kosofsky Sedgwick points out that in Gothic "it is the position of the self to be massively blocked off from something to which it ought normally to have access" (13). Eleanor is blocked off even as she is entrapped.

5. Sedgwick says that "to wake from a dream and *find it true*" is a common Gothic motif (31).

6. Many critics, for example Brian Docherty (8), regard Theo as a bisexual because she caresses Eleanor yet is attracted to Luke, and she lives back in the city with someone she calls a "friend" whose sex neither she nor the narrator specifies. However, what little actual sexuality (as opposed to sensuality) she expresses displays only the pregenital. As such, she is a figure of androgyny.

7. Burke said in a letter to Jackson and Stanley Edgar Hyman that Hill House is "midway between Hull and Hell."

8. Rosemary Jackson writes, "Gothic inverts romance structures: the quest, for example, is twisted into a circular journey to nowhere, ending in the same darkness with which it opened, remaining unenlightened" (101). *The Haunting of Hill House,* a Gothic fable of a woman being recycled back into the domestic trap, begins and ends with the same two sentences. Eugenia C. DeLamotte shows that ghosts figure the past surviving in the present, controlling the present: "Ghosts . . . are repetition: they are what has been lost but will not go away; what can neither be retrieved from the past nor exorcised from the present" (242).

9. Evidently done with a hard lead pencil pressed very lightly, her sketches are too light to reproduce without enhancing them, which would amount to modifying them.

10. The parodic surface sticks to the model that Chris Baldick outlines: "Typically a Gothic tale will invoke the tyranny of the past . . . with such weight as to stifle the hopes of the present. . . . Doubling as both fictional setting and as dominant symbol, the house reverberates for us with associations which are simultaneously psychological and historical" (xix–xx). Hill House exemplifies not only the historicization of subject formation, but does so by detailing the heteroglossic scrapbook that the patriarch assembled for his daughters' interpellation. See also David Punter for Gothic's historicization of the psychological.

11. Jackson's use of literal double-voicedness—Eleanor not knowing the voices inside her head from the voices outside—recalls Charles Brockden Brown. According to Sharon Cameron,

> In *Wieland,* voices heard from inside . . . are undifferentiated from voices heard from outside. . . . In fact, the phenomenon of the voice . . . offers an exemplification of why the self has trouble knowing the boundaries between itself and the world. . . . The split within the body (. . . between the body and the voice in the mind) generates a corollary split outside the body, between one entity and a separate other. (8)

Significantly, Eleanor hears a child's voice just before she awakes and asks, "Whose hand was I holding?"

CHAPTER TEN.
*WE HAVE ALWAYS LIVED IN THE CASTLE*

1. One of the most significant analyses of Shirley Jackson's oeuvre is Roberta Rubenstein's analysis of Jackson's recurrent mother-daughter theme. Rubenstein's article is particularly important when it addresses *We Have Always Lived in the Castle*.

2. Karen J. Hall contends that the murders occurred because each sister has been sexually abused. Although Hall admits there is little direct evidence for that assertion, she correctly points out that Merricat's behavior is like that of a sexual abuse victim. (And there are several such implied cases of sexual abuse in Jackson's fiction.) By contrast, Paul N. Reinsch states that "the reader would like to think Merricat has a reason for killing her parents though the text suggests childish madness is the only explanation" (93). As usual, the causes of behavior in Jackson's characters is undecidable.

3. Fiona Robertson relates "Gothic's dual preoccupations with history and narrative . . . to anxieties of literary origin by way of the figure of the recess" (17).

4. In one of his letters, Kenneth Burke asked her if she originated the term *neaten*. There is no record of her reply.

5. Along with Capote and Purdy, Poe was one of Hyman's least favorite writers, perhaps because Jackson's writing is so much like theirs. Chester E. Eisenger compares Jackson's fiction to that of not only Capote but also Paul Bowles, another gay writer (288–89).

6. For a discussion of Gothic as enabling absurdism, especially since Kafka, see Botting, 158–80.

7. Kari J. Winter writes, "Female writers of Gothic fiction fear the unchecked power of men and therefore explore possibilities of resistance to the patriarchal order. Female Gothic plots usually center on women trying to escape from decaying family estates and perverse patriarchs" (21–22).

8. For interesting discussions of food in this novel, see Carol Ames; Karen J. Hall. Food is a recurrent motif in Jackson, one that deserves detailed attention but is beyond the scope of this study.

9. In one of the most important readings of this text, Lynette Carpenter claims that the sisters accomplish "the overthrow of the Blackwood patriarchy" ("Establishment" 36) and now "live outside the boundaries of patriarchal society" (34) in "self-sufficiency" (34, 35). Carpenter is right that the sisters overthrow the Blackwood patriarchy. But the class system remains. The sisters are neo-aristocrats living on the inherited wealth that their patriarchs extracted from laborers—both male and female. And two of the people Merricat murders are women. As Karen J. Hall points out, the sisters' "resistance against the patriarchal order is readily contained" (118).

## AFTERWORD

1. For a study of some postmodernists as disruptive, see Maltby. See also McHale; Schaub.

2. Other recent studies that go far beyond the limits of older Jackson criticism include Drew; Egan; Joan Wylie Hall; Karen J. Hall; Kahane; Kosenko.

# WORKS CITED

Aldridge, John W. *After the Lost Generation: A Critical Study of the Writers of Two Wars*. New York: McGraw, 1958.

Alexander, Marguerite. *Flights from Realism: Themes and Strategies in Postmodernist British and American Fiction*. London: Edward Arnold, 1990.

Althusser, Louis. *Lenin and Philosophy and Other Essays*. Trans. Ben Brewster. New York: Monthly Review P, 1971.

Ames, Carol. "Love Triangles in Fiction: The Underlying Fantasies." Diss. State University of New York at Buffalo, 1973.

Atteberry, Brian. *Strategies of Fantasy*. Bloomington: Indiana UP, 1992.

Bachelard, Gaston. *The Poetics of Space*. Trans. Maria Jolas. Boston: Beacon, 1969.

Bailey, Dale Frederick. *American Nightmares: The Haunted House Formula in American Popular Fiction*. Bowling Green, OH: Bowling Green State UP, 1999.

Baldick, Chris, ed. *The Oxford Book of Gothic Tales*. New York: Oxford UP, 1992.

Baritz, Loren. *City on a Hill: A History of Ideas and Myths in America*. New York: Wiley, 1964.

Barrows, Marjorie Wescott et al., ed. *The American Experience: Fiction*. New York: Macmillan, 1968.

Bellah, Robert. *The Broken Covenant: American Civil Religion in Time of Trial*. New York: Seabury, 1975.

Bercovitch, Sacvan. *The American Jeremiad*. Madison: U of Wisconsin P, 1978.

———. *The Puritan Origins of the American Self*. New Haven: Yale UP, 1975.

———. *The Rites of Assent: Transformations in the Symbolic Construction of America*. New York: Routledge, 1993.

Berlant, Lauren. *The Anatomy of National Fantasy: Hawthorne, Utopia, and Everyday Life*. Chicago: U of Chicago P, 1991.

Botting, Fred. *Gothic*. London: Routledge, 1996.

Boyer, Paul. *By the Bomb's Early Light: American Thought and Culture at the Dawn of the Atomic Age*. New York: Pantheon, 1985.

Bradbury, Malcolm. *The Modern American Novel*. New York: Oxford UP, 1983.

Brooks, Cleanth, and Robert Penn Warren. "Interpretation." *Understanding Fiction*. 2nd ed. New York: Appleton-Century-Crofts, 1959. 72–76.

Cameron, Sharon. *The Corporeal Self: Allegories of the Body in Melville and Hawthorne*. Baltimore: Johns Hopkins UP, 1981.

Caminero-Santangelo, Marta. *The Mad Woman Can't Speak: Or Why Insanity Is Not Subversive*. Ithaca: Cornell UP, 1998.

Campbell, Jane. *Mythic Black Fiction: The Transformation of History*. Knoxville: U of Tennessee P, 1986.

Carby, Hazel. W. *Reconstructing Womanhood: The Emergence of the Afro-American Woman Novelist*. New York: Oxford UP, 1987.

Carpenter, Lynette. "Domestic Comedy, Black Comedy, and Real Life: Shirley Jackson, a Woman Writer." *Faith of a (Woman) Writer*. Ed. Alice Kessler-Harris and William McBrien. New York and Westport: Greenwood, 1988. 143–48.

———. "The Establishment and Preservation of Female Power in Shirley Jackson's *We Have Always Lived in the Castle*." *Frontiers* 8.1 (1984): 32–38.

Carroll, Paul. "In a Garden of Eden." Rev. of *We Have Always Lived in the Castle,* by Shirley Jackson. *Binghamton Sunday Press* 31 Mar. 1963: 16–B.

Chaucer, Geoffrey. "The Knight's Tale." *Canterbury Tales,* lines 2777–79. *The Riverside Chaucer*. Ed. Larry D. Brown. 3rd. ed. Boston: Houghton, 1987. 62.

Christensen, Inger. *The Meaning of Metafiction: A Critical Study of Selected Novels by Sterne, Nabokov, Barth and Beckett*. Bergen, Norway: Universitetsforlaget, 1981.

Chodorow Nancy. *The Reproduction of Mothering: Psychoanalysis and the Sociology of Gender*. Berkeley: U of California P, 1978.

Clark, John R. *The Modern Satiric Grotesque and Its Traditions*. Lexington: U of Kentucky P, 1991.

Clayton, John J., ed. *Heath Introduction to Fiction*. 4th ed. Lexington, Mass.: Heath, 1992.

Daiches, David. "Samuel Richardson." *Twentieth-Century Interpretations of Pamela*. Ed. Rosemary Cowler. Englewood Cliffs, NJ: Prentice, 1969. 14–25.

Davenport, Guy. "Dark Psychological Weather." Rev. of *Come Along with Me: Part of a Novel, Sixteen Stories, and Three Lectures*, by Shirley Jackson. Ed. Stanley Edgar Hyman. *New York Times Book Review* 15 Sept. 1968: 4.

——. "The Dust Witch, the Red October Moon." Rev. of *In Any Case*, by Richard G. Stern, *We Have Always Lived in the Castle*, by Shirley Jackson, and *Something Wicked This Way Comes*, by Ray Bradbury. *National Review* 31 Dec. 1962: 515–17.

Day, William Patrick. *In the Circles of Fear and Desire: A Study of Gothic Fantasy*. Chicago: U of Chicago P, 1985.

DeLamotte, Eugenia C. *Perils of the Night: A Feminist Study of Nineteenth-Century Gothic*. New York: Oxford UP, 1990.

Derleth, August. Rev. of *Hangsaman*, by Shirley Jackson. *Chicago Sunday Tribune* 29 Apr. 1951: 6.

Dewey, Joseph. *In a Dark Time: The Apocalyptic Temper in the American Novel of the Nuclear Age*. West Lafayette, Ind.: Purdue UP, 1990.

Didion, Joan. *Slouching Towards Bethlehem*. New York: Farrar, 1968.

Docherty, Brian, ed. *American Horror Fiction: From Brockden Brown to Stephen King*. London: Macmillan, 1990.

Douglas, Christopher. *Reciting America: Culture and Cliché in Contemporary U. S. Fiction*. Urbana: U of Illinois P, 2001.

Drew, Lorna Ellen. "The Mysteries of the Gothic: Psychoanalysis/Feminism/'The Female Gothic'." Diss. University of New Brunswick, 1993.

Egan, James. "Sanctuary: Shirley Jackson's Domestic and Fantastic Parables." *Studies in Weird Fiction* 6.1 (1989): 15–24.

Eisenger, Chester E. *Fiction of the Forties*. Chicago: U of Chicago P, 1963.

Ellis, Kate Ferguson. *The Contested Castle: Gothic Novels and the Subversion of Domestic Ideology*. Urbana: U of Illinois P, 1989.

Faulkner, William. *As I Lay Dying. The Corrected Text*. 1930. New York: Vintage, 1987.

Fedorko, Kathy A. *Gender and the Gothic in the Fiction of Edith Wharton*. Tuscaloosa: U Alabama P, 1995.

Fitzgerald, F. Scott. *The Great Gatsby*. 1925. New York: Scribner's, 1953.

Fleenor, Juliann E., ed. *The Female Gothic*. Montreal: Eden Press, 1983.

Fletcher, Angus. *Allegory: The Theory of a Symbolic Mode*. Ithaca: Cornell UP, 1964.

Fox-Genovese, Elizabeth. *Feminism without Illusions: A Critique of Individualism*. Chapel Hill: U of North Carolina P, 1991.

Freud, Sigmund. "The Uncanny." 1919. 17:217–52. *The Standard Edition of the Complete Psychological Works*. Ed. and trans. by James Strachey. London: Hogarth, 1953. 24 vols.

Friedman, Lenemaja. *Shirley Jackson*. Boston: Twayne, 1975.

Fryer, Judith. *The Faces of Eve: Women in the Nineteenth Century American Novel*. New York: Oxford UP, 1976.

Fuller, Edmund. "Shirley Jackson's New Novel Her Best." Rev. of *The Bird's Nest*, by Shirley Jackson. *Chicago Sunday Tribune* 27 June 1954: 4.

Gallop, Jane. *The Daughter's Seduction: Feminism and Psychoanalysis*. Ithaca: Cornell UP, 1982.

Geismar, Maxwell. "Annals of Magic." Rev. of *The Haunting of Hill House*, by Shirley Jackson. *Saturday Review* 31 Oct. 1959: 19+.

Gilbert, Sandra M., and Susan Gubar. *Madwoman in the Attic: The Woman Writer in the Nineteenth-Century Literary Imagination*. New Haven: Yale UP, 1979.

Gilman, Charlotte Perkins. "The Yellow Wall-Paper." *New England Magazine* Jan (1892): 647–56. *"The Yellow Wall-Paper" and Selected Stories of Charlotte Perkins Gilman*. Ed. Denise D. Knight. Newark: U of Delaware P, 1994. 39–53.

Girvin, Peter. Rev. of *The Sundial,* by Shirley Jackson. *New York Herald Tribune Book Review* 16 Feb. 1958: 5.

Goddu, Teresa A. *Gothic America: Narrative, History, and Nation*. New York: Columbia UP, 1997.

Goldman, Eric. *Rendezvous with Destiny: A History of Modern American Reform*. New York: Knopf, 1952.

Grebstein, Sheldon. "12 Plan for World's End." Rev. of *The Sundial*. *Sunday Herald Leader* 23 Feb. 1958: 37.

Greenblatt, Stephen. *Renaissance Self-Fashioning: From More to Shakespeare*. Chicago: U of Chicago P, 1980.

Grixti, Joseph. *Terrors of Uncertainty: The Cultural Contexts of Horror Fiction*. London: Routledge, 1989.

Haggerty, George E. *Gothic Fiction/Gothic Form*. University Park: Pennsylvania State UP, 1989.

Halberstam, Judith. *Skin Shows: Gothic Horror and the Technology of Monsters*. Durham, N.C.: Duke UP, 1995.

Hall, Joan Wylie. "Fallen Eden in Shirley Jackson's *The Road Through the Wall*." *Renascence* 46 (1994): 261–70.

——. *Shirley Jackson: A Study of the Short Fiction*. New York: Twayne, 1993.

Hall, Karen J. "Sisters in Collusion: Safety and Revolt in Shirley Jackson's *We Have Always Lived in the Castle*." *The Significance of Sibling Relationships in Literature*. Ed. JoAnna Stephens Mink and Janet Doubler Ward. Bowling Green: Bowling Green State U Popular P, 1993. 110–19.

Hammond, Arthur. "Poe in Petticoats Has Tall-Tale Art." Rev. of *We Have Always Lived in the Castle*, by Shirley Jackson. 8 Dec. 1962. Newspaper clipping in SJP Box 29 without place or page number.

Hassan, Ihab. "Three Hermits on a Hill." Rev. of *We Have Always Lived in the Castle*, by Shirley Jackson. *New York Times Book Review* 23 Sept. 1962: 5.

Hawthorne, Nathaniel. *The House of the Seven Gables*. *The Complete Novels and Selected Tales of Nathaniel Hawthorne*. Ed. Norman Holmes Pearson. New York: Modern Library, 1937.

Heller, Tamar. *Dead Secrets: Wilkie Collins and the Female Gothic*. New Haven: Yale UP, 1992.

Heller, Terry. *The Delights of Terror: An Aesthetics of the Tale of Terror*. Urbana: U of Illinois P, 1987.

Hemingway, Ernest. *The Green Hills of Africa*. New York: Scribner's, 1935.

Hicks, Granville. "A World of Everyday Demons." *Saturday Review* 14 Sept. 1968, 33+.

Highet, Gilbert. Rev. of *We Have Always Lived in the Castle*, by Shirley Jackson. *Book-of-the-Month Club News* 18 Dec. 1962: 8.

Hirsch, Marianne. "Spiritual *Bildung*: The Beautiful Soul as Paradigm." *The Voyage In: Fictions of Female Development*. Ed. Elizabeth Abel, Marianne Hirsch, and Elizabeth Langland. Hanover, NH: UP of New England for Dartmouth College, 1983. 23–48.

Holquist, Michael. *Dialogism: Bakhtin and His World*. London: Routledge, 1990.

Hume, Kathryn. *American Dream, American Nightmare: Fiction since 1960*. Urbana: U of Illinois P, 2000.

Hurley, Kelly. *The Gothic Body: Sexuality, Materialism, and Degeneration at the Fin de Siècle*. Cambridge: Cambridge UP, 1997.

Hyman, Stanley Edgar. *The Armed Vision: A Study in the Methods of Modern Literary Criticism.* New York: Knopf, 1948.

———. *Nathanael West.* Minneapolis, U of Minnesota P, 1962.

———. *Poetry and Criticism: Four Revolutions in Literary Taste.* New York: Atheneum, 1961.

———. *The Promised End: Essays and Reviews, 1942–1962.* Cleveland: World, 1963.

———. *Standards: A Chronicle of Books for Our Time.* New York: Horizon, 1966.

———. *The Tangled Bank: Darwin, Marx, Frazer and Freud as Imaginative Writers.* New York: Atheneum, 1962.

Jackson, Rosemary. *Fantasy: The Literature of Subversion.* London: Methuen, 1981.

Jackson, Shirley. *The Bird's Nest.* New York: Farrar, 1954.

———. *Come Along with Me: Part of a Novel, Sixteen Stories, and Three Lectures.* Ed. Stanley Edgar Hyman. New York: Viking, 1968.

———. "Go Down, Faulkner (in the Throes of William Faulkner's *Go Down, Moses*)." *The Best of Bad Faulkner.* Ed. Dean Faulkner Wells. San Diego: Harcourt, 1991. 129–32.

———. *Hangsaman.* New York: Farrar, 1951.

———. *The Haunting of Hill House.* New York: Viking, 1959.

———. *Just an Ordinary Day.* Ed. Laurence Jackson Hyman and Sarah Hyman Stewart. New York: Bantam, 1996.

———. *Life among the Savages.* New York: Farrar, 1953.

———. *The Lottery or, The Adventures of James Harris.* New York: Farrar, 1949.

———. "The Lovely House." *American Gothic Tales.* Ed. Joyce Carol Oates. New York: Penguin, 1996. 204–25.

———. *The Magic of Shirley Jackson.* Ed. Stanley Edgar Hyman. New York: Farrar, 1966.

———. "Notes on an Unfashionable Novelist." *Shirley Jackson: A Study of the Short Fiction,* by Joan Wylie Hall. New York: Twayne, 1993: 109–111.

———. *Raising Demons.* New York: Farrar, 1957.

———. *The Road Through the Wall.* New York: Farrar, 1948.

———. *Shirley Jackson Reads "The Lottery."* Folkways Recording #9728.

———. "Strangers in Town." *The American Experience: Fiction*. Ed. Marjorie Wescott Barrows. New York: Macmillan, 1968. 445–59.

———. *The Sundial*. New York: Farrar, 1958.

———. *We Have Always Lived in the Castle*. New York: Viking, 1962.

———. *The Witchcraft of Salem Village*. New York: Random, 1956.

Jameson, Fredric. *The Ideologies of Theory: Essays 1971–1986*. 2 vols. Minneapolis: U of Minnesota P, 1988.

Joshi, S. T. "A Modern-Day Bierce." *Necrophile: The Review of Horror Fiction* 9 (Summer 1993): 22–23.

———. "Shirley Jackson: Domestic Horror." *Studies in Weird Fiction* 14 (1994): 9–28.

———. *The Weird Tale*. Austin: U of Texas P, 1990.

Kahane, Claire. "The Gothic Mirror." *The (M)other Tongue: Essays in Feminist Psychoanalytic Interpretation*. Ed. Shirley Nelson Garner, Claire Kahane, and Madelon Sprengnether. Ithaca: Cornell UP, 1985. 334–51.

———. "The Maternal Legacy: The Grotesque Tradition in Flannery O'Connor's Female Gothic." Fleenor 232–56.

Kavanagh, James H. *Emily Brontë*. London: Basil Blackwell, 1985.

Kelley, Theresa M. *Reinventing Allegory*. Cambridge: Cambridge UP, 1997.

Kennedy, William. "Sampling of Stories Carries an Antique Quality." Rev. of *The Magic of Shirley Jackson,* by Shirley Jackson. *National Observer* 14 Oct. 1968: 23.

King, Debra Walker, ed. *Body Politics and the Fictional Double*. Bloomington: Indiana UP, 2000.

Koenen, Anne. *Visions of Doom, Plots of Power: The Fantastic in Anglo-American Women's Literature*. Frankfurt: Vervuert, 1999.

Kolodny, Annette. *The Lay of the Land: Metaphor as Experience and History in American Life and Letters*. Chapel Hill: U of North Carolina P, 1975.

Kosenko, Peter. "A Marxist/Feminist Reading of Shirley Jackson's 'The Lottery.'" *New Orleans Review* 12.1 (1985): 27–32.

Kristeva, Julia. *Powers of Horror: An Essay in Abjection*. Trans. Leon S. Roudiez. New York: Columbia UP, 1982.

Kuehl, John. *Alternate Worlds: A Study of Postmodern Antirealistic American Fiction*. New York: New York UP: 1989.

Kunitz, Stanley J. "Shirley Jackson." *Twentieth Century Authors*. First Supplement. New York: Wilson, 1955. 483.

LeCroy, Anne. "The Different Humor of Shirley Jackson: *Life among the Savages* and *Raising Demons*." *Studies in American Humor* 4 (1985): 62–73.

Lentricchia, Frank. *Ariel and the Police: Michel Foucault, William James, Wallace Stevens*. Madison: U of Wisconsin P, 1988.

Lethem, Jonathan. "Monstrous Acts and Little Murders." *Salon* Jan. 1997: 1–8. *Salon.com*. Online. 19 Dec. 1997.

Lewis, R. W. B. *The American Adam: Innocence, Tragedy, and Tradition in the Nineteenth Century*. Chicago: U of Chicago P, 1955.

Limon, John. *Writing after War: American War Fiction from Realism to Postmodernism*. New York: Oxford UP, 1994.

Lloyd-Smith, Allan Gardner. *Uncanny American Fiction: Medusa's Face*. London: Macmillan, 1989.

Lootens, Tricia. "'Whose Hand Was I Holding?': Familial and Sexual Politics in Shirley Jackson's *The Haunting of Hill House*." *Haunting the House of Fiction: Feminist Perspectives on Ghost Stories by American Women*. Ed. Lynette Carpenter and Wendy K. Kolmar. Knoxville: U of Tennessee P, 1991. 166–92.

MacAndrew, Elizabeth. *The Gothic Tradition in Fiction*. New York: Columbia UP, 1979.

Macpherson, Pat. *Reflecting on The Bell Jar*. London: Routledge, 1991.

Maltby, Paul. *Dissident Postmodernists: Barthelme, Coover, Pynchon*. Philadelphia: U of Pennsylvania P, 1991.

Manning, O. Rev. of *The Bird's Nest*, by Shirley Jackson. *Punch* 228 (1955): 271.

Marchalonis, Shirley. *College Girls: A Century in Fiction*. New Brunswick, N.J.: Rutgers UP, 1995.

Marx, Leo. *The Machine in Garden: Technology and the Pastoral Ideal in America*. New York: Oxford UP, 1964.

Masse, Michelle A. *In the Name of Love: Women, Masochism, and the Gothic*. Ithaca: Cornell UP, 1992.

McCafferey, Larry. *The Metafictional Muse: The Works of Robert Coover, Donald Barthleme, and William Gass*. Pittsburgh: U of Pittsburgh P, 1982.

McHale, Brian. *Postmodernist Fiction*. New York: Methuen, 1987.

Meindl, Dieter. *American Fiction and the Metaphysics of the Grotesque*. Columbia: U of Missouri P, 1996.

Melley, Timothy. *Empire of Conspiracy: The Culture of Paranoia in Postwar America*. Ithaca: Cornell UP, 2000.

Meyers, Helene. *Femicidal Fears: Narratives of the Female Gothic Experience.* Albany: State U of New York P, 2001.

Michie, Helena. *Sororophobia: Differences among Women in Literature and Culture.* New York: Oxford UP, 1992.

Miller, Nolan. "Mr. Jones and Others." Rev. of *Hangsaman,* by Shirley Jackson. *The Antioch Review* 11 (1951): 237–41.

Miller, Perry. *Errand into the Wilderness.* Cambridge: Harvard UP, 1956.

Mishra, Vijay. *The Gothic Sublime.* Albany: State U of New York P, 1994.

M. M. "A Talk with Shirley Jackson." *New York Post* 30 Sept. 62. Newspaper clipping in SJP Box 29 without page number.

Murphy, Richard. "In Print: John Barth." *Horizon* 5 (Jan. 1963): 37.

Nardacci, Michael L. "Theme, Character, and Technique in the Novels of Shirley Jackson." Diss. New York U, 1980.

Nash, Christopher. *World-Games: The Tradition of Anti-Realist Revolt.* London: Methuen, 1987.

Nemerov, Howard. "Poet Nemerov Appraises Shirley Jackson's Works." *Bennington Banner* 9 Aug. 1965: 10.

Newman, Judie. "Shirley Jackson and the Reproduction of Mothering: *The Haunting of Hill House.*" Docherty 120–34.

Nichols, Lewis. "In and Out of Books." *New York Times Book Review* 7 Oct. 1962: 8.

Noble, David W. *Death of a Nation: The End of American Exceptionalism.* Minneapolis: U of Minnesota P, forthcoming.

——. *The End of American History: Democracy, Capitalism, and the Metaphor of Two Worlds in Anglo-American Historical Writing, 1880–1980.* Minneapolis: U of Minnesota P, 1985.

——. *The Eternal Adam and the New World Garden: The Central Myth in the American Novel Since 1830.* New York: Braziller, 1968.

——. *Historians against History: The Frontier Thesis and the National Covenant in American Historical Writing Since 1830.* Minneapolis: U of Minnesota P, 1965.

Oates, Joyce Carol. Rev. of *Just an Ordinary Day,* by Shirley Jackson. *New York Times Book Review* 29 Dec. 1996: 10.

——. "Writing as a Natural Reaction." *Time* 10 Oct. 1969: 108.

O'Donnell, Patrick. *Latent Destinies: Cultural Paranoia and Contemporary U.S. Narrative.* Durham: Duke UP, 2000.

Oehlschlaeger, Fritz. "The Stoning of Mistress Hutchinson: Meaning and Context in 'The Lottery.'" *Essays in Literature* 15 (1988): 259–65.

Olster, Stacey. *Reminiscence and Re-Creation in Contemporary American Fiction.* New York: Cambridge UP, 1989.

Oppenheimer, Judy. *Private Demons: The Life of Shirley Jackson.* New York: Putnam's, 1988.

Parker, Dorothy. "Shudders Quiet and Cumulative." *Esquire.* Dec. 1962: 40–44.

Parks, John G. "Waiting for the End: Shirley Jackson's *The Sundial.*" *Critique* 19.3 (1978): 74–88.

Pease, Donald E., ed. *National Identities and Post-Americanist Narratives.* Durham, N.C.: Duke UP, 1994.

Peden, William. "The 'Chosen Few.'" Rev. of *The Sundial,* by Shirley Jackson. *Saturday Review* 8 Mar. 1958: 18.

Pettingell, Phoebe, ed. *The Critic's Credentials: Essays and Reviews by Stanley Edgar Hyman.* New York: Atheneum, 1978.

Pickrel, Paul. "Outstanding Novels." Rev. of thirteen books, including *Hangsaman,* by Shirley Jackson. *Yale Review* 40 (1951): 765–67.

Plath, Sylvia. *The Bell Jar.* London: Faber and Faber, 1963.

Plumley, William. "An Interview with John Barth." *Chicago Review* 40.4 (1994): 6–18.

Poe, Edgar Allan. "Masque of the Red Death." *The Collected Works of Edgar Allan Poe: Tales and Sketches, 1831–42.* Ed. Thomas Ollive Mabbott. Cambridge: Harvard UP, 1969. 670–78.

Poovey, Mary. "Ideology and *The Mysteries of Udolpho.*" *Criticism* 21 (1979): 307–30.

Prince, Morton. *The Dissociation of a Personality: A Biographical Study in Abnormal Psychology.* New York: Longmans, Green, and Co., 1906.

Punter, David. *The Gothic Tradition.* Vol. 1 of *The Literature of Terror/ A History of Gothic Fictions from 1765 to the Present Day.* London: Longman, 1996.

Putz, Manfred. *The Story of Identity: American Fiction of the Sixties.* Munich: Wilhelm Fink Verlag, 1987.

Pynchon, Thomas. *The Crying of Lot 49.* New York: Lippincott, 1966.

Rabkin, Eric S. *The Fantastic in Literature.* Princeton: Princeton UP, 1976.

Rabkin, Eric S., Martin H. Greenberg, and Joseph D. Olander. *The End of the World.* Carbondale: Southern Illinois UP, 1983.

Reinsch, Paul N. *A Critical Bibliography of Shirley Jackson, American Writer (1919–1965): Reviews, Criticism, Adaptations.* Lewiston, N.Y.: Mellen, 2001.

Rev. of *The Haunting of Hill House*, by Shirley Jackson. *Virginia Quarterly Review* 38 (Winter 1962): x.

Rev. of *We Have Always Lived in the Castle*, by Shirley Jackson. *New Yorker* 13 Oct. 1962: 231–32.

Rich, Adrienne. *Of Woman Born: Motherhood as Experience and Institution.* New York: Norton, 1976.

Richter, David H. *The Progress of Romance: Literary Historiography and the Gothic Novel.* Columbus: Ohio State UP, 1996.

Robertson, Fiona. *Legitimate Histories: Scott, Gothic, and the Authorities of Fiction.* Oxford: Clarendon P, 1994.

Robinson, Douglas. *American Apocalypses: The Image of the End of the World in American Literature.* Baltimore: Johns Hopkins UP, 1985.

Roth, Philip. "Writing American Fiction." *Commentary* 1 Mar.1961: 223–33.

Rubenstein, Roberta. "House Mothers and Haunted Daughters: Shirley Jackson and Female Gothic." *Tulsa Studies in Women's Literature* 15 (1996): 309–31.

Russ, Joanna. Introduction. *The Penguin Book of Modern Fantasy by Women.* Ed. A. Susan Williams and Richard Glyn Jones. London: Penguin, 1996.

Russo, Mary. *The Female Grotesque: Risk, Excess and Modernity.* New York: Routledge, 1995.

Safford, Edwin. "A Sunny, Cheery Horror." Rev. of *We Have Always Lived in the Castle*, by Shirley Jackson. *Providence Sunday Journal* 28 Oct. 1962: W-18.

Salinger, J. D. *The Catcher in the Rye.* Boston: Little, Brown, 1951.

Saltzman, Arthur M. *Designs of Darkness in Contemporary American Fiction.* Philadelphia: U of Pennsylvania P, 1990.

Sanford, Charles. *The Quest for Paradise: Europe and the American Moral Imagination.* Urbana: U of Illinois P, 1961.

Scharnhorst, Gary. "Fiction: 1930s to the 1960s." *American Literary Scholarship: An Annual,* ed. David J. Nordloh. Durham, N.C.: Duke UP, 1991. 225–50.

Schaub, Thomas Hill. *American Fiction in the Cold War.* Madison: U of Wisconsin P, 1991.

Schmitt, Cannon. *Alien Nation: Nineteenth-Century Gothic Fictions and English Nationality*. Philadelphia: U of Pennsylvania P, 1997.

Scholes, Robert. *The Fabulators*. New York: Oxford UP, 1967.

Schopp, Dale Frederick. "Sites of Control/Stress of Contest: The Deployment of Fear in 20th Century Narrative." Diss. U of Rochester, 1995.

Scott, Evelyn. "Blighted by Inner Tyrannies." Rev. of *The Bird's Nest,* by Shirley Jackson. *New York Times* 20 June 1954: 4.

Seaver, Edwin, ed. *Cross-Section: A Collection of New American Writing*. New York: L. B. Fischer, 1944.

Sedgwick, Eve Kosofsky. *The Coherence of Gothic Conventions*. New York: Arno, 1980.

Shakespeare, William. "O Mistress Mine." *Twelfth Night or What You Will*. Ed. Elizabeth Story Donno. Cambridge: Cambridge UP, 1985. 2:3:33–38, 41–46. 74–75.

Shelton, Wendy. "The Image of Shirley Jackson's World." Rev. of *The Bird's Nest. Washington DC Star*. Newspaper clipping in SJP Box 21 without date or page number.

Siebers, Tobin. *The Romantic Fantastic*. Ithaca: Cornell UP, 1984.

Slethaug, Gordon E. *The Play of the Double in Postmodern American Fiction*. Carbondale: Southern Illinois UP, 1993.

Slotkin, Richard. *The Fatal Environment: The Myth of the Frontier in the Age of Industrialism, 1880–1890*. New York: Atheneum, 1985.

———. *Gunfighter Nation: The Myth of the Frontier in Twentieth-Century America*. New York: Atheneum, 1992.

———. *Regeneration through Violence: The Mythology of the American Frontier*. Middletown, Conn.: Wesleyan UP, 1973.

Smith, Henry Nash. *Virgin Land*. Cambridge: Harvard UP, 1950.

Sternsher, Bernard. *Consensus, Conflict, and American Historians*. Bloomington: Indiana UP, 1975.

Stevick, Philip. *Alternative Pleasures: Postrealist Fiction and the Tradition*. Urbana: U of Illinois P, 1981.

Stoltzfus, Ben. *Lacan and Literature: Purloined Pretexts*. Albany: State U of New York P, 1996.

Stonehill, Brian. *The Self-Conscious Novel: Artifice in Fiction from Joyce to Pynchon*. Philadelphia: U of Pennsylvania P, 1988.

Sullivan, Jack. *The Penguin Encyclopedia of Horror and the Supernatural*. New York: Viking, 1986. 214, 226–29.

Swados, Harvey. "What Is This World?" Rev. of *The Sundial,* by Shirley Jackson. *New Republic.* 3 Mar. 1958: 19–20.

Tanner, Tony. *City of Words: American Fiction 1950–1970.* New York: Harper, 1971.

Tate, Lisa. "Werewolf in Lamb's Clothing." Rev. of *We Have Always Lived in the Castle,* by Shirley Jackson. *Bennington Banner* 22 Sept. 1962: 12.

Terral, Rufus. "Between Book Ends: Miss Jackson Reconsidered, with Reflection." Rev. of *The Magic of Shirley Jackson,* by Shirley Jackson. Ed. Stanley Edgar Hyman. *St. Louis Post Dispatch* 9 February 1967. Newspaper clipping in SJP Box 24 without page number.

Tuveson, Ernest L. *Millennium and Utopia: A Study in the Background of the Idea of Progress.* Berkeley: U of California P, 1949.

——— . *Redeemer Nation: The Idea of America's Millennial Role.* Chicago: U of Chicago P, 1968.

Untermeyer, Louis. Rev of *We Have Always Lived in the Castle,* by Shirley Jackson. *New York Times Book Review* 23 Sept. 1962: 9.

"U.S. Literature—Alive and Kicking," *Richmond News Leader* 10 Nov. 1955: Newspaper clipping in SJP Box 20 without page number.

Varnado, S. L. *Haunted Presence: The Numinous in Gothic Fiction.* Tuscaloosa: U of Alabama P, 1987.

Vonnegut, Kurt. *Timequake.* New York: Putnam's, 1997.

Walker, Nancy A. *A Very Serious Thing: Women's Humor and American Culture.* Minneapolis: U of Minnesota P, 1988.

Wardrop, Daneen. *Emily Dickinson's Gothic.* Iowa City: U of Iowa P, 1996.

Waugh, Patricia. *Feminine Fictions: Revisiting the Postmodern.* London: Routledge, 1989.

Westling, Louise Hutchings. *The Green Breast of the New World: Landscape, Gender, and American Fiction.* Athens: U of Georgia P, 1996.

Weston, Ruth. *Gothic Traditions and Narrative Techniques in the Fiction of Eudora Welty.* Baton Rouge: Louisiana State UP, 1994.

Whittier, Gayle. "'The Lottery' as Misogynist Parable." *Women's Studies* 18 (1991): 353–66.

Wilbur, Richard. "The House of Poe." *Poe: A Collection of Critical Essays.* Ed. Robert Regan. Englewood Cliffs, NJ: Prentice, 1967. 98–121.

Wilde, Alan. *Horizons of Assent: Modernism, Postmodernism, and the Ironic Imagination.* Baltimore: Johns Hopkins UP, 1981.

Winter, Kari J. *Subjects of Slavery, Agents of Change: Women and Power in Gothic Novels and Slave Narratives, 1790–1865.* Athens: U of Georgia P, 1992.

Wolff, Cynthia Griffin. "The Radcliffian Gothic Model: A Form for Feminine Sexuality." Fleenor 207–23.

Wolff, Geoffrey. "Shirley Jackson's Magic Style." Rev. of *Come Along with Me: Part of a Novel, Sixteen Stories, and Three Lectures,* by Shirley Jackson. Ed. Stanley Edgar Hyman. *New Leader* 9 Sept. 1968: 18–19.

Wolstenholme, Susan. *Gothic (Re)Visions: Writing Women as Readers.* Albany: State U of New York P, 1993.

Wojcik, Daniel. *The End of the World as We Know It: Faith, Fatalism, and Apocalypse in America.* New York: New York UP, 1997.

Wyatt, David. *The Fall into Eden: Landscape and Imagination in California.* New York: Cambridge UP, 1986.

# INDEX

223

Hughes, Langston, 1
humor, critical studies of Shirley
Jackson's, 12; parody, 67, 68, 76;
in *The Sundial*, 137, 140, 142,
145, 146; in *We Have Always
Lived in the Castle*, 175. *See also*
comic, parody
Hurley, Kelly, 203n. 1
Hyman, Stanley Edgar, abuse of
Shirley Jackson, 17–18, 23; *The
Armed Vision*, 13; depicted in
Shirley Jackson's fiction, 19, 103,
119–20, 155, 181; financial
exploitation of Shirley Jackson,
18–19; homophobia of, 17; hostility of, 17; influence on Shirley
Jackson, 15–18, 24, 97; literary
reputation of, 15; promotion of
Shirley Jackson's literary career,
16–17; *The Tangled Bank*, 19;
undermined in Shirley Jackson's
fiction, 46

ideology, 77, 136, 173–74, 175,
197n. 11; allegorical representation of, 9; and character, 7, 35,
62; depicted in Shirley Jackson's
works, 4, 42, 45–46, 53, 58, 68,
85, 97, 145, 187–89; domestic,
55, 102, 161. *See also* Marxism
Imaginary, 2, 6, 7, 84, 99, 173; and
characterization, 6, 51, 60, 123,
134; and interpellation, 7; as narrative device, 168; defined, 196n.
7; depicted in Shirley Jackson's fiction, 63–64
interpellation, and characterization,
4, 6, 83, 85, 88, 171; and text, 89,
168; depiction of, 7, 10, 65, 161,
155; metonymic, 88, 94, 197n. 11
intertextuality, fairy tales and nursery
rhymes, 181–82; in Shirley
Jackson's works, 3–5, 10, 116,
119, 130–33, 135, 140, 142–43,
147, 148, 151, 155, 161, 165–71,
173–74, 188–89

Jackson, Geraldine, described as
"phallic mother, 11, 23; influence
on Shirley Jackson, 23–25; interested in spiritualism, 11; Shirley
Jackson's relationship with,
reflected in fiction, 84; suggested
in *The Bird's Nest*, 128
Jackson, Leslie, 24; described as
"feminized," 24
Jackson, Rosemary, 3, 111, 196n. 6,
197n. 12, 199n. 4, 200n. 6, 201n.
7, 206n. 8
Jackson, Shirley, Life and Themes:
alcoholism of, 19–20; alienation,
in adolescence, 25; attitude toward
the supernatural, 8–9, 10, 16, 137,
198n. 17; autobiographical elements in writing, 84, 88, 99, 103,
162, 164–65, 188–89; 175, 176,
180, 181, 188–89; characteristics
of narrative style, 4; characterization in Shirley Jackson's works
(general remarks), 3, 26; colitis of,
22; conflicts within, 25–27; dependency on Hyman, 22–23; depression, 18; diary, 23, 27; dislike of
provincialism, 21; domestic narratives of, 19, 25, 73; drug dependency, 20–21, 199n. 5; editors and
publishers of, 2; financial success,
18, 19; hints of early sexual abuse
by male relatives, 26; hints of multiple personality in, 26–27, 189;
historicization in Shirley Jackson's
works, 4; influenced by Morton
Prince, 16; influenced by Stanley
Edgar Hyman; interest in myth
and ritual, 16; interest in psychology, 16; lifestyle of, 19–20, 24, 25;
literary agent of, 19; literary out-
put, 29; literary reputation and
critical appraisal, 1–2, 7–8, 11–13,
29, 132–33, 137, 152–53,
170–71, 180–81, 189, 191–93,
195n. 4 (*see also* individual titles);
married life with Stanley Edgar